Fortunate Sons

ALSO BY LIEL LEIBOVITZ AND MATTHEW MILLER

Lili Marlene: The Soldiers' Song of World War II

Fortunate Sons

The 120 Chinese Boys Who
Came to America, Went to School, and
Revolutionized an Ancient Civilization

Liel Leibovitz & Matthew Miller

W. W. Norton & Company
New York • *London*

For information about permission to reproduce selections from this book,
write to Permissions, W. W. Norton & Company, Inc.,
500 Fifth Avenue, New York, NY 10110

For information about special discounts for bulk purchases, please contact
W. W. Norton Special Sales at specialsales@wwnorton.com or 800-233-4830

Manufacturing by Courier Westford
Book design by Chris Welch
Production manager: Julia Druskin

Library of Congress Cataloging-in-Publication Data

Leibovitz, Liel.
Fortunate sons : the 120 Chinese boys who came to America, went to school, and
revolutionized an ancient civilization / Liel Leibovitz & Matthew Miller. — 1st ed.
p. cm.
Includes bibliographical references and index.
ISBN 978-0-393-07004-0 (hardcover)
1. China—History—1861–1912. 2. China—History—Reform Movement, 1898.
3. China—Politics and government—19th century. 4. China—Education—19th
century. 5. Chinese Educational Commission—History. 6. Chinese students—
United States—History—19th century. 7. Yung, Wing, 1828–1912.
I. Miller, Matthew I., 1979– II. Title.
DS761.2.L45 2011
951'.035—dc22

2010037724

W. W. Norton & Company, Inc.
500 Fifth Avenue, New York, N.Y. 10110
www.wwnorton.com

W. W. Norton & Company Ltd.
Castle House, 75/76 Wells Street, London W1T 3QT

1 2 3 4 5 6 7 8 9 0

To Lisa, evermore. —L.L.

To the girls of C.G., ever-victorious. —M.M.

CONTENTS

INTRODUCTION

Attempting to write even a slice of Chinese history is a monu-
mental challenge, requiring patience and untangling. The task
grows more complex when, in addition to recording the nation's
intricate past, one focuses on the biographies of 120 men, many
of whom led China during the final days of its empire and
attempted to shepherd it through ambitious reforms. For us,
the undertaking often seemed doomed. Yet, something about
the story of the Chinese Educational Mission compelled us to
persevere.

Despite its considerable implications for China, the United
States, and the relations between the two nations, the story of
the mission is not well known today. We came across it while
watching television on a rainy afternoon in Beijing: suddenly,
the screen was filled with creased and yellowing photographs of
young Chinese boys wearing voluminous silk robes, standing in
the midst of austere New England landscapes. The boys were
sent to the United States in 1872, during the twilight years of

the Qing Empire, in the hopes that a few years in America's leading schools would produce a band of leaders capable of rescuing China from its technological and military stupor. In the high schools and colleges of Connecticut, Massachusetts, New Jersey, and New York, the sons of the world's oldest surviving empire and the sons of an ascendant young republic met, played games, and exchanged ideas. In many ways, their interactions would shape both their nations in the decades and centuries to come.

While this book is primarily a work of history, it may also be read as a primer on the present. Had they strolled down the main street of contemporary Zhuhai, for example, or enjoyed a meal in Harbin, the men whose stories this volume tells would have likely recognized many of the same challenges and some of the same opportunities that had baffled and enticed them as they struggled to push and pull their ancient nation into the modern era. In America, too, they would probably have encountered the same enthusiasm and the same prejudices that at times served to promote them and at other times blocked their way. Although much has happened in Chinese history over the course of the last 100 years—too much for this book to attempt to describe—the fundamental challenge facing China has not changed since the boys first tackled it.

It is a challenge that starkly defined the lives of the Chinese Educational Mission's graduates. On the one hand, the students were infatuated with the promises inherent in modern machinery, in global commerce, in Western interpretations of innovation and progress. On the other, they were loyal sons of China who, even as they fought for sweeping reforms, revered the rituals of the past and took immense pride in their heritage and tradition. In resisting the clarion call of either ideology, they achieved, if only for a few passing years, a kind of harmonious balance between East and West, past and future, self and nation.

We hope that those who today call on China to abandon its essence and take up foreign ideas, and those who reject America out of hand and deny its virtues, will read this book. In it, they will find a brief retelling of China's struggle to become a modern nation, as well as the beginnings of America's rise to the pinnacle of international influence. Most importantly, however, they will find a story about men from two countries, two cultures, two worlds, who met in friendship and tried to craft a better future. This, we believe, offers a universal lesson, timeless and true, which we would do well to recall.

Part I

The Freshman

D espite the long marches and great leaps forward, China's slow stumble toward modernity, still very much a work in progress, may just as well have begun with a single touchdown at Yale College.

It was October of 1850, and the campus was swept up in the annual football game between the freshman and the sophomore classes. With the ground still soggy from the fall's first rains, dozens of students were wrestling one another to the ground, shoving, tackling, and grappling for the ball.[1]

For the students on the field, the game was more than just an athletic competition. Yale, which had originally been founded by Harvard graduates seeking to create a more theologically austere academic environment than the one they had found in Massachusetts, was, by the middle of the nineteenth century, undergoing a radical transformation. The school's initial commitment to divinity studies and ancient languages remained strong, but a modern spirit of professionalism and specialization had begun to ignite changes. In 1810, the college inaugurated its school of medicine, followed by the school of law in 1843, and, four years later, by the graduate school of arts and sciences and the Sheffield Scientific School. These new cathedrals of modernity called for new men, different from the previous erudite scholars not only in mind but in body as well: athletics, as one prominent critic of the period wrote, offered "that experience of pain and endurance necessary to bring out the masculine qualities,"[2] which a burgeoning nation needed in order to assert itself in the world. Unlike their more humble forefathers, schooled with the pulpit in mind and trained for a life of quiet reflection, the Yale men of the mid-nineteenth century were expected to show the kind of virility necessary in order for America to fulfill what the *Democratic Review* editor John L. O'Sullivan, acutely attuned to the zeitgeist, referred to as the young republic's "manifest destiny."

To meet that destiny, one needed cunning, speed, and bravery, qualities more evident on the playing field than in the lecture hall. Sports had become an increasingly important part of a young man's education, football in particular. Inklings of that fervor were evident in Yale's big game of 1850: with intercollegiate leagues not yet in existence, and concrete rules of play not yet written, the annual October match pitted the underclassmen in a contest of clashing bones and bruised skin. That day, the freshmen showed up in full force with 126 men, a slight advantage over the sophomores' 123. As the students took their place on the Green, the large public square that lay just opposite the college's gray buildings, nervous chatter echoed off the grand marble steps and the portico of the State House, where the local women were waving flags in support of their teams. This year, perhaps, the freshmen would win.

It seldom happened, for understandable reasons. Having had an additional year to practice and being more familiar with the rules of the game, the sophomores were the perennial favorites. They also tended to see themselves as zealous guardians of the unwritten hierarchy of collegiate life, the one that regarded newly minted students as unworthy of respect until proven otherwise. They weren't afraid to play dirty to protect their laurels; on one occasion, several years prior, one of their ranks had pulled out a knife and tried to stab a rushing freshman in a desperate effort to halt the boy's advance. But 1850 was no ordinary year. The freshmen were not only more numerous but also physically larger and blessed with a handful of determined young men bent on victory. Some members of the faculty, fearing severe injuries, tried to cancel the competition, but the game's appeal was already too great. With an unusually large crowd in attendance, the game was set to begin.

The contest started with the two sides lining up opposite each other, each charged with driving the ball to a respective goal lying fifty yards away. The most athletic man on each side, a rough equivalent of the modern-day quarterback, was entrusted with "canting" the ball, or setting the ball in play by throwing it to the player most likely to deliver it to its destination. For the freshmen, that man was L. M. Dorman, strong and committed to victory, the most exciting player, some said, to grace Yale's ranks in years. A coin toss was called, the winning side awarded an additional twenty yards, and the game was underway.

One of the freshmen on the field, Charles Hallock, recalled what happened: "From cant to finish, there was a surging conglomeration of arms and legs, amidst which the ball was seldom visible. . . . When the huge knot of players was unraveled it generally looked as though it had passed through a cotton gin."[3] The din was punctured by loud grunts and the sharp sound of ripping shirts, because canvas uniforms were still years away.

After a successful cant, the freshmen lost track of the ball, which was now buried somewhere beneath a writhing heap of thrashing limbs. Dorman and his friends frantically shoved and pulled, plunging themselves into the melee. They saw nothing— nothing but the sophomores heading toward them for a tough and determined counteroffensive. The upset everyone had been predicting seemed unlikely.

An unusual-looking freshman stood nearby. Significantly shorter than Dorman, and wearing his hair in a long braided ponytail, which he tucked beneath a straw hat, the boy stood out in his silk robe, the traditional attire of a Confucian scholar. This unlikely spectator was Yung Wing, a member of the freshman class who had been brought to the United States a few years earlier by missionaries returning from a lengthy stay in China. Yung was one of a handful of foreigners in the school and the first Chinese man ever to study at Yale. The game and its violence were unlike anything his countrymen back home would have associated with schools and study, and Yung tried to make sense of the unfolding scene.

A few days before the game, his curiosity had led him to a meeting in which members of the faculty discussed the athletic program at Yale. There, he had watched as a fellow freshman, an Armenian named Seropyan, rose up and denounced football as a "barbarous custom." Yung, who knew little about the sport, listened as another student, the youngest in a long lineage of Yale graduates, stood up and berated the Armenian for "coming all the way from the benighted region of Asia Minor" to slander the favorite pastime of "good old Yale." The tartness of the response, uncommon in the otherwise accepting and open collegial community, stuck with Yung and was still in his mind when, standing on the sidelines and watching his classmen huddle and shove, he suddenly spotted the ball rolling his way.

He picked up the odd object and tucked it under the long sleeve of his robe. He looked ahead and saw the goal lying in front of him, in Chapel Street. He didn't hesitate. He began to run as fast as he could.

The Chinese man speeding away, his silk robe billowing like a sail, was enough of a vision to distract the entangled mob on the field for an instant, but soon a burly sophomore was giving chase. The goal lay just a few yards ahead. An observer wrote that Yung's queue, the braid that all Chinese subjects were required to grow as a demonstration of loyalty to their emperor, went "flying in the air like a pump handle."[4] Desperate to stop the runaway freshman, the sophomore reached for Yung's hair and tugged on his queue. Yung felt a sharp pain, dropped the ball to the ground, and kicked it as hard as he could. It sailed over the goal line, giving the freshmen an upset victory. The spectators on the steps shrieked. The sophomores sighed. Yung's classmates huddled around their new hero and carried him off on their shoulders. For the first time since arriving in America, Yung Wing felt at home.

Although he had been educated by Westerners his entire life and immigrated to America when he was nineteen, Yung was very much a son of imperial China. The customs and habits of Connecticut were still foreign to him, irreconcilably different from those of Nam Ping, the small hamlet on the shores of the South China Sea where he was born and raised.[5]

From an early age, Yung had been exposed to Americans by the Reverend Samuel Brown—the teacher who had met him as a boy in China and brought him to the United States. Still, he found the entire concept of a Western education strange and powerfully moving. For all the familiarity his primary education at a missionary school in China had afforded him with American pedagogy, the American educational system presented nearly insurmountable challenges to the Chinese scholar. It adhered to a logic unlike anything that would have made sense to a subject of the Qing Empire.

By the time Yung had arrived in America, education in the United States was becoming rapidly institutionalized, with elementary schools, academies, and colleges established in nearly every county. According to the 1840 census, more than 55 percent of the youth aged five to fifteen attended a primary or grammar school.[6] The state of Connecticut, influenced by the work of the education reformer Horace Mann, had by then established a system of "common schools"; based on the Prussian model of education, these institutions were dedicated to the principle that all students, regardless of background or social standing, were entitled to the same uniform curriculum, and that only by a standardized educational agenda could society's socioeconomic gaps be bridged.

Nothing could be more foreign to a Chinese student reared, as Yung would inevitably have been, on Confucius's famed adage "Teach according to the student's ability."[7] Unlike America, with its democratic emphasis on equalizing large swaths of the population through a common curriculum, China nurtured an educational tradition asserting that collective harmony was possible only if the nation's best and brightest were isolated from their less capable peers and guided through classical studies refined over the course of many centuries.

The key word that obsessed each Chinese student was *cai*, which translates loosely as talent. While the United States has always been dependent on the rule of law—a concept sanctified in the Constitution—China relied on the rule of men, the imperial court and the regional governors they appointed. The elevation of worthy people imbued with *cai* to key positions was therefore paramount to the success of the state, and recognizing talent became a foremost political necessity. Students spent their formative years pondering their *cai* or lack thereof, and many found themselves despondent as a result of going unnoticed or being passed over.

No fate was worse for an aspiring Chinese scholar than to possess a modicum of talent and yet be ignored by higher-ups. Without recognition, without being allowed to put one's skills to the service of the state, there was little to live for. Generations of Chinese poets wrote about this sad occasion in the same tremulous tone their Western counterparts used to describe unrequited loves. Wang Wei, for example, wrote several poems in the eighth century that captured the existential despair a student felt when unappreciated and ignored. One of his best-known poems, used much later by Gustav Mahler in *The Song of the Earth*, deals with the self-imposed exile of a dejected scholar:

> *I get off my horse and drink your wine*
> *I ask where you're going*
> *You say things have not gone your way*
> *You're off to South Mountain for a long, long rest*
> *Off you go, I will ask no more*
> *White clouds till the end of time.*[8]

To locate the empire's most brilliant students, an imposing battery of examinations was created, established in the seventh century C.E. and refined by each new dynasty.[9] The intricate system of tests, known commonly as the civil service examinations, was free and open to all members of the public. Success came with a guarantee of a prestigious and lucrative position in the regional or imperial government, regardless of a student's lineage or status, and ensured, theoretically, that the son of a farmer and the son of a nobleman alike could have a chance to rise to prominence.

The system was not without its flaws. While the test was free to take, the expenses associated with traveling to the regional seats where the exams were conducted—as well as an ancient tradition that called on successful students to shower their examiners with lavish gifts—made passing an expensive proposition. Furthermore, with so many applicants competing for so few spots, the exam's authors gradually found themselves writing questions designed not to spot the most capable students but to stump the vast majority of applicants. It was not uncommon for examiners to break out in song in the examination hall upon learning that a certain question left all the students baffled. Naturally, with competition so fierce, a black market soon prospered; professional students offered to take the test on behalf of the few who could afford to pay their exorbitant rates. Aware of such cheating, the Qing officials added a number of precautionary steps, requiring, for example, that students recite the first few lines of the preliminary essays that they had written days earlier before being allowed to move on to the later stages of the test. This only added to the confusion and helped turn China's well-meaning institution into a dreaded and byzantine ritual.

Still, the exams were open to all, and that fact alone inspired China's youth to look to the system with hope. Growing up in Nam Ping, Yung Wing, like all other students, saw the test as providing his sole chance to live a meaningful and satisfying life. He watched as his older brother, a bright student in the village's best Confucian academy, prepared for his examination, a process that involved memorizing no fewer than 431,286 characters and learning by heart lengthy passages from China's most-revered classical texts. Renzong, an emperor of the Song dynasty, expressed his thoughts about the traditional methods of study and schooling in a poem he wrote during the eleventh century: "A boy who wants to become a somebody / devotes himself to the classics, faces the window, and reads."[10]

Writing in his later years, Yung expressed a nostalgic fondness for this system. It suffered, as he was the first to admit, from its share of setbacks, but was still governed by a spirit that inspired young men to apply themselves in the service of their empire. Neatly capturing the essence of Confucianism in form as well

as content, Chinese education rested on the sacred philosopher's
two most prominent tenets: *li*, ritual, and *ren*, the moral obligations inherent in all relationships. Both were strongly manifested
in the examination system, a ceremonial construct that, with
its rigid hierarchy, clearly dictated the obligations members of
society had toward one another.

At Yale, that ascetic spirit was nowhere in evidence. Yung's
new academic environment was an odd inversion of the Chinese
imperial system. Whereas in China young men of all classes
struggled for an opportunity to rise above the rest and join the
ranks of the nation's governing elite, in New Haven the children
of privilege came to mingle with one another and reassert their
good fortune. Whatever Yale lacked in an egalitarian sense of
national service, it more than made up for in energy. "College life
is something new to me," Yung wrote to his friend Samuel Wells
Williams. "One has no time to think or analyze except study.
There is also great excitement among the students themselves . . .
mental excitement. Old Yale is surrounded with an atmosphere
of ambition. I never was subject to such excitement. I enjoy its
influence very much."[11]

Excitement and enthusiasm, though, did not necessarily lead
to good grades: despite spending all of his time studying, Yale's
sole Chinese student finished his first semester with an average
of 2.12, barely above the 2.0 mark required to pass. By the end
of his freshman year, he had managed to improve only slightly,
rising to an average of 2.45, but flunking calculus and just barely
mastering Greek. The one thing that saved Yung was his talent for English composition.[12] Possessing, perhaps, something
of the classical Chinese scholar's predilection for elegant prose,

he wrote poignant works that displayed strong arguments and won him attention and respect. He was awarded first prize in composition and, on the strength of his writing, avoided being dismissed from school altogether.

More than calculus or Greek, though, it was sport that baffled Yung the most. As the emperor Renzong's poem suggests, Chinese scholars were expected to sit by the window and read, taking great pride in their sedentary life, while the less fortunate, those lacking *cai* or luck, would be the ones sweating in the fields. Arriving at Yale, Yung had a hard time adjusting to the robust physicality that often distinguished students far more than their agile minds. In his letter to Williams, he addressed this point. "To enjoy college," he observed, "a person must have a firm fit, or else endeavor with indomitable energy and perseverance to drive his studies along."[13] The tone, like Yung's disposition, was understated, but the demand for "a firm fit" continued to haunt him. His celebrated touchdown provided an early reprieve: his classmates would forgive him his foreign features, his braided queue and his silk robes, his mellifluous speech and his strange history, but they would not forgive him his weakness. To be a Yale man in 1850 was to be rugged and rough, a man of action. Yung Wing was not yet that man.

With great effort, Yung managed to improve his grades. And while he was never again a hero on the football field, he exercised regularly, developed muscle, and felt more and more like one of the students with each passing semester. To supplement his meager income, he took a position as the steward of a boarding club consisting of sophomores and juniors, where, in return for food, he served the club's twenty residents, shopping for their supplies and bringing them their meals. If Yung found the position humiliating, he left no record of it in his journal.

Finally, in 1854, the time came for Yung to graduate. Like college graduates before him and since, he was overcome with melancholy and doubt, uncertain of what to do next. He missed home immensely, but was equally enamored with America and the opportunities it offered to a bright, hardworking young man. Later in life, Yung described his dilemmas. The United States beckoned, but China, he wrote, "had never escaped my mind's eye nor my heart's yearning for her welfare." He explained:

> I wanted very much to stay a few years longer in order to take a scientific course. I had taken up surveying in the Sheffield Scientific School just as that department was starting into existence under Professor Norton. Had I had the means to prosecute a practical profession, that might have helped to shorten and facilitate the way to the goal I had in view; but as I was poor and my friends thought that a longer stay in this country might keep me here for good, and China would lose me altogether, I was for this and other reasons induced to return. The scientific course was accordingly abandoned.[14]

As Yung Wing prepared for the long journey home, he hoped that he had acquired the talent and ability to ably serve his emperor. But imperial China in the mid-nineteenth century was very different from the puritan world of New England's elite universities, and it would take all of Yung's *cai* to prove himself a worthy servant to the suspicious mandarins of the Celestial Court.

The Qing

As soon as Yung Wing stepped down to the docks on New York's East River and walked toward the ship that was going to take him back to China, he could sense that his journey home was not going to be a pleasurable one. He had hoped that the friends he made at Yale, the families with whom he had stayed, and the Americans he felt had become a part of his life would come to see him off. He imagined teary farewells and white handkerchiefs waving in the wind and final, kind words of goodbye shouted over the howls of wind and crew. But the docks were empty.

Walking briskly, the chilly mid-November gusts lashing at his face, he strode over to the commercial clipper *Eureka*, bound for Hong Kong. Ahead of him were nearly five months of lonely days and tight quarters. But it wasn't all a wash: he was happy to hear that another passenger was on the ship, and pleasantly surprised when he saw that the man was someone he had known from China. The Reverend William Allen Macy, the missionary who had replaced the Reverend Brown as the headmaster of Yung Wing's old school in Hong Kong, was also returning to the East. In his school days, Yung never cared much for Macy; whereas Brown was a veteran educator who dispensed stern sermons and silly jokes in equal measure, Macy was young, reserved, and aloof. He spoke of his ideals and his ideas as if both existed in some faraway realm inaccessible to anyone but him, an affectation that grated on his young charges. Seeing Macy stumble over his luggage in *Eureka*'s narrow passageways, though, gave Yung tremendous relief. In situations such as these, he thought, anyone familiar was a friend.

Just how important Macy's companionship would prove became evident a few moments later, when Yung met the ship's crew and captain. Over a gruff coterie of Swedish and Norwegian sailors towered a Philadelphian, Captain Whipple, who possessed at once a strong stutter and an air of insanity. A tugboat hauled *Eureka* to Sandy Hook, New Jersey. There, it was set to begin its journey east, via the Cape of Good Hope to Hong Kong, a distance of thirteen thousand nautical miles.

Upon hitting open water, the crew of the *Eureka* came to understand the magnitude of Whipple's madness. Owing to his careless calculations, the men soon found themselves sailing into the shrieking wind. That forced the sailors to jibe vigilantly and made the journey difficult for the ship's seamen and nauseating for its two passengers.

To make matters worse, the demented captain would pace up and down the quarterdeck each morning, stopping every few steps to look heavenward and, as if following some strange ritual, would scream, curse, spit, and resume his pacing. As the sun climbed in the sky, the captain's performance grew more erratic: by midday, he would take to pantomiming a duel with the wind, jabbing away at the emptiness and erupting with laughter. Years later, Yung recalled the spectacle:

> All at once, he halted, stared at the quarter of the sky from whence the malicious head wind came. With a face all bloated and reddened by intense excitement, his eyes almost standing out of their sockets, and all ablaze with uncontrollable rage, with arms uplifted, he would clutch his hair as if plucking it out by the roots, gnash his teeth, and simultaneously he would jump up and down, stamping on the deck, and swear at the Almighty for sending him head winds. The air for the moment was split with his revolting imprecations and blasphemous oaths that were ejaculated through the laborious process of stammering and stuttering, which made him a most pitiable object to behold.[1]

By the afternoon, the madman's powers were all spent, and he would collapse on the deck and mutter to himself a medley of bitter words and self-pitying condolences.

The wind, however, was too ethereal and indifferent a target to contain Whipple's fury, and the stuttering skipper soon searched for a more substantial scapegoat. The lanky foreigner on board was a perfect target. One afternoon, as the ship docked some- where in the tropics, Whipple approached the Reverend Macy and struck up an awkward conversation about the Bible. Macy was surprised; the captain was neither an educated man nor, given his severe speech impediment, much of a conversationalist, and he had never before made any holy overtures. But Whipple kept on babbling about the Lord, until he hit on a statement that seemed to please him immensely. The ship had been experiencing bad luck, he told Macy, because there was a Jonah on board. The allusion to the accursed biblical prophet, whose vessel was assaulted by storms until he was tossed overboard by the ship's fearful crewmen, wasn't lost on the reverend, nor was the identity of the modern-day Jonah to whom Whipple was referring. With trepidation, the reverend watched as the captain, now staring openly at Yung, repeated his mantra again and again: "Jonah on board," he stammered, "Jonah on board."[2]

Yung was livid. On the playing fields of New Haven, such an insult would have been reason enough to punch a man in the face; yet Yung's peculiar circumstances on board *Eureka*, stuck at sea and very much beholden to the captain's good graces, were enough to persuade him to forgo physical violence. But the slight still needed to be addressed. After the ship passed the Makassar Strait, not far from Borneo, Whipple, still yowling at the wind, seemed unable to point his vessel in the direction it needed to go. Yung smiled mischievously and said, in a voice just loud enough for the captain to hear, "If I had charge of the vessel, I could take her through in less than ten days."[3] Whipple's cheeks grew red. His eyes bulged. But he didn't say a word.

In time, Whipple managed to guide the ship into Hong Kong's harbor. Within sight of the teeming city, a tugboat was sent to drag the clipper into port, and its captain, a convivial Chinese man, climbed aboard *Eureka* to meet its crew and deliver his instructions. Perpetually terrified of his surroundings, Whipple ran up to Yung, and told him to ask the Chinese captain whether any dangerous rocks and shoals were around. Yung opened his mouth. He tried to form the sentence in his native tongue. He tried to remember the words. However, he had been in the United States for eight years, during which time he had had little opportunity to speak Chinese. He arrived in New England at the age when the mind begins to harden rapidly into the patterns that serve it for a lifetime to come. Yung's mind was set on the English language, on British literature and American idioms. He opened his mouth again, but nothing came out. Looking at the captain shamefully, he had to admit that he had no idea how to say "dangerous rocks and shoals" in Chinese.

Hearing this, the Chinese captain burst out laughing and, speaking perfect English, taught Yung the phrases he needed.[4]

Whipple, Macy, and a few crewmates standing by began to chuckle. Yung did too, but his laughter slowly gave way to unease. He was returning home, he had told himself nearly every day of the long and arduous journey, but just what sort of home would it be? Not knowing the language, not knowing the conditions, not having had any of the traditional education or training, he faced a precarious future.

Yung grabbed his possessions, strode off the clipper, and made his way uphill, where his old school still stood and where he had a few friends, mainly American missionaries, whom he wanted to see. He spent a day or two with Andrew Shortrede, the editor and proprietor of the influential newspaper *China Mail* and a philanthropist who had sponsored some of Yung's American education. Yung was grateful to Shortrede and excited to spend time in his presence and discuss all that he had done at Yale.

It softened the blow of being reintroduced into his now foreign native land. Thus fortified, Yung returned home to his mother.

As he embarked on the boat that would take him to Macao, where his mother lived, Yung was anxious. In his rush to see her, he had neglected to buy traditional Chinese clothes, and, dressed in an American suit, he looked more like a Western businessman than the distinguished scholar he knew she was expecting. Making matters worse was his mustache—neatly trimmed whiskers were all the rage in America. Yung, enough of an odd man out by virtue of his race at Yale, was quick to grow one in an attempt to fit in where he could. In China, however, a mustache had symbolic meaning, announcing to the world that its wearer was married. A mustachioed bachelor was considered foolish or, worse, insolent.

Without knowing what to expect, he entered his mother's house. As he walked in, she looked at him for a few moments. She said nothing to this tall gentleman in a blue suit. Yung, too, said nothing. She would be right to reject him, he thought nervously. She would be right to turn away. But she did no such thing. As soon as her shock subsided, she rushed over to her son and, crying, began to caress him. Still weeping after many minutes, she asked him to sit down and tell her all about his time in America.

Yung obliged. He spoke of Yale, of his job at the boarding club and of the generosity of the New Englanders, of his struggles with mathematics and his sudden star turn on the football grid. His mother listened attentively, but as the stream of stories slowed, she interjected with the question she found most important.

"What degree did you receive?" she asked Yung.[5] He replied it was called a bachelor's degree, the equivalent, roughly, of the Chinese title of *xiucai*, literally meaning elegant talent, the degree bestowed upon those young men who had successfully taken the imperial test. It was a great honor, he continued, and was inscribed ceremoniously on a parchment made of sheepskin.

"And how much money," the mother asked pointedly, "does this degree confer?"

Painstakingly, Yung explained that the American system operated very differently from China's. Successful test takers were not guaranteed positions in the government. American schools conferred nothing on their graduates but an education, and expected the carefully groomed young men to find a position and a salary on their own. This, he sensed, did not impress the old woman in the least. Nonplussed, he told her that Americans believed that men who had been educated could make money faster and easier than men who had not been so fortunate, that an educated fellow, if he possessed the right character, could easily become a leader of men, that a leader of men, almost by definition, made a lot of money, and that he, Yung, was certain that he would be able to earn a nice living. Still eliciting no response, he resorted to flattery.

"Knowledge," he spoke slowly, as if reciting a poem, "is power, and power is greater than riches. I am the first Chinese to graduate from Yale College, and that being the case, you have the honor of being the first and only mother out of the countless millions of mothers in China at this time, who can claim the honor of having a son who is the first Chinese graduate of a first-class American college. Such an honor is a rare thing to possess."

The language of honor was one Yung's mother understood. She smiled at her son and nodded her head. Still, there were pressing matters to address. "I see you have already raised your mustaches," she said. "You know you have a brother who is much older than you are; he hasn't grown his mustaches yet. You must have yours off."

It was, Yung realized, a test. Deep in his mother's eyes, he could sense maternal discomfort. She spoke softly, but the meaning of her words was clear: shave off your mustache, she was telling her son, and show me that in all those years in America you haven't forgotten your basic obligation to honor your family and observe your tradition. Making a show of his subservience, Yung rose to his feet, hurried out of the room, and returned a few minutes later, bowing and clean-shaven. The old woman clasped her hands, smiled widely, and hugged her son once more. Full of emotion, he promised her that he was back for good and that, from now on, he would see to her every need.

Leaving his mother's house with a renewed sense of his identity as a son of China, Yung decided that his first priority lay in restoring his lost language. That, he realized, couldn't be done in Macao, the small island where his mother lived and which was populated largely by foreigners. If he stayed there, he would quickly gravitate toward the Americans and English. To truly relearn Chinese, he needed to be among his own people, to live in a city that drew its rhythms not from the stentorian symphonies of Western merchants and missionaries, but from the subtle inflections of traditional China. Still, having spent most of his life in the company of Westerners, he had no close Chinese friends or acquaintances with whom he could reside, and, having barely been able to afford Yale, he had no money to pay for any other form of residence. Yung reached out to an American missionary, the Reverend Daniel Vrooman, for a touch of charity. A few days later, in the summer of 1855, Yung made his way to Vrooman's residence in the city of Canton, ironically a place, like Macao, brimming with foreigners. No matter. It would have to do. The largest city in the province of the same name, Canton was also the seat of the local government. Vrooman lived in a district called Ham La Han, on the southern end of town, near the Pearl River and directly across from the vast field that served as the government's official execution ground. And just as Yung arrived in town, the local authorities were putting the ground to use.

Yung himself took a long while to ascertain the causes of the turmoil that was gripping Canton. He had left China as a boy, ignorant of its politics, and came of age more aware of Millard Filmore and Franklin Pierce than about the obscure mandarins who ran the imperial court. But as soon as Yung was hit by the putrid stench wafting off of the killing field in the oppressive heat, he was forced to confront the cruel realities he had thus far managed to ignore, the attendant horrors of the Qing dynasty's slow descent into oblivion.

On the throne since 1644, China's ruling clan entered the nineteenth century with what its members recognized, much too late, to be insurmountable difficulties. Natural processes, simple economics, foreign intervention, and internal strife were constantly putting new strains on the ancient imperial order. In almost every area of Chinese life, obsolescent technology and approaches to governance were responsible for spectacular failures.

The most elementary problem was the rapid growth of the
Chinese population. In 1400, a census pegged China's population at 100 million people. Under Qing rule, that number had
grown to 450 million by the time of Yung Wing's birth.[6] The
Chinese Empire covered 7 percent of the planet's surface and
was home to almost a fifth of its people, most of whom were
concentrated not in the cities but in the surrounding areas. And
whereas food was plentiful and employment guaranteed in the
early years of the Qing dynasty, the quadrupling of the population had taken its toll on China's agrarian society: between 1753
and 1812, to cite just one gloomy statistic, the average plot of
land each Chinese farmer could expect to cultivate shrank by
more than 43 percent, to less than half an acre per person.[7] As
a result, the standard of living in China, considered generally
high throughout most of the Qing's reign, encountered strong
downward pressures at the dawn of the modern age. In the West,
the limitations of agricultural production and exploding popula-
tions were offset by the Industrial Revolution, where inventions
in the fields of manufacture and mining were able to siphon off
excess personnel into productive new enterprises. But China, the
nation that had invented gunpowder, the compass, the printing
press, and the abacus, found the expressive limitations of its
character-based language and the weight of Confucianism too
difficult to reconcile with the exponential growth of ideas and
concepts that marked the onset of scientific modernity.[8] The
imperial court, its days of innovation behind it, had, by Yung
Wing's time, retreated into an existence governed by rituals and
isolation.

China's emperors lived in ceremonious seclusion from the

vast and disparate lands under their care, ensconced, since 1420, in the Forbidden City, nestled behind a 170-foot-wide moat and a three-story wall that stretched for more than two miles. Reporting directly to the emperor were two select groups of scholars, known as the Grand Council and the Grand Secretariat, as well as six boards and nine ministries. Altogether, the cloistered emperor administered his enormous domain through no more than 40,000 civilian and military officials who were tasked with ruling nearly half a billion people. He concerned himself with little more than levying the occasional tax and keeping a small regular army, which answered directly to him.[9] Innovative measures and social reforms were avoided at all costs, as the Qing ruling class cherished the harmony of the existing order above everything else. The toxic disruptions of unruly new technologies and ways of thinking were left for the barbarian West to fiddle and experiment with. One contemporary British observer summed up his impression of the court of Emperor Tongzhi, who ascended to the throne in 1861, with unflattering words: the regime's perception of its responsibilities, he wrote, "seems to be to keep records of past occurrences, legalise *faits accomplis*, and strangle whatever comes before it in embryo. It recognises the grand truth that eyes have two uses—to see, and not to see; and it, as a rule, pins its faith to not seeing."[10]

The disinterested rituals of imperial governance, in large part, had to do with the fact that the residents of the Forbidden City understood their mission as originating not from the earthly needs of its citizens but from the celestial mandate awarded it from above. The emperors considered themselves the Sons of Heaven, not in themselves divine but trusted with keeping the all-important balance between heaven and earth. Such balance was best preserved when thought and action alike focused on harmony and the maintenance of the sacred order. Thus, the Chinese scrupulously avoided anything—industrialization and foreign intercourse, for example—that might upset the existing way.

Over the centuries, the Qing had brought harmony to an enormous landmass that stretched from frozen mountains to balmy ports, with scorching deserts and fertile river valleys in between. The very notion of the "Chinese" people was a misleading one, for the Qing subjects comprised a number of different nationalities and feuding religions, a polyglot people speaking seven main languages—Mandarin, Shanghainese, Cantonese, Hunan, Hakka, Gan, and Min—each as different from the other as German is from French. Inherent in this artificial construction of nationality were numerous fissures that the Qing had managed to stabilize in the course of their reign. Thus, unlike Westerners, who welcomed the opportunities presented by a climate of perpetual motion and change, the Chinese preferred to hold everything in a state of delicate suspension. To them, the greatest danger of all was to be found in *luan*, or chaos. In order to preserve the balanced system that they had inherited from their ancestors, the Qing preferred to govern with extreme caution, when they chose to govern at all. Nothing was done spontaneously, and everything adhered to the principles laid down ages ago. One Chinese scholar, a contemporary of Yung's, ably captured this ultra-conservative spirit: "Generation after generation has upheld Confucian teachings, proper human relationships, between ruler and minister, father and son, superiors and subordinates, the high and the low," he wrote. "All in the proper place, just as hats and shoes are not interchangeable."[11]

Still, the daily demands of China's civil society needed addressing, and where the imperial authority would not interfere, an extraordinarily intricate network of local fiefdoms was established to govern in its name. The Qing awarded near-total autonomy to eighteen regional governors, men who assumed powers usually reserved for ruling heads of state, such as the right to send embassies to foreign countries or negotiate military and economic treaties, as if there were no central authority in Beijing. The more mundane aspects of regional government—collecting taxes, paving roads, upholding law and order, settling disputes—fell to 1,300 district magistrates. As these districts, however, were too large for any one official to oversee single-handedly, a separate bureaucratic class of clerks grew up beneath them, men who themselves relied on the many heads of households who were required to submit regular reports on the activities of their families. Thus the empire kept its affairs in order.

Crucial to Qing governance was the all-important rule of avoidance. In order to safeguard the system against the undue influence of tribal loyalties, the court required magistrates to serve three-year terms in districts far removed from their native regions. Good intentions aside, the rule of avoidance had a devastating impact on China's political culture: thrust into a remote corner of the country, unfamiliar with the local language, and required to leave office after a relatively short period of time, many magistrates opted for the path of least resistance, idling away their days and avoiding any sudden movements that might anger or pique the citizens. Magistrates settled into lives of pleasant corruption, and dikes up and down the Yellow River were perpetually left unattended so as to guarantee officials regular repair work and the attendant commissions when the annual rains inevitably flooded neighboring villages. The Grand Canal, the thousand-mile-long artery of commerce that dated back to the fifth century B.C., crumbled under the weight of such imperial inefficiency and neglect.

Although it had sustained China for centuries, this elaborate system of government was splendidly inept at meeting the growing challenges it faced. Starting from the second decade of the nineteenth century, it began to unravel. To the lofty occupants of the walled palace, always in search of celestial patterns, it sometimes seemed as if the challenges buffeting the empire at the dawn of the modern age were guided by a heavenly hand. Nowhere was this felt more acutely than in the realm of finance: China's economy was sent into a tailspin when copper, the metal used by the imperial court to mint its coins, began to grow scarce.[12] The mandarins in Beijing, none too practiced in the study of markets, took the shortage to be a sign of cosmic imbalance. But the actual reason was more earthly: concerned primarily with its own needs, the court instituted a rigid mining policy, demanding that each copper mine sell Beijing a specific allotment of the metal at a fixed price, after which the mine could offer the remaining copper to the public at the normal market rate. As the mines exhausted their initial supplies, though, the ore became less accessible, extraction costs grew rapidly, and many mines, constantly losing significant portions of their production to the undervalued imperial contracts that the Qing refused to adjust, were forced to shut down. This, in turn, led to a shortage of currency and, almost immediately, to inflation. Embarrassingly for the Qing, foreign denominations were quick to fill the void: the British pound, the French franc, the Portuguese real, and the Russian ruble were all soon in circulation, introduced by the hordes of Western merchants who were invading China's shores with increasing ferocity. By the middle of the nineteenth century, even Qing officials were paid in foreign coin.

Ultimately, however, the Western merchants who came bearing hard currency, and the armies that followed them, were the Qing's undoing. Once shielded from foreign intrusions by the Great Wall, China was rapidly learning that the shifting realities of economics, technology, and modern statehood made isolation impossible. And as China lacked a central body that dictated its foreign policy, the Westerners who arrived at its shores were received by the aptly named Ministry of Rituals. At the ministry, foreign traders were instructed to perform ceremonial prostrations to the emperor, the famous kowtow, and to acknowledge the superiority of the Qing in all matters temporal and celestial. In exchange for the acceptance of these conditions, the visiting merchants were allowed to conduct a small, supervised amount of business. For the Qing, this was the extent of foreign exchange. Developments a world away, though, would expose the limits of this myopic system.

Following the Napoleonic Wars, Europe refashioned itself into a constellation of independent nation-states, each considered to be a part of the "comity of Christian nations." No longer singularly obsessed with slaughtering one another, these nation-states looked at the larger map of the world and saw ripe opportunities for economic and territorial expansions. Hegel would later write that the Chinese saw the sea as "only the limit, the ceasing of the land," whereas the Europeans were eager to extend their influence and dominion beyond their own maritime borders, unfettered by what he called the "infinite multitude of dependencies" that shackled any culture rooted solely in its own soil.[13] The West was also invigorated by the edicts of economic liberalism, and moved by Adam Smith and other thinkers to replace their traditional mercantilist view—the belief that the global volume of commerce is unchangeable and that each nation must strive to keep its transactions positively balanced—with the vigorous philosophy of free trade, which argued that more trade, regardless of the direction of currency flow, is the ultimate goal. Under these conditions, China shone as a particularly desirable destination: as early as the turn of the nineteenth century, talk of "opening up China," with its fabled riches and enormous base of consumers, became the bon ton among Europe's capitalists. Though bandied about as a purely financial mission statement, the idea of "opening up China" never disguised its cultural and moral underpinnings. To Hegel and his contemporary European thinkers, China represented all that was archaic and outmoded about the Orient, where emperors ruled by caprice over people who "believe that men are born only to drag the car of Imperial Power." It was a culture that existed "outside the World's History," as Hegel wrote, and that would require the enlightened guidance of the West in order to see the light.[14]

With this perspective in mind, the West's view of China began to change rapidly. Whereas in 1749 William Douglas, a writer from Boston, rhapsodized about the Chinese as "the elder brother of all the nations of mankind," by 1800 a fellow Bostonian working in China as a commercial emissary stated that, among expatriate Westerners, "the knavery of the Chinese, particularly those of the trading classes, has become prover- bial."[15] Of the Qing government, the emissary wrote, "It may perhaps be questioned whether there is a more oppressive one to be found in any civilized nation upon the earth. All offices in the provinces are bestowed upon such as can make most inter- est for them with great mandarins at court, in consequence the subject undergoes every species of oppression. He is squeezed by the petty mandarins, these again by the higher, [and] they in turn by their superiors, the governors and viceroys."[16]

As soon as the West began to perceive China as a destination for trade and a partner in the rapidly globalizing network of exchange, the ancient empire's deficiencies became stark. The amalgam of assorted provinces held together by loose threads to a timid and inefficient imperial government both infuriated and delighted the Westerners, who soon began pressing on the Middle Kingdom with growing tenacity, amazed at the ease with which its fruits could be plucked but also bewildered by the complex choreography of Chinese officialdom.

Fearing that the enterprising merchants would upset the deli- cate balance of the harmonious empire that had taken centuries to stabilize, the Qing court tried to keep the Westerners in strict seclusion. At first, the imperial officials hoped to limit the scope of Western influence by designating specific areas in which for- eigners were permitted to trade; in 1760, they established the Canton system, named for the city where foreign commerce was largely centered. It opened up a limited number of ports for importing and exporting goods and established a Chinese merchant monopoly, known as the Cohong, to supervise all dealings with the foreigners. Unlike the earlier caravans and smaller trade delegations that could be easily managed by the Ministry of Rituals, the Europeans now arriving were hungrier for goods and market share, buccaneer capitalists more numerous and persistent than any Occidentals the Chinese had seen before.

From the outset, the most lucrative item for the foreigners was tea, which had gone from being an unobtainable luxury to being a staple of life in Great Britain, commanding nearly 5 percent of the annual income of the average British household by the mid-1800s. In the late seventeenth century, England's East India Company imported around 200 pounds of Chinese tea leaves a year; within a few decades, that number rose to 400,000 pounds, and it had jumped past the 28,000,000-pound mark by the time Yung Wing was born.[17] To pay for such massive imports, the East India Company had first sold China raw Indian cotton, but by the early nineteenth century the Chinese appetite for imported cotton had died down. Reviewing its options, the company looked at other desirable commodities to trade. Among the first that it considered was silver from the New World. British merchants had historically re-exported Chinese tea to their colonies in North America, getting silver in return and using it to pay the Qing for more tea—it was Chinese tea, after all, that the American colonists dumped overboard during the Boston Tea Party. But in the early nineteenth century, the Bolivarian revolutions halted access to South American silver, leaving the East India Company scrambling in search of another product with which to pay for the unquenchable British thirst for tea.

The opium poppy, which grew abundantly in certain regions of India, seemed to provide a perfect solution. Opium, introduced to China by the Arabs sometime between the fifth and eighth centuries, had since been used only as a medicine and even then only under strict conditions. Yet when the British marketed it to the Chinese as a consumer product—extolling its virtues and mentioning none of its hazards—opium quickly caught on and soon made addicts out of large numbers of Chinese. According to some accounts, 45 million Chinese citizens were dependent on the drug by 1850.[18] The highest rates of addiction were registered among the military and official classes, the two sectors that regulated trade with England and therefore had unfettered access to everything passing through the port of Canton. These addicts, now hopelessly tethered to the Westerners, were the same bureaucrats originally entrusted by the imperial court with the limiting of foreign influence.

Concerned, the Qing outlawed the drug, but that did little to wean the addicts; underground criminal networks soon sprang into existence, smuggling opium to all corners of the kingdom. The Qing protested, and the British became testy; without opium, they had nothing with which to pay for tea. Her Majesty's subjects realized the devastating outcome of their insistent trade: the East India Company, itself aware of opium's evils, had taken the unusual step of renting private vessels to deliver the drug to China's shores, thus sparing its ships and sailors the moral taint of the drug trade even as its directors continued their efforts to expand the sordid business. Collision was inevitable.

In early 1839, Lin Zexu, a high-ranking Qing official, arrived in Canton. Bearing the title of imperial commissioner, he had a single interest, to put an immediate end to the opium trade. He waited until late spring, and then ordered all foreign merchants to surrender all the opium in their possession. To signal his resolve, he had his small band of troops confine the Westerners in their compounds until they surrendered their supplies. Charles Elliot, the British superintendent of trade and a naval officer with a punctilious respect for rank and protocol, promptly ordered the merchants to comply with Lin's demands. Upon seizing the entirety of the stock, Lin ceremoniously dumped it into the South China Sea.

Drily, Elliot asked Lin to pay for the destroyed goods, imagining he might have stumbled upon a system that would give both sides satisfaction: the British would receive their payment without suffering the pangs of guilt associated with the consequences of the opium trade, and the Chinese would once and for all rid themselves of the drug's menace. But the obstinate Lin refused to pay. Opium, he told Elliot, was contraband, a fact clearly communicated to the British, and therefore no compensation was required. An officer by training and disposition, Elliot needed no further excuse. He declared war.

The news reached Beijing quickly. At first, Emperor Daoguang wasn't worried. The British, he said, were "an insignificant and detestable race."[19] But the tough talk soon gave way to terror, as British forces, equipped with modern weapons, routed the disorganized Chinese. By 1841, Elliot had occupied the island of Hong Kong, and then proceeded to capture the forts protecting Canton's harbor. By August of 1842, the bewildered Chinese had no choice but to surrender.

Meeting in the northern city of Nanjing to discuss a peace treaty, the Qing officials agreed to terms that would forever bind the empire. In addition to paying Britain the princely sum of $21 million in reparations, China ceded Hong Kong to the British crown, and agreed to accept a British "chief high officer" in Beijing. The treaty further stipulated that "the Subordinates of both countries [communicate] on a footing of perfect equality."[20] The Canton system was discontinued, the Cohong disbanded, and additional ports opened up for Western trade. The treaty also granted to British and American citizens "extraterritoriality" status, whereby those residing in China would be subject to their native laws and regulations and immune from the punishments and justice of Chinese magistrates. Finally, expecting the surge in commercial competition that the opening of new ports was likely to unleash, Britain insisted on being christened China's "most favored nation," so that "should the Emperor hereafter, from any cause whatever, be pleased to grant additional privileges or immunities to any of the Subjects or Citizens of such Foreign Countries, the same privileges and immunities will be extended to and enjoyed by British Subjects."[21]

This was the starting pistol that Europe's other nations were waiting to hear. The ravenous Westerners raced to China's gates. The following decades saw England, France, Germany, Russia, Portugal, Italy, and, to a lesser extent, the United States competing with one another in China, engaging in trade, as well as creating provocations and threatening the Qing with war in order to gain major concessions.

In the wake of the humiliating defeat, with the already wobbly Chinese economy further taxed by the ransom now owed the British, anti-Qing sentiments flared across the country. Dissidents easily struck the chord of ethnic resentment; whereas the majority of the population were Han Chinese, the Qing were Manchu, outsiders from the far north. In the seventeenth century, the founders of the Qing dynasty had come together under the Manchu banner, charged toward the capital, and eventually unseated the Ming emperor. Seizing power, the Qing forced their subjects to adopt their signature hairstyle, ordering all Chinese men to shave the hair above their foreheads and grow a long queue or face execution: "Keep your hair and lose your head," one popular saying advised, "or lose your hair and keep your head."[22] The Han had initially revolted against this foreign custom, but their resistance was quelled, and, for the most part, the Qing's ethnic identity did not present an issue, because the ensuing decades and centuries brought relative stability and prosperity.

As conditions deteriorated, however, it became increasingly fashionable to attribute China's misfortunes to the Qing's immigrant ancestry and the displeasure their foreign rule caused the heavens. No group capitalized on this ethnic mistrust better than the Taiping, a well-organized band of rebels who, between 1850 and 1864, nearly brought about the collapse of the imperial system.

The Taiping, a name that means Great Peace, was founded by Hong Xiuquan, a village teacher from the southern Canton Province who had repeatedly failed the imperial examination. Incensed at the Qing for failing to recognize his talent, Hong fell ill. When he rose from his sickbed, he claimed to have had a vision in which Jesus Christ appeared, identified Hong as his long-lost brother, and ordered him to rid China of the foreigners who bedeviled it, which Hong took to mean not the British but rather the interloping Manchu. Drawing on his own ethnic sub-group, the Hakka, for support, Hong's inflammatory anti-Qing rhetoric attracted converts to his movement, which advocated a potent ideological cocktail of Christianity and egalitarian ideas. The Manchus, railed one typical Taiping tract, wanted nothing more than to "reduce the number of us Chinese" and had "unleashed grasping officials and corrupt subordinates to strip the people of their flesh until men and women weep by the roadside . . . the rich hold the power and the heroes despair."[23]

In February 1850, Emperor Daoguang died. He was succeeded by Emperor Xianfeng, who inherited the mounting rebellion. By the end of the year, the Taiping had ten thousand troops at their disposal. The following January, on Hong's thirty-seventh birthday, he declared himself *tianwang*, or heavenly king, of a new dynasty he christened the Heavenly Kingdom of Great Peace. This flourish of imperial rhetoric was one his followers could easily understand. With Hong's radical advocacy of land collectivization and his fierce resistance to archaic customs like the binding of women's feet, the Taiping leader offered himself to his followers as another in a long line of providential monarchs, holier and more just than the hated Qing. The frequent references to the heavens were not lost on anyone; in declaring himself *tianwang*, Hong was attempting to snatch the divine mandate away from the corrupt hands of the emperor's wealthy mandarins. "Those with millions owe us their money," went one popular Taiping song, "Those who are half poor–half rich can till their fields. / Those with ambitions but no cash should go with us: / Broke or hungry, Heaven will keep you well."[24]

Such inspired lyrics, traditional enough to resonate with the uneducated and underprivileged, worked their religious magic on the disenfranchised masses. By 1853, the Taiping army numbered more than 700,000 soldiers. After a fierce battle, Hong and his men established control over the city of Nanjing, which they promptly renamed Tianjing, or Heavenly Capital. Hong was taken into his new fiefdom on a golden sedan chair carried by sixteen of his followers. He wore a crown and wrapped himself in a silk robe embroidered with a mighty dragon. He was surrounded by his four lieutenants, warriors who referred to themselves as the four kings. All were in their midtwenties or early thirties.

The scholars of the Forbidden City in Beijing searched for answers, scouring the ancient texts for solutions. Hong's forces seemed to grow exponentially, and his army seized some of China's wealthiest provinces, taking with them almost 90 percent of the empire's tax revenue. With the pendulum of war swinging wildly, granting victory now to this side and then to the other, China's towns and villages were rife with violence and suspicion. In Canton, the imperial governor, Ye Mingchen, won a reputation for brutality even by the standards of that vicious period. Morbidly obese and vindictive, Ye, who hailed from the inland city of Hankou, had been sent to govern the southern port city in accordance with the rule of avoidance. As he was settling in to his new position, the Taiping set fire to Ye's vast properties back in Hankou. Furious, Ye swore to take vengeance. Ye had control over areas that were the native districts of Hong and many of his most loyal followers, and he lost no time enacting his retribution. He accused a great number of citizens of sedition, sentenced them to death, and then offered them the opportunity to redeem their lives for a fee. Those who could, paid with silver, copper, real estate, and livestock; those who could not were killed.

By the time Yung Wing settled in at Vrooman's house in Canton, Ye's men had beheaded 75,000 people.

Yung stumbled onto the scene of this genocide almost by accident:

> One day, out of curiosity, I ventured to walk over to the [execution ground]. But, oh! What a sight! The ground was perfectly drenched with human blood. On both sides of the driveway were to be seen headless human trunks, piled up in heaps, waiting to be taken away for burial. But no provision had been made to facilitate their removal.
>
> The execution was carried on on a larger scale than had been expected, and no provision had been made to find a place large enough to bury all the bodies. There they were, left exposed to a burning sun. The temperature stood from morning to night in midsummer steadily at 90° Fahrenheit, and sometimes higher. The atmosphere within a radius of two thousand yards of the execution ground was heavily charged with the poisonous and pestilential vapor that was reeking from the ground already over-saturated with blood and from the heaps of corpses which had been left behind for at least two days, and which showed signs of rapid decomposition. It was a wonder to me that no virulent epidemic had sprung up from such

an infectious spot to decimate the compact population of the city of Canton. It was a fortunate circumstance that at least a deep and extensive ravine, located in the far-off outskirts of the western part of the city, was found, which was at once converted into a sepulchral receptacle into which this vast human hecatomb was dumped. It was said that no earth was needed to be thrown over these corpses to cover them up; the work was accomplished by countless swarms of worms of a reddish hue and of an appearance that was perfectly hideous and revolting.[25]

Seeing the rotting corpses, Yung walked home as quickly as he could, doing his best not to think about the horrors he had just witnessed. The images of the blood and the soil and the worms were too vivid for him to forget. That evening, he refused dinner. That night, he futilely tried to fall asleep. All he could think about were the headless bodies.

The Foreigners

With time, as the stark images of executed innocents receded, Yung's shock and anger gave way to more rational thoughts. The massacre, he was convinced, was indicative of the Qing's corrupt system, a lumbering bureaucracy that allowed demons like Ye to do as they pleased and that sentenced the vast majority of Chinese to live at the mercy of selfish, sadistic officials. Yung had never given much thought to the Taiping or their cause, but now he felt empathy for Hong and his men. "I thought then," he wrote later, "that the Taiping rebels had ample grounds to justify their attempt to overthrow the Manchu régime. My sympathies were thoroughly enlisted in their favor and I thought seriously of making preparations to join the Taiping rebels."[1]

For a few days, Yung toyed with the idea of heading west to Nanjing and offering his services to defend the Heavenly Kingdom. Standing in front of the mirror, he twirled his queue between his fingers and imagined what he would look like if he cut off the symbol of acquiescence to the Manchus and instead let his hair grow long like the Taiping, in accordance with ancient Confucian tradition. But Yung was no rebel; his collegiate affinity for composition had trained him to see all sides of any given issue and then argue his position with eloquence and reason. He was also a devoted son, who couldn't stomach the thought of telling his aged mother, who had been widowed when Yung's father was killed in the Opium War less than a decade ago, that she might be bereaved once again. The best way to overcome his rage, he told himself repeatedly, was to focus on the reason why he had come to Canton—namely, to relearn his language as quickly and as efficiently as he could.

For six months, Yung concentrated on the native tongue he had forgotten, its characters and phrasing and grammar. He studied furiously, taking pleasure in once again engaging in an academic pursuit, a fact that seemed to bring a measure of comfort and order to his otherwise unstable world. More than once, he peeked out the window at the sweltering city, closed his eyes, and imagined that he was again in Connecticut, where life had seemed full of possibilities. When he was finally able to chat with Canton's merchants in fluent Chinese without a trace of self-consciousness, he realized he was ready to pursue a career. But which one?

Yung considered his options. He was educated but poor, ready but uncertain as to what path to take. Had he had any money, he could have simply bought himself a title and grown rich: increasingly, more and more of the Qing's aspiring bureaucrats bypassed the dreaded imperial exam with a hefty bribe. Because he was a pauper, his choices were limited. More, however, than wondering what to do, Yung was troubled by the question of his personal allegiances. Much as he commanded himself not to dwell on the horrors he had witnessed at the execution grounds, certain thoughts took hold in his mind. He was a loyal son of China, of that he had no doubt, but if all China could present him with were the bumbling, murderous Qing on the one hand and the violent rebels on the other, he might as well cast his lot with the foreigners.

It was a sensible decision. Even having mastered Chinese, Yung was never as comfortable with his native tongue as he was with English; the New England lilt had become the natural inflection of his speech. His friends, with few exceptions, were all American or British, and he had grown closer to the Christian Gospels than to Confucianism's archaic texts and ancient edicts. Confucianism, he sometimes meditated, offered a life governed by ritual and burdened by deference to everyone from elders to emperors, while Christianity, for all of its riddles and difficulties, put the onus on the individual. It was China that was obsessed with *cai*, but America that allowed its sons to fully explore the true limits of their talent. Despite having lost a father to the Western invasion, Yung held no grudges. He decided to cast his lot with the Americans. And no man seemed better suited to help him than Dr. Peter Parker.

Parker was the closest thing the United States had to an official emissary to the Qing court. A Presbyterian minister and a physician, he received both his theological and his medical training at Yale. He considered his interests to be intertwined: medicine, he was fond of saying, was "the handmaid of religious truth."[2] Arriving in Canton immediately after his graduation in 1834, Parker opened an ophthalmic hospital, specializing in diseases of the eye and bodily tumors.

Two decades later, Parker, fluent in Chinese and highly regarded by some of China's most powerful officials on account of his medical pursuits, was appointed delegate to the Qing court by President Franklin Pierce, who instructed the doctor to try to get as many economic concessions out of the Chinese as they were willing to make. Parker, a devout Christian more interested in conversions than in currency, was not an especially hard-nosed negotiator; he found himself more focused on making the acquaintance of interesting people than on wrangling over treaties. When Yung introduced himself and asked for a job, Parker immediately agreed to hire him, even though there was little work for his fellow Yale man to do. Parker felt that Yung, comfortable in both cultures, might be a valuable asset. He offered him a modest salary of fifteen dollars a month, which Yung gratefully accepted. He was now Parker's personal secretary.

More than having the gainful employment, Yung was thrilled to be in the service of an influential man. He was still a product of the traditional Chinese system, and as such believed that the best way for a man with abilities and aspirations to advance in his pursuits was to be noticed by an established official who understood *cai* and could open doors. Working for Parker, Yung imagined, provided just such an opportunity. It would put him in touch with both the court's mandarins and the West's merchants and might lead to prospects down the line.

That dream, however, died quickly. For all of his goodwill, Parker simply hadn't enough to offer an ambitious and educated young man like Yung, who soon found himself eager to move on from secretarial work. With Parker's blessing, he left Canton and returned to Hong Kong, where he once again stayed with the newspaper editor Shortrede, his friend and benefactor. Through the latter's connections, Yung was awarded an internship at the Hong Kong Supreme Court, a position that paid seventy-five dollars a month and that promised more career possibilities.

The law, Shortrede advised Yung, was not a bad path for an enterprising young fellow to pursue. It was as good a route as any to government work and would allow Yung to meet a variety of influential people. The best way to learn the law and gain experience, Shortrede advised, was to closely study the practice of a local barrister; in addition to Yung's internship at the supreme court, Shortrede suggested an apprenticeship with Mr. Parson, an attorney with whom he was friendly. Delighted, Yung embarked on his new career with high hopes.

These, too, were soon shattered. No matter that he spoke perfect English and dressed in Western suits, never mind his love of Shakespeare or his knowledge of Greek history—when Hong Kong's British barristers looked at Yung, all they saw was a Chinese man butting his way into a club to which he could never belong. Taking out an ad in the *China Mail*, a group of prominent lawyers argued that Yung must not be allowed to practice law; if he became an attorney, they reasoned, he was all but guaranteed to secure both British and Chinese business, given his undue advantage as a bilingual practitioner. Their argument, of course, was not without its colonialist underpinnings: having won Hong Kong in battle, the resident British saw the

island as their exclusive property, not as a meeting place in which
to partner with the Chinese.

Devastated, Yung prepared to defend himself, to summon his
verbal skill and argue that it was preposterous to believe that one
man, no matter how gifted, could somehow deprive an entire
community of barristers of their jobs. But he lacked the time.
Other matters demanded his attention. The newly appointed
British attorney general, Thomas Chisholm Anstey, having
initially supported Yung's bid to become an attorney, quickly
turned into a bitter foe. The reason is not altogether clear: Yung
believed that Anstey wanted to secure his services himself, and
was livid when Yung apprenticed himself to Parson instead.
Whatever the cause, Anstey soon began to find fault with Yung's
work, claiming that his translations of legal documents were
subpar. A baffled and offended Yung had little choice but to quit.
He sought solace with Parson, telling himself that no matter the
loss of wages, he could at least count on the solid training given
him by the friendly attorney. But Parson was made of weaker
stuff; seeing his colleagues denigrate Yung, Parson didn't want
to be associated with Yung and soon let him go.

For the second time in a few months, Yung's hopes were
dashed. Even worse, the reconciliatory dream he had once had,
the one in which he could happily cast his lot with the foreigners,
was gone. From the moment he had caught that football at Yale
five years before, he increasingly imagined himself as belonging to the same caste as his classmates, the fortunate sons of
America's white, Protestant, affluent elite. But as the barristers
in Hong Kong were all too eager to remind him, he was none of

those things. Having been rejected in Hong Kong, Yung had no choice but to return once again to the mainland.

Walking purposelessly along Hong Kong's harbor before departing, Yung befriended a Bostonian sea captain who promised him a free trip to Shanghai. The city sounded like a perfect destination. Yung was well aware that his most, maybe his only, valuable skill was his command of English. He thought there was probably no better place on the mainland than Shanghai, with its many foreigners, for him to ply his trade.

Arriving in the city, Yung presented himself at the Imperial Customs Translating Department and was hired on the spot. His salary was small but sufficient, paid in Mexican dollars: valued for its purity and consistency, the foreign silver coin was the strongest currency in town. Despite the promise of steady employment, within a few days he was bored. There was not much he was required to do; frustrated, he resolved to hang on. Losing three jobs in one year was a bit too much, and he passed the hours reading British and American literary classics.

His colleagues, however, had other ideas about how officials should pass their time. In the fine tradition of low-level regional clerks, they supplemented their earnings with the systematic solicitation of graft. Yung was equally terrified, enraged, and driven to despair. For the first month or two, he did his best to politely skirt the issue and somehow avoid partaking in the scheme without appearing to disapprove of the avarice of his fellow translators. They, however, soon made it clear that if he wished to keep his position at the customs office, he had better forgo his principles and extend his hand.

Yung refused. He was raised to believe that proper government is selfless government, and feared nothing more than being tainted with corruption's stain. At wit's end, Yung called on the chief commissioner of customs, H. N. Lay, and asked him what the chances were for an American-educated Chinese man like himself to receive a promotion. No Chinese-born translator, Lay replied matter-of-factly, would ever be promoted to any position of power. Immediately, Yung handed in his resignation. The chief commissioner, however, refused to accept it. Thinking Yung was merely trying to negotiate for a hefty raise, he offered to double his salary. Years later, Yung wrote,

> It did not occur to him, that there was at least one Chinaman who valued a clean reputation and an honest character more than money; that being an educated man, I saw no reason why I should not be given the same chances to rise in the service of the Chinese government as an Englishman, nor why my individuality should not be recognized and respected in every walk of life. He little thought that I had aspirations even higher than his, and that I did not care to associate myself with a pack of Custom-house interpreters and inspectors, who were known to take bribes; that a man who expects others to respect him, must first respect himself.[3]

Dignified but once again unemployed, Yung was distraught. He allowed himself to entertain the bitterest thoughts. Perhaps he was too much of an idealist to survive in the competitive climate of the time. He couldn't imagine being any other way.

"We are not called into being simply to drudge for an animal existence," he wrote later. "I had had to work hard for my education, and I felt that I ought to make the most of what little I had, not so much to benefit myself individually as to make it a blessing common to my race."[4]

Members of his race having rejected him just as the foreigners had, Yung decided that his only chance at success lay not in attempting to ingratiate himself with one suspicious bureaucracy or another but in going into business for himself and amassing a fortune that would shield him from sharp tongues and narrow minds. A position with a small firm of British silk and tea merchants ended when the firm, mismanaged into bankruptcy, dissolved. Attending the auction of his former employer's furniture, Yung stood in the back of the room, looking sadly at the objects that had once represented, however briefly, the possibility of a new life for him. The crowd consisted of foreigners and Chinese. Standing next to Yung was a tall and boisterous Scotsman. Yung had seen the man before; he was employed by local British traders and was one of those boorish foreigners for whom China was a playground and its customs the source of dumb amusement.

Spotting Yung's queue, the Scotsman chuckled. He fumbled for something in his pocket, produced a few cotton balls, and tied them to Yung's carefully braided hair, snickering as he went along and motioning for his friends to observe the spectacle. Not one for confrontation, Yung smiled politely and asked the Scotsman to untie the cotton balls from his queue. But the Scotsman refused. A Chinese man, he believed, had no business addressing a Westerner as an equal. He turned his body toward Yung, folded his arms, and shot Yung a scornful look. Yung was no longer smiling. As calmly and firmly as he could, he repeated his request: untie my queue, untie it now.

The Scotsman punched Yung in the mouth. Though the Scotsman was large, his movements were clumsy. Yung struck back, hitting the Scotsman between the mouth and nose. Blood streamed down the man's face. Confused, the Scotsman stumbled about, finally managing to grasp Yung's arm. He squeezed Yung's wrist as tightly as he could, contemplating his next move. Yung prepared to kick the man away, ending the tussle once and for all.

Just then, the head partner of the dissolved firm entered the circle around Yung and the Scotsman and separated the two. "Do you want to fight?" yelled some rowdy Brit in the crowd. Yung turned around and, addressing no one in particular, said, "No, I was only defending myself. Your friend insulted me and added injury to insult. I took him for a gentleman, but he has proved himself a blackguard."[5]

It was a stinging indictment. Sensing danger, Yung slipped away. As he was leaving, he heard a voice he recognized as that of the British consul in Shanghai, saying, with more respect than rage, "The young man was a little too fiery; if he had not taken the law into his own hands, he could have brought suit for assault and battery in the consular court, but since he has already retaliated and his last remark before the crowd has inflicted a deeper cut to his antagonist than the blow itself, he has lost the advantage of a suit."[6]

A lawsuit, however, was far from Yung's mind. As the adrenaline rush faded, he realized the full meaning of what he had done. He hadn't been in Shanghai very long, but it was clear that the local Chinese population, awed by the foreigners in their midst, treated the Westerners with meek deference, and that the Westerners, in turn, came to view the locals as subservient creatures. Striking back at the Scotsman, therefore, was a radical act, an act of defiance, an act of liberation. "The time will soon come, however," Yung wrote in his diary, "when the people of China will be so educated and enlightened as to know what their rights are, public and private, and to have the moral courage to assert and defend them whenever they are invaded."[7]

Although he was still unemployed, Yung was no longer dismayed. His punch was the talk of Shanghai. The city's educated Chinese revered him, and its Western elite looked at him with a grudging respect. Everywhere he went, whispers followed. Merchants and officials alike were curious about this feisty new arrival, said to be well educated. When the head of one of Shanghai's leading British firms died, Yung was asked to translate his epitaph. "My name," he later wrote, "began to be known among the Chinese, not as a fighter this time, but as a Chinese student educated in America."[8]

Publicity is rarely without its perks, and Yung's desk was soon cluttered with solicitations. He received more offers for translation work than he could accept, and even though he had neither title nor fortune, he was welcomed among Shanghai's elites, Chinese and Westerner alike, as a desirable guest. One member of this elevated circle, the British director of a large tea-trading firm, approached Yung with a job offer. His firm, he told Yung, had just received new business exporting tea to the Japanese market and needed a comprador, a clerk who could serve as intermediary between the local farmers and the British merchants.

The prospect of a steady and considerable paycheck appealed to Yung, but the more he thought about the offer, the more he realized that he had to turn it down. He was a Yale man, he told himself, and he would discredit his alma mater if he were to accept a position, however profitable, that involved more than a bit of subservience. He was also a proud citizen of China, and a comprador, by definition, was an agent of the Western colonizers, "the head servant of servants," as he later put it, "in an English establishment."[9] Thanking the director profusely, Yung told the stunned Brit that he had to refuse the offer. There were cases, Yung told the man quietly but firmly, in which a man, subdued by circumstances, had to accept a menial position in order to survive; but that, he added, was not yet the case for him. Not quite knowing what to make of the strong-willed, independent Chinese man, the British director, curious, asked Yung whether there was any other position in the firm he would consider. Yung smiled shyly and replied he would like to trade tea and silk, either for a steady salary or on commission. The director listened intently. Yung, he later told a friend, was poor and proud, traits, he noted, that often went hand in hand. But there was no way to ignore his tenacity, confidence, and intelligence. Shaking Yung's hand, the director offered him a job as a trader.

Yung's new position sent him deep into the countryside, far from the port cities to which he was accustomed. On occasion, his path took him through provinces held by the Taiping rebels. There, he had an opportunity to witness firsthand the earthly failures of the Heavenly Kingdom. Often as cruel as the Manchus they fought so bitterly—Hong was fond of saying that all who resisted his soldiers were "idolatrous demons, and we kill them without sparing"[10]—the Taiping could also be just as incompetent as the empire when it came to erecting the necessary edifices of commerce and trade. With a great deal of tea in their possession and little knowledge of how to bring it to market, Hong's men consistently left millions of tons of leaves to rot. Yung took it upon himself to negotiate the purchase of these orphaned crops, package them, and ship them to the coast, where they would be loaded onto ships headed to England. To that end, he called on his early sympathies for the rebels, expressing an understanding for their cause that helped him succeed brilliantly in his trade.

Yung's attention, however, was soon drawn to the Taiping for other reasons. In 1856, a minor maritime scuffle led to a rapid conflagration that soon turned into the Second Opium War. During the new hostilities, Britain pummeled Canton, while a joint British and French force laid siege to Tianjin, just east of Beijing. Outflanking the Qing defenses, the foreigners had a clear path to Beijing. The emperor fled to his hunting grounds in Jehol, beyond the Great Wall, while the 80,000-men-strong army, unpaid and undisciplined, roamed the streets of the capital in confusion, with no clear orders and no one in charge. Approaching the imperial Summer Palace, just five miles outside the walls of the Forbidden City, British troops were ordered to burn the compound. One of the soldiers, Charles Gordon, who would later become a great ally of the empire, wrote to his mother from the palace's smoldering gardens, "You can scarcely imagine the beauty and the magnificence of the places we burnt. It made one's heart sore to burn them; in fact, these palaces were so large, and we were so pressed for time, that we could not plunder them carefully. . . . It was wretchedly demoralising work for an army."[11]

With the empire on its knees and the barbarians at its gates, the British could have easily laid claim to China as they had to India. But the Middle Kingdom, they realized, was too vast, too unruly, too desired by other nations for proper colonization. The British army was ordered to remain outside the Forbidden City's walls, and Emperor Xianfeng was entreated to return to the throne and negotiate yet another humiliating treaty. Only thirty years old, the monarch had seen more than he could take. By 1861, he was gravely ill. He had but one son, a five-year-old born to a lowly concubine. As he lay dying, the concubine rushed the toddler to the emperor's deathbed, where the fading ruler blessed the boy and named him the next sovereign. Moments later, Xianfeng drew his last breath and ceded power to the boy emperor Tongzhi.

For many Chinese, even those traditionally unconcerned with the goings-on in Beijing, the five years that separated the outbreak of the war and the death of the monarch were a particularly grim period. Radical ideas were once more in vogue. Yung, now a well-off and well-known merchant, was not immune to the mounting talk of revolution that stirred men of his class and education. The empire was in disarray. It was time, Yung decided, to consider the Taiping once again.

In the fall of 1859, Yung, accompanied by a few Western and Chinese friends, had set out on a trip to Nanjing, the Taiping capital. Gunboats lurked in the waters, and rumors of nearby atrocities frightened the crew. For a day or two, Yung and his colleagues sat perched on the deck, alert and sleepless. But nothing happened. With each boat they passed—some manned by scraggly rebels, others by slightly better equipped imperial troops—it became clear that, conflict or not, their journey would not be interrupted. Yung's relief soon turned to sarcasm: with the Chinese, even warfare was conducted with incompetence. With the threat of harassment dissipated, he was free to observe the countryside. All along the river's banks, fertile fields stood uncultivated, gathering moss, the sweet stench of decomposing crops permeating the air. Instead of young men working the land, Yung saw only old and bent peasants, baskets in hand, peddling eggs, oranges, small cakes, a few wilting vegetables, and a bit of pork. Their faces had been aged by war, by despair, by time. More even than the headless corpses he had seen in Canton, these villagers, the living dead, filled Yung with dread.

After nearly two weeks of sailing from port to port and appealing to a long succession of indifferent lieutenants for right of passage into the rebel capital, Yung and his entourage finally reached Nanjing. There, they had an appointment with Hong Rengan, Hong Xiuquan's cousin and one of the Heavenly Kingdom's most influential officials. Yung had met him years before, in Hong Kong, where they were both young men struggling to establish their careers. The years, Yung learned upon meeting his old friend, had been good to Rengan. He had exchanged his modest Western suits for princely robes, which was no mere affectation, for the heavenly monarch had given Rengan the title *ganwang*, or shield prince. Still, this newfound nobility did little to tame Rengan's jovial demeanor, and he greeted Yung warmly, eager to catch up with his old friend and interested to hear of Yung's ups and downs, his exploits and successes. They chatted for a long while, exchanging pleasantries, sharing anecdotes, and swapping stories of acquaintances from Hong Kong. Then the prince turned serious. He looked at Yung intently and asked him, quietly and directly, whether his allegiance lay with the Taiping or with the empire.

It was a loaded question. Yung looked around the room, pausing for a moment before he answered. If he sided with the Taiping, he would please the prince but put himself at risk. Some of his colleagues could easily return to Shanghai and let it be known, inadvertently or otherwise, that Yung was a rebel at heart. On the other hand, expressing loyalty to the Qing was sure to harden the protecting prince's heart and shut his mind. Yung chose the most difficult path of all: he told the truth. He was not casting his lot with any party, Yung told the prince, but he was nevertheless thrilled to pay his respects to the Heavenly Kingdom and wanted to find out for himself the conditions in Nanjing. The prince admired his friend's candor and asked him to speak frankly; what, he inquired, would Yung suggest the Taiping do in order to thrive and subdue the emperor?

It was the opportunity Yung had waited for. Having thought about this question often, he came equipped with a seven-point plan for the revitalization of the struggling rebellion, which he now produced from his pocket. Matter-of-factly, he read each point out loud:

1. To organize an army on scientific principles.
2. To establish a military school for the training of competent military officers.
3. To establish a naval school for a navy.

4. To organize a civil government with able and experienced men to act as advisers in the different departments of administration.
5. To establish a banking system, and to determine on a standard of weight and measure.
6. To establish an educational system of graded schools for the people, making the Bible one of the text books.
7. To organize a system of industrial schools.[12]

Yung, in other words, wanted Nanjing to become New Haven. If his proposal pleased the rebels, he told the prince, he would quit his profitable position as a trader and join the Taiping, overseeing the reforms himself. The prince nodded intently and asked for some time to consider Yung's proposals.

Two days later, they met again. This time, there was little need for small talk or loyalty tests. The prince was firmly convinced of the merits of Yung's proposal. Having himself resided in Hong Kong, he knew very well the full measure of foreign influence on China. He agreed with Yung wholeheartedly that the only way to defeat the colonizers was to educate the Chinese people in matters of technology and allow them to apply their talents in a well-organized and regulated marketplace. Yung's proposals were just what the Taiping, and China, needed, the prince said, but he added that he lacked the authority to approve such far-reaching measures on his own. His fellow Taiping princes were out fighting the imperials, but when they returned, he would put Yung's ideas before them and do his best to see them approved. To ensure his friend's safe passage back to Shanghai, the prince provided Yung with a silk document, an official passport of the Heavenly Kingdom, and promised to be in touch.

Returning home, Yung waited for weeks, then months, but no word came from Nanjing. The silk passport, however, served him well, allowing him to travel even deeper into Taiping territory, extract more tea, earn more money, and further bolster his reputation. His big break, he thought to himself, would come eventually. Until then, all he could do was work and wait.

Self-Strengthening

Yung's routine was soon interrupted by the arrival of a letter that terrified and intrigued him. In 1863, Yung was contacted by an old friend who informed him that Zeng Guofan had requested to see him immediately. That, Yung thought, was probably not good news. Zeng Guofan was the governor-general of Hunan and the leader of the imperial war on the Taiping. "On the receipt of the letter," Yung later wrote, "I was in a quandary and asked myself many questions: What could such a distinguished man want of me? Had he got wind of my late visit to [Nanjing] and of my later enterprise to the district of Taiping for the green tea that was held there by the rebels? . . . [D]id he want, under a polite invitation, to trap me and have my head off?"[1] Striking as deferential a tone as he possibly could, Yung wrote back. He thanked Zeng profusely for his invitation, but replied that since the high season for tea packing was upon him, he could not possibly abdicate his professional duties and make the trip to meet his excellency. Two months later, another letter arrived, this time from another of Zeng's underlings, he, too, an old acquaintance of Yung's. Sensing Yung's apprehensions, the man wrote that Zeng had heard of Yung's American education, of his loyalty to China, and of his desire to see the homeland thrive. Zeng, the letter stated, was interested in machinery and wanted Yung's help procuring and operating production facilities.

Some of Yung's anxieties were soothed, but he was still not altogether certain of the mandarin's intentions. He wrote back, again thanked Zeng politely, and once more promised that as soon as the tea season ended, he would report to Zeng in person and do his best to assist him.

Almost immediately, both of Yung's acquaintances in Zeng's service wrote Yung once more. The governor, they stated bluntly, was not asking for Yung's help; he was commanding his cooperation and expected him to abandon his trade and report immediately for government work. Yung had no choice. Besides, his acquaintances' tone suggested that Zeng, finally, might just be the patron whom Yung had always sought, an eminent and intelligent official who recognized Yung's talent and was willing to harness it in the service of reform.

As he traveled to meet the governor, Yung had plenty of time to deepen his familiarity with Zeng's reputation. Having passed the highest rank of the imperial exam at the uncommonly young age of twenty-seven, Zeng emerged almost immediately as one of China's most competent bureaucrats. Not long after embarking on his career as a Qing official, he wrote to the throne and suggested that the very system that had allowed his rise was flawed at its core. Officials, he wrote, were being appointed for their "smart demeanor and smooth speech"[2] rather than for any real abilities in the marketplace or on the battlefield. Faced with the great threat of the Taiping, he continued, many Qing official-scholars did little but devote themselves to the Confucian classics. "How can anyone who can read and write," he concluded, "remain quietly seated, hands in sleeves, without thinking of doing something about it?"[3]

But Zeng's passion for action never undermined his appreciation for the Confucian teachings he followed. This made him an unlikely mandarin; whereas most of his peers engaged in a merciless pursuit of wealth and did whatever they could to deflect any hint of blame, Zeng had very different advice for his lieutenants. "If you win a battle," he told them, reflecting his own unorthodox beliefs, "shift the praise to others. If they lose a battle, go to their aid."[4] The secret to military victory, Zeng wrote repeatedly, "lies in mind and not in weapons."[5]

A classic literary scholar, Zeng nonetheless proved himself a very adept military commander. He was fond of pincer moves, and, true to his Confucian faith, he obeyed the principle of *ren* and treated his soldiers with the obligation of a father to his children, demanding filial loyalty and lavishing subordinates with praise and care. Rather than recruit sycophantic strongmen and peasants, he stacked his council with thinkers and approached battles with a high degree of premeditation and analysis. His dedication and wisdom served to counteract the Taiping propaganda that the Qing acted against the interests of the Chinese nation. For all these reasons, Zeng was soon appointed governor-general of Hunan, a position he used to create a vast network of associates and underlings who would go on to fill some of China's highest-ranking positions.[6]

Arriving in Anqing, the town in Anhui where Zeng established his base, Yung was greeted by two of his old acquaintances, Zeng's lieutenants who had written and urged him to
come to meet their commander. Enthusiastically, the two told
Yung that Zeng had expressed the utmost interest in him and
had been talking about meeting him for the past six months.

This made Yung uneasy. Could it be, he wondered, that all
Zeng wanted was to satisfy his curiosity and meet, as Yung put it
years later, "a native of China made into a veritable Occidental"?[7]
Was he a mere object of amusement, to be put on display and
cast away soon thereafter? The familiar dread crept in. But it was
too late to do anything about it, Yung realized. He was already in
Zeng's quarters, and he might as well dispel all those worrisome
thoughts, at least until he met the man.

The day after his arrival in Anqing, Yung reported to Zeng's
compound. He presented the guard with his calling card and a
few moments later was ushered past the anteroom and into the
great man's chamber. The two exchanged ceremonial greetings.
Then Zeng sat down at his massive desk. Eyeing Yung silently,
he smiled. Yung could sense the governor's eyes scanning his
every inch, and he twitched uncomfortably in his seat, wondering whether anything about his appearance struck the governor
as odd or displeasing. Finally, Zeng looked Yung in the eye with
a steely gaze and began questioning him.

"How long were you abroad?"

"I was absent from China eight years in pursuit of a Western
education," Yung replied, formally, rigidly.

"Would you like to be a soldier in charge of a company?"

What, Yung wondered, was the right answer to that question?

"I should be pleased to head one," he answered, "if I had been fitted for it. I have never studied military science."

"I should judge from your looks," Zeng said, "you would make a fine soldier, for I can see from your eyes that you are brave and can command."

"I thank your Excellency for the compliment. I may have the courage of a soldier, but I certainly lack military training and experience, and on that account I may not be able to meet Your Excellency's expectations."[8]

The governor asked how old Yung was and whether he was married. Then Zeng began to sip his tea, which customarily meant that the interview had ended and the guest was at liberty to leave. Yung took a few sips from his own cup, then rose and bade Zeng farewell. On his way out, relieved of the pressures of the interview, he had time to consider Zeng's features. At around five feet, nine inches tall, muscular and broad-shouldered, he looked far more vigorous than his sixty years would suggest. The thick side-whiskers protruding from his beard gave him an air of gravity and authority. Yung returned to his room, not knowing whether he had impressed Zeng or disappointed him.

Almost immediately, Yung's old friends called on him and demanded an account of his interview with Zeng. He replied in detail, repeating to them the governor's questions as well as Yung's own answers. His friends smiled and laughed, telling him that the conversation seemed to have proceeded splendidly; by asking him whether he had any interest in the military, the friends told Yung, Zeng simply tried to gauge Yung's interest in becoming part of China's official class. By replying as he did, Yung presented himself as loyal, the sort of man who put the needs of the empire over his own aspirations. And that, they reassured him, was the sort of man Zeng respected above all.

Zeng himself, however, was silent for the next two weeks. Yung learned from his friends that Zeng's main interest was the establishment of a machine shop in China that could manufacture weapons to match or surpass those employed by the foreigners. But just what sort of machine shop none of Zeng's lieutenants knew. Implicitly at first, then bluntly, they asked Yung whether he had any idea.

In his memoirs, Yung recalls what happened next:

> I said, that as I was not an expert in the matter, my opinions or suggestions might not be worth much. . . . In a large country like China, I told them, they would need many primary or fundamental machine shops, but that after they had one (and a first-class one at that) they could make it the mother shop for reproducing others—perhaps better and more improved. If they had a number of them, it would enable them to have the shops co-operate with each other in case of need. It would be cheaper to have them reproduced and multiplied in China, I said, where labor and material were cheaper, than in Europe and America. Such was my crude idea of the subject.[9]

Yung's friends reported his answer to Zeng, and the governor soon summoned Yung to his office once again. The same ceremonial introductions took place, but this time, Zeng had only one question, blunt and pregnant. In his opinion, what would be the best thing for China to do at the present time?

Had he not been prepared by his friends, Yung would

probably have advocated a scheme similar to the one he offered the Taiping prince. But he knew the governor had his mind set on machine shops, and of machine shops Yung spoke.

"Well," Zeng said, "this is a subject quite beyond my knowledge. It would be well for you to discuss the matter with [your friends], who are more familiar with it than I am and we will decide what is best to be done."[10]

Another two weeks passed, in the course of which Zeng summoned each of Yung's friends for consultations. Finally, one of them, a man named Wha, was sent to tell Yung that the governor had given the plan the go-ahead, leaving its execution entirely up to Yung.

Wasting little time, Yung chose Kow Chang Meu, four miles northwest of Shanghai, as the location for his new shop. He received a commission as a low-level official, as well as the large sum necessary for the purchase. With that, it was time for Yung Wing to return to America.

Arriving in New York during the spring of 1864, Yung reflected on his last ocean crossing a decade earlier, at the mercy of ferocious winds and a demented captain. Now he was a wealthy merchant, relaxing aboard a comfortable steamer. More than that, Yung was traveling in the service of an important enterprise that, if carried to fruition, would reward his entire nation. Observers could conclude from the confident demeanor of the Chinese official looking over the railings of the ship that Yung Wing was, in short, a man in full.

Before leaving Shanghai, Yung had settled on a machine shop: the Putnam Machine Company of Fitchburg, Massachusetts. He assumed that he had little to do but stop by, arrange payment, and wait for the large, complex machines to be assembled. Larger events, though, intervened. Usually, Putnam's manager explained apologetically, an order like Yung's was simple enough to fill, but with the Civil War currently raging, the shop's men and assembly lines were working at full capacity on behalf of the Union army.

The war made him meditate on a fact he'd long forgotten: while at Yale, he had become a naturalized American citizen. At the time, he didn't think very much of it. China, after all, had never perceived itself as a nation-state, and citizenship was therefore a practical measure one undertook to cut down on bureaucratic wrangling. In China, his American citizenship mattered little to him, but in wartime Fitchburg, Yung thought, it carried with it a string of obligations. But duty was not the only motive for Yung: in the Southerners, he saw the torchbearers of the same narrow-minded xenophobia he had fought so bitterly in Shanghai and Hong Kong. If a fight for freedom was being waged, he decided after a few days of mulling over the issue, then he had to fight on the side of the free.

Yung had attended his ten-year college reunion soon after he had arrived in New York. There, he reacquainted himself with an old friend, William Barnes, a fellow library dweller and literary enthusiast. Yung learned that Barnes's father was James Barnes, a brigadier general in the Union army. He decided to seek him out and offer his services. While Yung was waiting for the war machinery he ordered on behalf of China, he'd fight for America. He went to Washington to offer Barnes his services as a soldier.

"Well, my young friend," Barnes said to Yung, "I thank you

very much for your offer, but since you are charged with a responsible trust to execute for the Chinese government, you had better return to Fitchburg to attend to it. We have plenty of men to serve, both as couriers and as fighting men to go to the front."[11]

A general refusing additional soldiers was a baffling thing. Yung offered Barnes some words of gratitude and returned to Massachusetts. In the spring of 1865, just a few weeks before the Civil War came to a close, the machines were built, and Yung, his contraptions in tow, boarded a ship headed home.

The China in which Yung disembarked had become a nation vastly different from the one he had left behind. During that time, Zeng had focused all of his efforts on eradicating the Taiping. He was aided by a fellow mandarin, Li Hongzhang, a stocky man with a passion and penchant for warfare. In the mannered world of Qing officialdom, Li was an anomaly, a hard-nosed achiever whose passion was strictly business.

When rebels laid siege to Shanghai in 1861, Li, unimpressed with his own motley crew of Chinese fighters, tapped an American, Frederick Townsend Ward, to aid in the city's defense. Ward raised his own army, recruiting every able-bodied Western fighter he could find. Many, like himself, were mercenaries who saw China as a vast field of conflicting, meaningless interests and an easy place to earn hard currency. Ward, who rode into battle smoking a cheroot and armed only with a riding crop, used Li's money to outfit all of his men with green turbans and spent weeks training his troops in marksmanship, a foreign concept on China's freewheeling battlefields. As they gained success after success, Ward's soldiers were soon dubbed

the Ever Victorious Army, attracting eager hordes of adventurous, unemployed local Chinese with each new conquest.

Li looked on in awe: "The rifles and cannon of several thousand foreign troops go off at the same time," he wrote to Zeng
shortly after winning the battle against the Taiping for Shanghai,
"and whatever is in the way is immediately destroyed. The shells
that explode [before] touching the ground are indeed a device
of the gods!"[12] Yet these very weapons, he realized, could be
used to suppress China. If the empire was ever to thrive, it had
to free itself from any dependence on foreigners. It needed its
own godly devices. It needed to become stronger.

From these sentiments was born the self-strengthening movement, a tide that, sometimes ebbing and sometimes flowing,
swept China through space and time, westward and forward,
away from its ritual-ridden isolation and closer to an increasingly
globalized world. A new vision of Chinese modernity emerged,
one neatly captured in the phrase *ti-yong*, a combination of the
characters for "essence" and "practical use." Li himself was a most
passionate advocate of this new philosophy of *ti-yong*, whereby
China would modernize on its own terms, incorporating the
cream of Western ingenuity and technology while maintain-
ing its own cultural sensibilities. The Chinese, he wrote to
Zeng, had "to strive for self-strengthening and not to mix with
foreigners."[13]

A few months later in Ningbo, Li became furious upon hearing that the local Chinese merchant community invited the
British and French forces to protect them against the Taiping.
He told Zeng to send Qing soldiers to Ningbo to provide security
so that the locals did not give themselves over to the Westerners.

"If China failed to strengthen itself," he warned his elderly mentor, "the calamity for the future is unthinkable."[14]

With such potential dangers in mind, Li redoubled his modernizing efforts. Within a year, he had managed to amass a force of forty thousand men, ten thousand rifles, and numerous cannons stocked with 36-pound shells. Li's new soldiers were winning the war: mismanaged and exhausted, Hong's Heavenly Kingdom suffered defeat after defeat. By June 1864, with a prolonged siege condemning Nanjing, the Taiping capital, to starvation, even Hong was reduced to clawing the earth in search of hidden roots and rotten vegetables to eat. One such bit of refuse caught his hungry eye. He ate it, fell ill, and died of food poisoning after three weeks. Despite pitched battles and ferocious skirmishing, it was a legume, and not a legion, that claimed the life of the Taiping leader. A few days after his death, the imperial forces stormed the city. On Zeng's command, they exhumed Hong's body, burned it, and shot the ashes from a cannon. It was the ultimate inglorious send-off to a war that lasted fourteen years and claimed more than twenty-five million lives. Decades later, the Taiping spirit of social revolution would resurface to inspire a new cadre of revolutionaries, led by Mao Zedong; for the moment, however, it was subdued.

Yung heard the news of the Taiping's collapse shortly after he returned home. Whether he mourned the demise of the egalitarian-minded rebels or rejoiced in the stellar victory of his new benefactor, Zeng, is impossible to tell; his diary and correspondence leave little evidence. He arrived at Zeng's headquarters, where the old general welcomed Yung warmly, complimented him on a job well done, asked a few questions about the machines, and then announced that he intended to make Yung's mission to Massachusetts the subject of a special memorial to the throne.

Yung gasped. For a Qing official, there was nothing that expressed one's status as powerfully as the ability to send a memorial to the emperor. The correspondences that went through were often the sole sources of information that penetrated the glorious isolation of the palace. To have one's name mentioned in a memorial guaranteed immediate recognition by the Qing's highest officers, and that almost always translated into a prestigious position. In Yung's presence, Zeng dictated the memorial to his secretary.

> Yung Wing is a foreign educated Chinese. He has mastered the English language. In his journey over thousands of miles of ocean to the extreme ends of the earth to fulfill the commission I entrusted to him, he was utterly oblivious to difficulties and dangers that lay in his way. In this respect even the missions of the Ancients present no parallel equal to his. Therefore, I would recommend that he be promoted to the expectancy of one of the [Jiangsu] subprefects, and he is entitled to fill the first vacancy presenting itself, in recognition of his valuable services.[15]

The secretary finished drawing up the document, copied it out, and handed it to Yung, who took it, mumbled a few breathless words of thanks, and left the room.

A few weeks after he returned home to Shanghai, a letter from Zeng arrived, confirming Yung's appointment as a full-fledged mandarin and awarding him an uncommonly large salary. In 1867, with Zeng growing even more powerful in the Qing hierarchy, the old general decided to embark on a tour of his jurisdiction and to pay his protégé Yung a visit. Together, the two traveled to the arsenal where Yung's American-bought machine shop was now serving China's self-strengthening effort, producing guns and cannons. Visiting the factory, Zeng "stood and watched its automatic movement, with unabated delight, for this was the first time he had seen machinery, and how it worked."[16] Fascinated, he asked Yung what else could be done to improve the enterprise. It was a question Yung had pondered for more than a decade, discussing it with rebels and viceroys alike. Calmly and eloquently, he told the general that purchasing Western technology was one thing, but knowing how to replicate it, even improve on it, was something else. The solution was to establish an engineering school near the arsenal, where local Chinese students could train in designing, building, and operating machines like the ones spinning away before Zeng's awestruck eyes.

Unbeknownst to Yung, his answer of educating China's youth touched upon a conclusion Li had made earlier. When Yung left on his American purchasing trip, an ecstatic Li had written Zeng, stating that Yung's machinery would mark "the beginning of self strengthening on our coasts."[17] Shortly thereafter, however, Li qualified his enthusiasm, writing Zeng to say that weapons were useless without men who knew how to operate them. He suggested setting up a network of English-language schools, in which young men would be taught "that which the foreigners are good at, such as mathematical studies, the principles of science, and the techniques of manufacturing and

astronomy. . . . Can the Chinese be inferior to the Westerners
in ingenuity and intelligence? If there are men well versed in the
Western language and one person can teach another, then all
the skillful techniques of steamships and firearms can be gradually mastered."[18] Li's new motto, repeated incessantly, made his
intentions clear: "learn their methods without having always to
use their men."[19]

When Yung suggested schooling the arsenal's staff, Zeng
therefore agreed before Yung could even finish his sentence. In
Yung, Zeng realized, he had found the passionate and capable
administrator who could bring his and Li's vision of a modern
China to life. He invited Yung to set up a school.

Yung's academy, housed near the arsenal, was small, and its
interests were limited. Within months, the arsenal's employees
were being schooled in the principles of physics, mathematics,
and warfare. Emboldened by this success, Yung pushed his educational experiment further. What China needed was a new
educational framework that would allow many young and talented
men to broaden their horizons and sharpen their minds.

As he was toying with these thoughts, Yung was approached
by Ding Richang, a good friend who was at the time leaving
Shanghai after being appointed governor of Jiangsu Province.
Ding was an avid believer in self-strengthening and an able
bureaucrat, but not a man of vision. He came to Yung in search
of projects and told him that if he had any specific proposals,
he would memorialize them to Beijing and campaign on their
behalf. Yung accepted the generous invitation and drafted a program of four core ideas.

The first was the organization of an exclusively Chinese

steamship company, which could efficiently transport rice across the nation and stem the famines caused by the Qing's inefficient agricultural policies. Another called on the government to open up mines and fully utilize China's mineral resources. A third took aim at the growing influence of Catholicism in China and called on the court "to prohibit missionaries of any religious sect or denomination from exercising any kind of jurisdiction over their converts, in either civil or criminal cases."[20] All of these were sound ideas. But it was the final part of the proposal that expressed Yung's deepest hopes.

In order to reform its educational system, he wrote, China should send students to America and pay for their education at the finest colleges there. Yung Wing was proposing, in other words, the creation of more Yung Wings. Allowing young men to come of age in the classrooms and playing fields of New England's colleges could create a core group of future leaders unburdened by antiquated thinking and superstitions. Yung did his best to cement his idea with many specific details. The boys would be aged twelve to fourteen. There would be 120 of them, shipped to America over the course of four years, with 30 boys arriving annually. They would remain stateside for fifteen years. If they came back proven leaders, the program would be expanded dramatically to include as many young men as the empire could afford to send.

Yung sealed his proposal and sent it to Ding, who supported Yung's ideas wholeheartedly. Ding's patron in Beijing was Wen Xiang, a very senior minister in the emperor's immediate circle. With Wen's approval, Yung's educational mission would be underway before too long.

Just as Ding was drafting his memorial to the throne, though, Wen's mother died, and the minister was obliged, according to the customs of Confucianism, to retire from office and go into mourning for twenty-seven months, abstaining entirely from all public affairs. Yung felt his project undermined by this ridiculous system of bureaucrats and their rituals. He had no choice but to wait until someone in a position to promote such an ambitious scheme came along.

That someone was Zeng.

After an international incident in Tianjin involving the British and the French, a small delegation of high-ranking mandarins, including both Zeng and Ding, was dispatched to negotiate a resolution. In need of a good translator, Ding asked Yung to come immediately.

In Tianjin with the two officials most likely to assist him, Yung once more made the case for his proposals, speaking first to Ding, who promised to take the proposal up with Zeng before leaving Tianjin. Ding took his leave, and Yung went to bed.

He was awakened by a servant in the middle of the night. Ding had to see him right away. Yung rushed to his sitting room, where his friend Ding was smiling widely. That night, he told Yung, he had discussed Yung's ideas with Zeng and a few other viceroys, all of whom thought they were excellent. Zeng agreed to memorialize the throne. With his support, the emperor would most likely grant quick approval.

"This piece of news was too much to allow me to sleep any more that night," Yung wrote later; "while lying on my bed, as wakeful as an owl, I felt as though I were treading on clouds and walking in air."[21]

Two days later, Zeng, Ding and the other viceroys sent Yung's four-pronged proposal to Beijing, recommending that Yung head the educational mission to America. A short while after that, Beijing wrote back approvingly, with two caveats: first, that the mission be financed by a portion of Shanghai's tax intake, and, second, that another mandarin, Chen Lan Pin, be named codirector alongside Yung. As he read Chen's name, Yung immediately understood Beijing's concerns. Chen was as much a man of the rigid Confucian system as any Yung had known, and in appointing him, the court sought to balance Yung's enthusiastic spirit of innovative reform with someone who would make sure that the Chinese students sent abroad would be constantly reminded of their traditions and ritual obligations.

But even having to share the platform with Chen failed to dampen Yung's spirits. As a student at Yale, he had entertained the idea of a hundred other Chinese students enjoying New Haven. And now he was about to make it happen.

The signing in 1868 of the Burlingame Treaty, which established friendly diplomatic relations between China and the United States, would make his mission easier. Article 7 stated, "Citizens of the United States shall enjoy all the privileges of the public educational institutions under the control of the government of China, and, reciprocally, Chinese subjects shall enjoy all the privileges of the public educational institutions under the control of the government of the United States."[22] All Yung had to do now was announce the initiative and select the best candidates among the thousands who would doubtlessly apply.

Yet the recruitment process proved more difficult than Yung had initially imagined. Li Hongzhang, who oversaw the mission on behalf of the court, gave Yung a list of requirements that the prospective students would have to meet. The boys had to be able to spend the entire period of their education abroad, and commit to serving the state upon their graduation. Since the students would be representing the Qing empire in America, they had to be "pleasant to look at," and if they were "ungracefully named, they would need to be renamed gracefully."[23] It further complicated Yung's task that China had no national newspapers or popular means to disseminate official decisions, and when Yung's emissaries locally advertised an officially sponsored, all-expenses-paid, fifteen-year educational mission to America, they were met by suspicion and often promptly turned away by uninterested parents who doubted the veracity of the offer. It didn't help matters that the scheme appeared to contradict one of Confucianism's key tenets, filial loyalty, in calling for a son to be separated from his parents for the duration of his childhood. Finally, because most Chinese either had never met a foreigner or knew about the West only through the humiliating Opium Wars, mistrust of the invaders was deep-seated. One boy who eventually joined Yung's mission recalled, decades later, the intense pressure applied to dissuade him from signing up with Yung. Local elders terrified him with tales of America's horrific ways, insisting that "the wild men over there would skin us alive, graft the skin of dogs onto our bodies and exhibit us as they would some uncommon animal."[24]

Disheartened, Yung focused his efforts on his own province, Canton. There, at least, he knew many influential people and enjoyed enough of a reputation to overcome prejudice and dispel myths. From the days of the Canton system, the people of this region had interactions with foreign merchants and understood, to some degree, what the West had to offer. For months, he traveled from cities to villages, presenting the plan. By the time he had managed to find 120 willing candidates, more than 70 percent of them came from Canton, and more than a third from his own district, Xiangshan.

It wasn't exactly the diverse group Yung had hoped for, and he worried that his mission, designed as a beacon for all of China, would be perceived as nothing more than a southern affectation. But he had no time to lose: he set up a preparatory school, hired teachers and translators, and prepared to send his young charges on the same path he himself had traveled many years before. The first detachment, Yung had planned, would leave for America in the summer of 1872; he himself would travel to Connecticut a few months in advance and arrange for foster families and adoptive schools.

As he was about to set sail, news arrived that Zeng had died. "Had his life been spared even a year longer," Yung later wrote of his patron, "he would have seen the first installment of thirty students started for the United States—the first fruit of his own planting. But founders of all great and good works are not permitted by the nature and order of things to live beyond their ordained limitations to witness the successful developments of their own labor in this world; but the consequences of human action and human character, when once their die is cast, will reach to eternity."[25]

Part II

The Arrival

After a twenty-five-day journey, the *Spirit of Peking* ended its voyage across the Pacific Ocean and eased its way into the industrious and hilly San Francisco Bay area in September 1872, delivering the first detachment of Yung Wing's Chinese Educational Mission students to American shores.

As the boys made their way off the ship and onto the streets of the bustling city, they were struck by the urban panorama unfolding before their eyes, dramatically different from anything they had known back home. San Francisco was not a quiet village with working beasts and vast rice fields. It was a metropolis, with six-story buildings, sturdy ships, and a churning sea of Caucasian faces. People here walked at a brisk pace down paved boulevards or hopped on and off the streetcars clattering up and down the roads. To the boys, none of it made any sense. All they could see was a storm of human movement; all they could hear were the incomprehensible shouts and chatter of a modern city.

Their amazement only grew when they arrived, a little while

later, at the entrance to their hotel. In China, most of the boys had been accustomed to mud huts with paper windows. Here was a five-story building, a place of luxury and wonder, adorned with fluted columns and wide, regal arches. The hotel's amenities captured the boys' imaginations. Heat emanated from coiled radiators, water flowed out of metal pipes, and light shone brightly even though not a single lantern was in sight. Some of the boys had previously glimpsed the trappings of modern technology, but for most, the sons of poor families from the south of China, the hotel was a revelation.

Boys being boys, the idle hours were spent in exploration. They could never, it seemed, ring an electric bell often enough and giggle as it emitted its metallic trill, or turn on a faucet and stare, hypnotized, at the never-ending stream of fresh water. They rode the elevator, up and down and up again.

In time, Yung Wing's students settled in and began paying serious attention to their surroundings. What first caught their eyes was how strangely the people of San Francisco dressed. The boys, wearing uniforms of maroon robes with blue silk coats and round, short hats, couldn't make sense of the Western fashions. Looking outside the hotel's windows, they saw men in tight pants and coarse, form-fitting jackets. Whereas in China people wore loosely draped clothing, here everything seemed designed to cling to one's body. Back home, only the women had their feet bound, yet in America even the men wore laced shoes and boots, footwear that seemed impossibly restrictive to boys used to plain, padded slippers. The sexes acted nothing like the Chinese, either: instead of remaining docile and sweet, women here seemed to mix freely with men, as if little difference existed between them. The boys were deeply confused.

Further exploration produced more startling discoveries. There were, the boys noticed, Chinese people already present in San Francisco, callused and sun-bitten men who moved through the city like ghosts, never appearing at home amid its modern marvels. While San Franciscans were excited to make the acquaintance of Yung Wing's students, the locals were much less interested in the lives of the Chinese who had already made California their home. The *New York Times* neatly captured this distinction. "The thirty Chinese students who arrived yesterday are very young," the newspaper reported. "They are fine intelligent . . . gentlemen, and of much fairer complexion than any of their countrymen who have heretofore visited the United States."[1]

The boys, of course, had neither the wherewithal nor the leisure to learn it at the time, but the Chinese already living in San Francisco had come for very different purposes than to attend America's best schools. Ever since the first gold nuggets had been sifted out of the Sacramento River in 1848 at Sutter's Mill, tens of thousands of ambitious Chinese immigrants had flooded California's shores; particularly attractive was San Francisco, known as Gold Mountain, a city that assumed a mythic character among the peasantry of South China's impoverished villages. To these poor peasants, the allure of San Francisco was enough for them to sell their possessions and raise enormous sums of money for the singular privilege of toiling in mines and living in dangerous conditions surrounded by gamblers and thieves. These men were called *k'u-li*, Chinese for hard strength. To the coolies, as these Chinese workers became known in America, Gold Mountain promised the material wealth and financial prosperity that eluded them in the rigid caste system of agrarian China.

When the Chinese workers began to arrive in San Francisco, they found a town every bit as kinetic as their expectations. From a dusty military post with barely 500 residents just three decades earlier, San Francisco had grown into a teeming city of almost 200,000 by the time the boys arrived in 1872.[2] The same rapid growth was true of the city's Chinese population: before the news of California's gold reached China, there had been only 50 Chinese living in the United States, and 7 in all of California. With gold came many more Chinese men. One broker in Hong Kong, hoping to entice his countrymen on the mainland to emigrate, vowed in an advertisement that America was a nation free of mandarins and marauding soldiers, a haven of equality in which all who were willing to work hard would thrive.[3] In 1852 alone, 20,000 Chinese men would heed the call.

While most laborers wound their way through the hills and brush to the various mining camps around the region, those who chose to remain in San Francisco established a budding Chinatown centered on Dupont and Sacramento Streets. Among the men who headed out of the city, the first step was to swap their cotton slippers for leather boots and tuck their queues beneath cowboy hats. Life in the camps was rough and precarious, and an English phrasebook of the period given to the Chinese miners reflects the anxiety and dangers they faced:

He assaulted me without provocation.
He claimed my mine.

He tries to extort money from me.
He was choked to death with a lasso, by a robber.
She is a good-for-nothing huzzy.[4]

Mark Twain, writing of these hardworking men struggling in the unforgiving landscapes of an unfamiliar country, was thoroughly impressed: "They are quiet, peaceable, tractable, free from drunkenness. A disorderly Chinaman does not exist, and a lazy one is rare. So long as a Chinaman has strength to use his hands he needs no support from anybody . . . he always finds something to do."[5]

In San Francisco, the initial settlement of Chinatown eventually evolved into a vibrant, ten-block neighborhood. At the local grocers, cuttlefish, abalone, fruits, and bird's nests were all on display, stacked in reed baskets suspended from bamboo poles or splayed out on mats placed across the busy sidewalks. The first Chinese cafeterias, marked by triangular yellow silk flags—their dining floors littered with bones and gristle, their patrons gorging on all-you-could-eat feasts—were eventually joined by sumptuous marble palaces of Asian gastronomy, grand restaurants bedecked with red balconies and imported latticework screens, places where local Chinese and adventurous American diners could enjoy such exotic delicacies as shark-fin soup under ceilings strung with hanging lanterns and gas-lit chandeliers.[6]

Overseeing all of this growth were the Chinese benevolent associations that controlled almost every aspect of the community's social and business life. The six companies, as these associations became known, provided something essential to the Chinese worker arriving alone in a foreign land: a sense of family and community, and the necessary elements of Confucian ritual and theology. To start a family in America, of course, was out of the question, because few eligible Chinese women were able or willing to make the trip to the United States, and the immigrants who arrived were generally interested only in making their fortune and returning to China as wealthy men. The benevolent associations, at least, provided the new arrivals with a room to live in, a place to receive mail, and a social network.

Some of the Chinese immigrants found their way not into one of the six companies but into the tongs, the secret societies that made up the seamy underbelly of Chinatown. The tongs took to running rackets, serving as mercenaries for shady businessmen, and controlling lucrative and widespread prostitution rings. They gained notoriety for auctioning off girls to brothels in broad daylight on the docks; when mounting public outrage forced the constabulary to act, the tongs simply moved their operations into the secluded confines of the city's Chinese theaters and temples.

While lurid stories of tong immorality dulled the luster of the Chinese community, what presented a real danger to its integrity was the shifting tide of economy and industry. Although the transcontinental railroad, recently completed in 1869, had made millionaires of its principals in San Francisco, it had also sparked a depression in the city, as the massive flow of goods from the rest of the country into northern California allowed the more established eastern factories to undercut local manufacturing and put large numbers of people out of work. The teeming population of Chinese in San Francisco ensured that one out of every three job seekers in the city was Chinese, a statistic that only added to the rising ethnic tension. The first of many laws aimed at limiting the influence of the Chinese community had been passed two decades earlier—a punishing foreign miner's tax in 1852—and after that anti-Chinese rhetoric was common currency in the streets, in the press, and in the halls of power.

The arriving students, too young to appreciate the political and social currents, could be forgiven for naively believing that San Francisco was a paradise for the Chinese, a glittering city where self-exiled immigrants were able to enjoy mechanical elevators and electric bells whenever they pleased. And although Chinatown was not too far from their hotel, the boys had no desire to ponder the coolies' true situation. Instead, what interested them most during their brief visit to San Francisco was the railroad station. The boys had seen trains once before, when their ship had stopped in Japan, but the depot here was on an altogether different scale. Hundreds of people rushed in, nearly colliding with hundreds more rushing out. Trains—not one or two but many—came and went. While the boys' chaperones hoped to show them the city, all the boys wanted to do was look at the trains, which they called "fire-car roads."

They would eventually ride one. After a few days in San Francisco, they were shepherded to Sacramento, escorted to a reserved train car, and sent off on a great railroad journey across America's mountains, valleys, and yawning prairies, riding the transcontinental railroad toward their final destination in New England.

Their train followed a path inaugurated only three years earlier, tracing an overland route through the United States that had solidified the country both physically and culturally, linking the newly acquired western states to the well-developed eastern seaboard. During the railroad's construction, telegraph poles were erected alongside the tracks. The vast frontier was finally accessible, tamed, in a sense, by the passengers, goods, and information that could now cross it with speed and ease. Before the railroad, a coast-to-coast traveler had to make either a four-month trek through inhospitable routes over the Rocky Mountains, settle for a lengthy sea voyage around the Strait of Magellan, or risk their lives in the Comanche and Apache territories of the Southwest. The significance of the railroad to America's epic sense of its own destiny led the western poet Joaquin Miller to opine, "There is more poetry in the rush of a single railroad across the continent than in all the gory story of the burning of Troy."[7]

For the boys, the story of the railroad's creation could have contained many lessons about the contrasting outlooks of imperial China and the young American republic. Whereas the Chinese court, for the most part, avoided modernization and the disruptive influence of new technology at all costs, the Americans were only too happy to undertake massive projects in the messianic service of "progress." Not even the ongoing Civil War could check the American thirst for heroic expansion: it was in 1862, after all, that President Lincoln and Congress passed the Pacific Railway Act, whereby the American government ordained the construction of the route that was to cut through a thousand miles of wilderness. The Central Pacific Railroad soon began laying track east from Sacramento, slowly making its way through Nevada and Utah toward the Union Pacific company, which was building the midwestern portion of the line out of Omaha and across the plains.

For years, tens of thousands of men toiled in the American West, hammering spikes into railroad ties day and night, staving off privation and sickness, sometimes putting down four rails a minute far from the safety and pleasures of civilization. Crucial to the success of the railroad were the ten thousand Chinese workers of the Central Pacific. These were the same class of men that the boys had seen in San Francisco, loading carts and carrying bales of laundry, desperate men who took whatever jobs they could find, hard workers who in time acquired a legendary reputation for diligence and skill with explosives. They blew through some of the largest trees in the world with barrels of gunpowder, and chiseled through granite with hand drills and shovels. They blasted hills with nitroglycerin and survived landslides and loose boulders, boring through sections of the rugged Sierra Nevada at the agonizing rate of seven inches per day, at a cost of a million dollars per mile. During the winter of 1866—one of the most brutal in recorded history, nicknamed "the Homeric" for the scope of its punishments—they struggled under blizzard conditions that dumped forty feet of snow in their path, and worked beneath the surface by lantern light in tunnels, stairs, and workrooms dug out from under the massive banks of snow. In one instance, after an avalanche covered a Chinese camp, the remains of the workers were discovered only after the spring's first thaws, their corpses standing upright, tools still in hand.[8]

Despite their enormous sacrifices and efforts, the Chinese workers faced prejudice and resentment as construction progressed along the route. From the earliest days of the project, white Americans convinced of their racial supremacy laughed at the notion that Chinese workers, standing an average four feet

and ten inches tall,[9] would be able to handle the job. Though
these doubts were answered with the trenchant observation of
Charles Crocker, one of the Central Pacific's directors, who said,
"The people who built the Great Wall can build our railroad,"[10]
ethnic animosity was rife in the camps. In one instance, a group
of Irish laborers detonated mining explosives near some Chinese
tents, spurring the Chinese to retaliate with a bombing campaign of their own. Despite the abuse they received at the hands
of their fellow workers and from overseers who occasionally
resorted to whipping them, the Chinese eked out an existence as
they always did, by sticking together and adhering to their rituals; at least the Chinese practice of boiling water for tea spared
them from the dysentery that was rampant in the other camps.

Ensconced in their rumbling passenger car, their journey well
underway, Yung Wing's students had little to do but look out the
windows of the train as they hurtled toward Utah. The boys,
who could have hardly imagined the human struggles involved in
building the transcontinental railroad, might have noticed small
groups of Chinese men solemnly digging in the Sierra Nevada,
even though the work of the railroad was long finished. Here,
where the hard construction exacted such an enormous toll in
human lives, groups of Chinese men would come on pilgrimages
to search for the graves of their fellow workers. Beneath simple
wooden stakes lay bodies buried with wax-sealed bottles holding
pieces of cloth inscribed with the deceased's name and native
village. These remains, thus discovered, would be exhumed and
shipped back to China; in all, twenty thousand pounds of bones
would make this final journey.[11]

When the 1,776-mile-long railroad was finished in 1869,

Americans made the day one of national celebration. The country, still scarred after the devastation of the Civil War, had nevertheless been able to seize its manifest destiny, conquer the open plains, and impose an orderly system of modern technology on the wilderness that lay between its coastal belts. With high spirits, five hundred people stood in the soggy muck of Promontory Point, Utah, on May 10, 1869, to watch the final spikes being driven into the final tie of the transcontinental railroad.[12] The heads and high officials of the railroads were in attendance, and the Twenty-first Infantry Battalion was sent by the federal government to lend martial color, with musical accompaniment provided by the military band of Fort Douglas, Wyoming, and the Tenth Ward Band out of Salt Lake City. Brigham Young sent a bishop to represent the Mormon Church. Reporters circled the area, conducting interviews and taking notes, while photographers, having been given the freedom to shoot as they pleased by the event organizers, jostled each other in the mud for the best vantage points.

At noon, the Central Pacific's *Jupiter* and the Union Pacific's *119* faced each other across a narrow gap in the nearly completed railroad, while the infantry assembled along the western side of the tracks and waited. At twenty minutes past, the final tie, made of polished laurel wood, was placed into position. The Reverend Dr. John Todd of Pittsfield, Massachusetts, marked the occasion with a two-minute prayer service, after which Newton Watson Shilling sent notice down the telegraph lines from Maine to California: "We have got done praying. The spike is about to be presented."[13] First to be delicately sunk into the predrilled augur holes were the ceremonial spikes donated by Nevada and Arizona. Then, with the worshipful reverence of a holy relic being gently placed upon a sacred altar, the final, golden spike was lowered into its place. It was wired to the telegraph table, so that the entire nation could share in the triumphant sounds of its being hammered into position. The railroad men swung at it, missed, and missed again. No matter, Shilling tapped out three dots at 12:47, and the deed was consecrated.

The country erupted. The Liberty Bell was rung in Philadelphia. Two hundred and twenty cannons at Fort Point in San Francisco blasted their approval and one hundred in Washington, D.C., followed suit. It was said that more artillery was fired on May 10, 1869, than during the entire Battle of Gettysburg. Fireworks were set off in cities, while people in small towns gathered in churches and prayed. *Jupiter* and *119* unhooked themselves from their trains, inching so close to each other that the two enormous machines almost kissed. *Jupiter* gracefully reversed and allowed *119* to roll forward and christen those final inches of the transcontinental railroad. *Jupiter* then followed suit and crossed over the polished laurel tie. In Chicago, a celebratory parade stretched for seven miles; in the beaten cities of the defeated Confederacy, a renewed sense of American patriotism could be felt in the streets. There were festivities in Atlanta, New Orleans, and even the Confederate capital of Richmond, Virginia. With the transcontinental railroad set in steel, America had grasped its sense of purpose.

But for the Chinese employed by Central Pacific, there was little to celebrate. As construction came to an end, most workers were simply laid off, denied their promised return passage to

China, and shipped back to California. There, they competed for hard-to-find jobs with the Civil War veterans and others who were migrating to the American West along the metal artery that the Chinese had helped build. Prejudicial legislation soon followed: in 1870, San Francisco banned the use of poles to carry baskets on the streets—the traditional Chinese method for carrying groceries and goods—and imposed heavy taxes on Chinese laundries. The city also passed the Cubic Air Law, by which every lodging house was required to provide five hundred cubic feet of open space per person. The law was aimed squarely at the cramped residences of Chinatown, and those unable to pay the requisite fine were subject to the municipal "queue ordinance," whereby each male prisoner unable or unwilling to settle his account with the city would have his head shaved to within one inch of his scalp, a punishment meaningless to the white inmates but especially devastating to the identity of the Chinese, whose queues were worn as marks of fealty to the emperor in the wilds of the western United States.

Simmering racial tensions continued to mount and often boiled over into outright violence. In October 1871, two policemen responding to an outbreak of tong violence in Los Angeles were shot and killed. Seeking revenge, an angry mob dragged dozens of Chinese residents out of their homes and murdered nineteen of them in the course of the night. An observer recounted the death of one unfortunate Chinese boy who was caught by the crowd: "The little fellow was not above twelve years of age. He had been but a month in the country, and knew not a word of English. He seemed paralyzed by fear—his eyes were fixed and staring, his face blue-blanched and idiotic. He was hanged."[14]

While the realities of life in California were growing increasingly painful for the Chinese community, developments throughout America's fertile central plains, which the boys' train was racing across, had helped shape the country's mythology and mission-ary sensibilities during the nineteenth century. Passing through the vast prairies, the boys witnessed, from the seats of their passenger car, some of the soon to vanish icons of the legendary West, including herds of mustangs and lumbering buffalo.

Li En Fu, a student who arrived with the second detachment of boys a year later, took the same transcontinental railroad jour-ney to New England. Aboard the train, he was captivated by the sight of Native Americans, eagle feathers sticking out of their jet-black hair, riding through the countryside with bows and arrows, a vision that brought to his mind traditional Chinese actors with their boldly painted faces.

Adding to the romance and adventure of the journey east was his witnessing of that seminal plot point in so many dime-store western novels and the cowboy films of the future: a train rob-bery. He recounted the event in his memoirs:

> The train suddenly bounded backward, then rushed for-ward a few feet, and, then meeting some resistance, started back again. Then all was confusion and terror. Pistol-shots could be made out above the cries of frightened passengers. Women shrieked and babies cried. Our party, teachers and pupils, jumped from our seats in dismay and looked out through the windows for more light on the subject. What we saw was enough to make our hair stand on end. Two ruffianly men held a revolver in each hand and seemed to

be taking aim at us. . . . [D]oubtless many prayers were most fervently offered to the gods of China at that time. Our teachers certainly prayed as they had never done before. One of them was overheard calling upon all the gods of the Chinese Pantheon to come and save him.[15]

Following a few harried moments of panic and action, calm returned to the train. The wrecked locomotive was replaced with a fresh one, and the boys were once again on their way.

Of course, the West was slowly being civilized by the settlements transforming many of the open ranges of the continent into farms, towns, and regional centers. As elsewhere in the United States, it was modern technology that had led the charge of progress across the Midwest. The great agricultural potential of America's central expanses had always been limited by its difficult soil; when worked with traditional iron plows, it would indifferently and unhelpfully slink right back into the furrows wrought by the farmers' simple tools, refusing to turn over and share its fertile bounty. The thick prairie sod would adhere to the underside of plows and make it necessary to clean the blades every few steps, making profitable farming a tedious affair.

These simple facts of western life impeded development of the region until the decades following 1837, when John Deere, a Vermont transplant living in Grand Detour, Illinois, engineered a revolutionary plow that eventually made massive cultivation of the prairie a reality. Deere, a blacksmith by trade, had analyzed the flaws in the various implements brought to him by his customers for repair and devised a much improved version of the mangled, heavy plows that filled his workshop. His design,

made of modern steel, carried a circular saw blade that made
short work of the prairie sod, allowing farmers to easily create
deep and consistent furrows. Deere's invention was light enough
to be drawn by a horse, freeing farmers from the lumbering
oxen required to pull iron plows. In 1848, Deere opened a factory in Moline, Illinois, which produced thirteen thousand steel
plows annually within a decade of operation. By the time of the
Civil War, 150 varieties of plows were being advertised, and
experimentation was underway on steam-powered versions that
promised the possibility of digging six furrows simultaneously.

Crucial to the booming agricultural empire of the Midwest
was wheat, a crop whose harvest was radically transformed
through mechanization. A few years before Deere invented his
plow, Cyrus Hall McCormick of Virginia and Obed Hussey of
Ohio both developed, independently of each other, steel-toothed
reapers, revolutionary devices that changed the landscape of the
American plains. McCormick, the son of a farmer and mechanic,
was a natural tinkerer who spent his youth playing with farm
equipment and observing agricultural production. He realized
that the limiting factor in harvesting wheat was time, because
wheat had to be collected almost as soon as it ripened. Working
with hand tools, a farmer could profitably grow only as much
wheat as he could manage to harvest by hand, an amount that
worked out to about an acre per day. McCormick, however,
developed a machine that could tackle eight acres a day, as much
wheat as a team of men with scythes. His invention opened
the way for the massive wheat farms of the midwestern plains:
in 1839, eighty bushels of wheat passed through the city of
Chicago, ten years later, that number had exploded to twenty

million bushels. With the aid of the "American system" of interchangeable parts, McCormick was making five hundred reapers a month, and barely keeping up with demand. In 1851, he exhibited his reaper at the Great Exposition of London, the first world's fair. Initially, the *Times* of London looked disdainfully on what it deemed "an extravagant Yankee contrivance, huge, unwieldy, unsightly and incomprehensible."[16] Following a demonstration in an English wheat field, though, the paper reversed its verdict, now declaring, "The reaping machine from the United States is the most valuable contribution from abroad to the stock of our previous knowledge. . . . It is worth the whole cost of the Exposition."[17] The technologies developed by men like McCormick and Deere, combined with the growth of agricultural colleges after the Civil War and the Homestead Act of 1862, led to the largest growth of agricultural production in human history.

As the boys drew nearer to their destination, they whittled away the repetitive hours of travel playing games with one another and exploring the different sections of the train. Having passed through Albany and rapidly approaching Springfield, Massachusetts, one of the boys made his way out of the car specially designated for the use of the Chinese Educational Mission. He stepped into the choking haze of the smoking car, where men accustomed to the dull entertainments of these long journeys were sitting at tables, concentrating on the cards in their hands. Seeing a young Chinese boy with a billowing silk robe sidling up to join them in a game of euchre, the men didn't quite know how to react. Won over, perhaps, by a smile they later described as "childlike and bland,"[18] the Americans dealt the young student into their game, eyeing him with polite suspicion, sure that winning cards must be hidden, somewhere, in the enormous sleeves of his robe. But when he continued to lose hand after hand, it was clear that the young scholar had no idea how to play. Before long, it was time for him to disembark from the train and begin his American education.

The Forbidden City
of Willard Street

n New England, the boys learned that the cultural differences between the Pacific and the Atlantic coasts of the United States were as profound as their landscapes were dissimilar. As the train rolled into Massachusetts, the boys saw colonial houses and church steeples and neatly groomed people exuding a sense of propriety and purpose. What they didn't see were their fellow countrymen. Unlike California, the East was home to so few Chinese that, as late as 1880, New York City, then a metropolis of 1.2 million people, had fewer than 800 Chinese residents. More than the strange dress of the Americans, more than all the technology that had amused and delighted them in San Francisco, it was the towns and schools of New England that would truly bewilder the boys. Back in Hong Kong, Yung Wing had endeavored to teach his young charges the basics of American life, everything from the foundations of English grammar to the intricacies of social interactions. But as the train slowed down in Springfield, many of the boys stared out the

window and perhaps sensed that they were thoroughly unpre-
pared for what came next. There, at the station, gathered an
odd-looking crowd, men in stern collars and top hats, women
in bonnets and caged crinoline dresses. They, it was plain to see,
were no California prospectors in dirty work boots. They were
America's mandarins.

Before the boys had a chance to properly disembark, these
mandarins moved as one, circling them, cooing and staring and
waving hello. Like that out west, the local press considered the
new arrivals bona fide celebrities. Few bothered to ask questions
or compose an accurate portrait of the mission; instead, the local
papers let their imaginations run wild and reported that the
boys were the sons of wealthy Shanghai merchants, privileged
youth who moved effortlessly between the rarefied airs of China
and America's uppermost echelons. The visitors had arrived,
explained one newspaper, to learn from America in order "to
shine as stars in the galaxy of wise and intelligent Chinamen."[1]
Unable to read anything beyond very basic English, the boys
had no chance to savor the irony of an American reporter's
using the same celestial terminology so beloved by the imperials back home.

Looking at the spectacle from the side was Yung Wing, who
had arrived in Springfield a few weeks earlier to prepare for the
boys' arrival. If he was moved, watching his students about to
embark on the same path he himself had taken all those years
earlier, his diary doesn't say. All it conveys is the sense of a man
gripped by the mechanics of a complex operation. The mission,
after all, was Yung's to run; his aloof codirector, Chen Lan Pin,
knew little English and no Americans, leaving Yung to search

single-handedly for foster families, make arrangements with schools, introduce the endeavor to local politicians and clergy- men, and prepare to erect a permanent home in which the boys could regularly congregate and practice their Confucianism. Still, the memory of himself as a young boy, anxious and at a loss in a strange new place, had never grown dull in Yung's mind. He remembered how distressed he felt when he was surrounded by examining throngs, how much he hated all that attention. To acclimate the boys as quickly as possible, he organized a brief introductory tour of the American Northeast, taking the whole detachment to see such local attractions as the Hartford armory and the town hall.

Wherever the students ventured, though, the locals' curiosity was hard to curb. This group of boys, dressed in silk gowns, their queues flapping, was too much for New Englanders, be they small-town folk or city dwellers, to ignore. In Springfield, for example, the boys' dinner at a local hotel was interrupted when an American woman, dining at a nearby table, stood up and wordlessly approached the Chinese youths and started dreamily fondling their queues. She was shown out by the staff, leaving the boys to laugh the whole thing off. They were less amused a few days later when, while visiting Hartford, American children chased them down the street, pushing and shoving each other for a better glimpse of the strange, new breed of humans that had arrived on their shores. The staring was more than the boys could take. The more fearful among them recalled the horrific stories circulated back home about Americans and their desire to turn the Chinese boys into sideshow curiosities. Some of the boys were unsure how to dispel the mob of children ogling them; others, however, were not. Searching their pockets for pennies, they threw them at the Americans. The local children were dazzled by the prospect of free money and fell over themselves to collect the change being tossed their way. Hartford's gentry were amused. "Think of it!" declared the *Harford Evening Post*. "The 'heathen Chinese' tossing coppers to the children of Puritan and enlightened New England!"[2]

Shortly after the boys' arrival, Yung moved the mission's base of operations from Springfield to Hartford. Perhaps it reminded him of Shanghai: the city, located on the banks of the Connecticut River, was a haven for merchants, men who, like Yung himself, made their fortune by trading goods with markets the world over. It was also the center of the American insurance industry and could lay claim to being the wealthiest city, per capita, in the United States. Equally as resonant was Hartford's stature as a bastion of men and women committed to change and progress: it was here, in 1639, that a group of English settlers became the first to establish a government by the consent of the people; here, in 1814, that delegates from across New England convened to mull over a possible secession from the union in protest against the raging war with Britain; here, in 1844, that the nation's oldest public art museum, the Wadsworth Athenaeum, was inaugurated. It was home to abolitionists and artists. Harriet Beecher Stowe, not long after completing *Uncle Tom's Cabin*, moved into a spacious cottage on Asylum Hill, next to the home of Mark Twain, who had arrived in town an impoverished unknown and left, nearly two decades later, the revered author of such American classics as *The Adventures of Tom Sawyer*, *Adventures of Huckleberry Finn*, and *A Connecticut Yankee in King Arthur's Court*. "Of all the beautiful towns it has been my fortune to see," Twain wrote of Hartford, "this is the chief."[3]

Most importantly, in Hartford, Yung Wing had a supportive community. A few were old friends, like Eunice Capron, the girl he had taken to his senior year prom at Yale twenty-two years earlier. Others were new acquaintances, like B. G. Northrop, Connecticut's superintendent for education. Quite a few, like the Reverend Joseph Twichell, were excited to impart the Christian gospel to the Chinese without having to travel across the Pacific Ocean. "Lo," Twichell wrote, "God has brought the work to my very door."[4] Yung's friends were affluent, influential, and infatuated with the goals of his mission. All vowed to do whatever they could to help.

As soon as the boys arrived in Connecticut, foster families stepped forward, making room in their homes for pairs of Chinese boys and investing considerable time and effort in teaching the newcomers the language and customs. Yet for all their goodwill, the New Englanders were just as ignorant of Chinese culture and customs as the boys were of American ways. The hosts, then, did what came naturally to them and were often puzzled when things went awry.

Li En Fu, the eloquent chronicler of the train robbery, wrote that when he was first introduced to the woman under whose care he was to remain, she immediately bent down and gave him a kiss, that singularly embarrassing gesture of Western affection, so different in practice from the austere familial relations he and the other boys were used to in China. Back home, one of the boys' farewells to his mother had consisted of four deep bows of the head, which was considered a suitable goodbye for a journey of fifteen years. Seeing Li receive a kiss from this unknown woman was too much for his friends to bear silently. Unable to stifle their giggles, the other boys burst out in laughter. Li would write that it was the first kiss he had been given since he was an infant.

Other miscommunications, however, were harder to laugh off. On the first Sunday of his stay in Springfield, Li and the boy with whom he was paired were instructed to prepare for Sunday school. The two were thrilled—they had come to America to get an education and were eager to begin as soon as possible. They wrapped up their books, dressed in their best clothes, and, chatting happily, followed their family to what they believed was their new school. Gradually, it dawned on them that something wasn't right. The building had a steeple. A cross. They walked in: it was a church, with pews and people now standing to stare at them. Sunday school wasn't a school at all. They froze, petrified, unsure of what to do. Back in China, they had been warned—by relatives, by friends, and by Yung Wing's co-commissioner Chen Lan Pin— that some Americans might try to convert them to Christianity. Was this, they wondered, what was happening to them right now? Were they being forced to adopt a new religion? Not knowing the language, and having no idea of the church's centrality to the communal life of pious New England, they nervously exchanged hushed words. Then, without thinking twice, they started running. They ran as fast as they could, out of the church, down the street and back to their room, where they hid, cowering, until their American foster parents came home and convinced them that no one was trying to make them abandon their faith and that attending church was a normal part of the week's routine.

The spiritual panic abated, only to be replaced by sartorial issues. When the boys began attending local schools, their colorful robes and long braided hair caused their American peers, in the time-honored tradition of schoolyard malice, to refer to them as "Chinese girls." This naturally upset the boys, and they sought solace in Yung Wing. He, they hoped, would understand, having doubtlessly encountered similar harassment in his days as a student in America. Yung was sympathetic; almost immediately after receiving the first complaints, he was inclined to allow the boys to abandon their traditional dress for Western clothes, maybe even cut off their queues for the duration of their stateside stay. But Yung's partner at the mission's helm, Chen, sent by the imperial officials to ensure that the boys stayed true to their Confucian heritage, was appalled by such talk. To him, clothes made the man; if they removed their robes, the very uniform of the classical Chinese scholar, he believed the boys would become nothing more than a gaggle of Americans. Chen, who had spent twenty years as an official with the Imperial Board of Punishments, ignored pleas for empathy almost as a matter of course: the boys would dress as they were supposed to. Patiently, Yung explained that different clothes were necessary if the boys were to receive an American education to its fullest extent. If they spent their days defending themselves against taunts, he argued, they would have little time and energy left for math and science. Begrudgingly, Chen agreed to a compromise. The boys would be permitted to don suits. But the queue had to stay. The boys could tuck it beneath their jackets, but never cut it off. It was a symbol of loyalty, and no dutiful subject of the Son of Heaven, he warned, could ever consider doing away with it.

In their new outfits, the boys looked less and less like foreigners every day. They were also picking up English at so fast a pace that even the optimistic Yung Wing was pleasantly surprised. This, Yung acknowledged, had just as much to do with the boys' talent as with their hosts' tenacity. Stern disciplinarians for the most part, God-fearing people who believed in hard work and heavenly rewards, the families hosting the boys often employed harsh measures to ensure that their young charges acquired the new language quickly. "We learned English by object-lessons," Li En Fu recalled. "At table we were always told the names of certain dishes, and then assured that if we could not remember the name we were not to partake of the article of food. Taught by this method, our progress was rapid and surprising."[5]

Y. T. Woo, a student who lived with the Bartlett family of Hartford, remembered similar instructions in the ways of New England. The lady of the house was "a strict disciplinarian. When we held our knives and forks too low at meals, she would correct us. When she heard us talking in our rooms in the attic after nine or ten p.m., she would shout from below, 'Boys, stop talking, it is time to sleep.'"[6]

Once each of the mission's four detachments had arrived from China, and Yung Wing's 120 students had become accustomed to life in New England, their true personalities began to emerge. After they had studied together in Hong Kong, and crossed the world together by ship and train, the boys were finally getting to know one another.

At the center of the group was Tong Shao-yi. Studying Greek in school, the boys read the *Iliad*, and when they did, they had little doubt what nickname to give their friend: they called him

Ajax, after the hero of the Trojan War. Tong, while neither the strongest nor the tallest of the group, was, like his Achaean namesake, athletic and brave; most important, he shared with the legendary Ajax a natural inclination for leadership. He was the one whose advice the boys sought and whose approval they craved. It helped that he came from a very wealthy clan—the Tongs had catapulted their shrimp sauce business to fame, fortune, and influence back in China—but Tong's charisma had little to do with his lineage. It was innate. Ajax the Greek was the only major protagonist in the epic poem to triumph without any help from the gods; Ajax the Chinese seemed to be equally blessed, triumphing on the playing field and in the classroom without any help from adults.

Sharing Tong's room at the Gardner family home in Hartford was his cousin, Liang Ju-hao. Liang could hardly have been more different from his popular relative. Whereas Tong had an easy manner and a talent for conversation, Liang was introverted; when he did come into contact with friends, it was often to point out their flaws. The boys, then, were far less generous with Liang than with his cousin, naming the poor young man Cold Fish Chalie.

Whenever Tong found Liang's company bothersome, he, like the mission's other boys, had only to call on Yung Leang. A nephew of Yung Wing's, Yung Leang was nothing like his highminded uncle. Perpetually at the ready with a wisecrack, and always eager to joke around, he soon became known as By-jinks Johnnie. Yung Leang's capacity for mayhem was rivaled only by that of Tsai Ting Kan. Short, stout, and smiling, Tsai would nevertheless explode in anger at the slightest provocation. He never

seemed to miss an opportunity for a scuffle and took great pleasure in pounding his fists into the chest of some taller, stronger
boy. Tsai's combative attitude won him the nickname Fighting
Chinee.

Rounding up the small group of boys who were most visible among their peers were two serious-minded youths, Jeme
Tien-yau and Liang Dunyan. Jeme—who was soon rechristened
Jimmy—was perhaps the mission's sharpest student. While all the
boys were quick to pick up English and most excelled at school,
Jeme did so with astonishing grace, revealing, in particular, a
keen mind for mathematics. Coming from a poor family, he was
also humble and pleasant, which made his talents shine all the
more brightly. Finally, there was Liang Dunyan. Even though the
students, in their boyish zeal to blend in, were constantly amus-
ing themselves by making up clever American nicknames for one
another, Liang Dunyan was one of the very few boys who never
inspired such familiarity. He preferred to be alone and seemed
to always be immersed in intense self-improvement. He was
left-handed, and worked his arm tirelessly to become an expert
baseball player whose pitches were nearly impossible for opposing batters to hit. He exercised his mind with equal rigor; after
eighteen months in America, he was comfortable enough with
English to inscribe the following poem in a classmate's yearbook:

I am a pretty little kitten
My name is tabby gray
I live out in the country
Some twenty miles away
My eyes are black and hazel

My fur is soft as silk
I am fed each night and morning
With a saucer full of milk.[7]

The boys, with their leaders, their followers, and their clowns, were free to rush along on their quest to fit in with their new American friends. Like Yung Wing at Yale, the boys, too, soon learned that their American counterparts revered strength, speed, and dexterity, qualities that, in China, were deemed highly inappropriate for serious scholars. But the boys, being younger than Yung had been when he first entered college, were thrilled to seize any opportunity to run around. The students were especially drawn to the baseball diamond, and soon arranged for uniforms to be sewn, tucking their queues underneath their caps as they sped and slid from base to base. When there wasn't enough time to arrange a game, chasing pigs on nearby farms was a popular alternative.

Robust exercise, coupled with a rich diet, did wonders for the boys' well-being. Back home, most of them—the sons of simple families of modest means—could count on little but rice to satisfy their hunger and, if they were lucky, some chicken or an orange. In New England, however, they were fed rich and fattening foods: meat and potatoes, bread and cheese, lots of cream. Even the smallest and sickliest of the boys were now in excellent health. Writing two years after the boys' arrival, the *Hartford Evening Post* took pride in the town's good stewardship of its young guests and reported that, collectively, the boys had taken no more than two weeks of sick time and incurred less than fifty dollars in doctors' bills.[8]

Completing this picture of well-being was the boys' academic distinction. Even though they had shed the traditional dress, the boys were, at heart, Chinese scholars in the ancient mold. They all believed, following the ancient imperial dictum, that a boy who wanted to become somebody faced the window, sat down, and studied. Even though their American peers praised physical prowess and measured men by their charisma and charm, the boys still saw schoolwork as their paramount duty. Shortly after their arrival, nearly all of the boys ranked at or near the top of their class.

One, however, did not take very well to his schooling. The pugnacious Tsai Ting Kan, Fighting Chinee, was deemed too unruly for the quiet classrooms of New England. He wasn't too clever, his teachers reflected, and lacked the discipline to overcome his own flaws. Still, they searched for a place for him in America. Shortly after his arrival, Tsai was sent not to school but to a machine shop. So that his queue didn't accidentally become caught in the heavy industrial equipment, Tsai was given special dispensation to cut it off, further differentiating him from his friends. Soon, among the boisterous clatter of noisy cogs and gears, Tsai was happy.

Living in Hartford, and seeing the boys thrive in body and mind, Yung was delighted. In private visits and conversations, he encouraged them to further explore their surroundings, to spend their afternoons—as he once had—in libraries, to dance, and to participate in sports. Chen, on the other hand, remained unimpressed and perpetually suspicious. In his eyes, every small step the boys took toward academic or athletic excellence was a step out of the emperor's long reach. He watched with growing horror as the robe-wearing Chinese boys he had escorted off the ship became, within months, young American men in dark blue flannel suits and crisp white shirts. Chen did not keep his frustrations private: with General Zeng dead, the mission's patron in the Qing court was Li Hongzhang, and it was to Li that Chen dispatched lengthy reports lamenting the boys' wanton behavior. These reports, Chen hoped, would be enough to end the mission. But Li had different designs. As far as he was concerned, he had sent the boys to America to become mechanics and military men, and no sartorial slipup was about to change his mind. He needed modern weapons, and the people to work them, and ordered Chen to proceed as instructed.

Grumbling, Chen consented. Still uncomfortable with America and its ways, he sought to replicate, as much as possible, the conditions a man of his stature would enjoy back home. He moved into a large house in Hartford along with two of the group's teachers, a cook, laundryman, houseboy, and tailor. Whereas the boys under his charge tried their best to assimilate in their new surroundings, Chen did his utmost to stand apart, turning his home into an extraterritorial bit of China, a Forbidden City of Willard Street.

The neighborhood children were entranced by Chen's house. In the residence, they found all of the exotic charms and mysteries that the boys, with their American nicknames and improving English and passion for baseball games, were increasingly failing to provide. One after the other, the children of Hartford's best families would sneak up to the front door of Chen's home, ring the doorbell, and wait for the taciturn servants in strange robes who would unfailingly come to answer the door. Then the children would crane their necks and peek inside: while from the outside the house resembled that of any other in the neighborhood, Chen's interiors suited his traditional sensibilities. In the entry hall, there were no chairs, only huge tapestries on the wall and, in the northeast corner, a shrine to Confucius.

But if Chen's simple decorating dazzled the local youth, it was his unfailing hospitality that won him the most admiration. Clara Capron, then an eight-year-old girl whose family lived adjacent to Chen, recalled the generous habits of the foreigners next door:

> At the top of the front staircase was a hall closet. In our house, we used it for coats and hats, but the Chinese had filled it with boxes, and boxes, and boxes of nuts and sweetmeats. We were conducted solemnly up the stairs and each of us was presented with a sweetmeat. These were delicious and we went often. We were always received with politeness and it never occurred to us that we were a nuisance or bore.[9]

In addition to the perpetual snacks, Capron enjoyed sitting at the top of her fence and yelling out words to the laundryman washing clothes in Chen's backyard. Although she was almost close enough to touch him, she shouted each word as loudly as she could so that he could feel the full force of the English language. The man, perpetually smiling, indulged her, repeating each word after her and triggering wild bursts of laughter from his little neighbor whenever he stumbled over the letter *r*. Unlike the good-natured laundryman, though, the boys bristled when they were teased in class on account of their foreign accents. A local newspaper lent them a helping hand when it addressed the issue, scoring points for compassion but perhaps losing some marks for faulty geography:

> It may be mentioned, for the benefit of sundry young persons at the High School who find the imperfect pronunciation of its young Japanese students there a cause of merriment, that said students are exceedingly sensitive about the matter, and that they have expressed themselves to friends outside as cut to the heart because of laughter of scholars during recitations. Some of the Hartford juveniles are evidently in condition to be taught good breeding by these children of the land of the sun.[10]

In some ways, this earnest appeal to common decency captured the attitude of the New Englanders toward the Chinese visitors: while perfectly civil and exceedingly friendly, the locals found little to be curious about in the newcomers' history, rituals, and traditions. The Chinese were encouraged and embraced by the evangelizing natives when they took pains to fit in, and gently prodded when they did not. Manifest destiny had little room for cross-cultural pollination; it rewarded deference, invited emulation, and ignored the rest.

Hartford's notables were impressed by the boys' adjustment. Largely overlooking the natural desire of children to fit in and find comfort in a dramatically new environment, they interpreted the quick learning of English and other signs of assimilation as an affirmation of the potent American spirit and its triumph over

the becalmed and ineffectual traditions of China. As they saw
it, the Chinese were being civilized. In a letter written to all the
families that had taken Yung's students into their homes, the
Reverend B. G. Northrop, Connecticut's superintendant of education and a friend of Yung Wing's, outlined the broad principles
of the mission and the expectations of his office in regard to the
boys' education. While respecting the Chinese students' "cheerful obedience," Northrop noted that it was imperative that they
learn, in time, "self-reliance, self-denial, self-command, energy
and perseverance," and other typically Puritan virtues. They
were to be educated toward a "love of country and an ambition
to become the exponents of our science and culture, and thus
the benefactors of their own land." America being what it is,
the boys' progress was not to be left unmeasured: at Northrop's
insistence, daily records of the boys' activities and grades were to
be kept, and any lag in study or spirit promptly reported to the
mission. Especially important, according to Northrop's instructions, were English, geography, and arithmetic, and the "mental
combinations" thereof.[11]

Chen, though, ensured that a steady diet of Chinese instruction was fed to the boys to help them fend off this creeping
Americanization. He ensured that a separate letter was sent to
the boys' teachers, informing them that the mission students
under their supervision were required to study Chinese for one
hour each day. He also required that every three months the
boys were sent to the mission headquarters for two weeks to
undergo extensive instruction in their native language and literature. Yung, reflecting on these conservative measures, was
not opposed: remembering his own efforts to relearn his mother

tongue after his Yale days, he wanted to be certain that the boys' eventual reintroduction to China would be as smooth as possible, and here, at least, Chen had crafted a wise and forward-thinking policy.

The boys, however, viewed practicing Chinese as an unnecessary burden. Although most of them could grudgingly tolerate the daily hour of language class during the school year, they thoroughly detested the summer sessions. With their American peers enjoying a three-month vacation—swimming in the creek, playing ball, chasing pigs, or just lazing about—the mission's students bristled at having to spend their summers under Chen's supervision, subjected to a grueling schedule. For six weeks, they would rise at eight o'clock in the morning and study Chinese from nine until noon, from two to four in the afternoon, and from seven until nine in the evening. In addition, the boys were recalled to the mission headquarters on days deemed auspicious by traditional Chinese astrological calculations to hear Chen read the Kangxi emperor's Sacred Edict and then perform rituals of obeisance to the reigning sovereign. Such ceremonies, Chen believed, would satisfy the imperial demand that the boys not become "enclosed by foreign learning"[12] and instill in them the proper respect for their traditions.

In reality, of course, the opposite was often true. Genuflecting before a shrine to a monarch reigning thousands of miles away struck most of the boys as an inane gesture. What they learned in class made sense: math, science, navigation, even Latin and English composition. These were subjects that lent themselves to demonstrable, practical usage. They helped create engineers and orators, lawyers and generals. The Sacred Edict's sixteen moral maxims, a collection of Confucian reflections on the desired life, made little sense. They evoked a world that seemed, to the boys, extremely distant in both space and time. With every day that passed, they were assuming the mind-set of modern Americans; to the dismay of Chen, ancient China was increasingly looking incomprehensible and irrelevant.

Following their new American instincts, the boys soon formed their own baseball team. With a touch of humor and irony, they christened themselves the Orientals. The students took to football as well. Deng Shicong, who an American classmate later wrote was "built like a hound and dodged like a cat,"[13] was always the first choice when teams were being drawn up on the gridiron.

The boys also continued to excel in their studies: two years after Clara Capron had first educated her neighbor's laundryman in the finer points of English pronunciation, the now ten-year-old girl found herself under the careful instruction of the West Middle Public School in Hartford, sharing a classroom with Cai Shaoji. At first, Clara was at the very top of her class, earning an 8.5 in scholarship, while Cai, although five years her senior, mustered only a 7.9. One year later, though, he had bested her and all of the other Americans with an 8.8, followed closely by the 8.5 scored by Huang Kaijia. The boys were adjusting socially as well, taking to the time-honored traditions of American schools with increasing ease. A jealous American classmate at Hartford Public High School recalled later that "at dances and receptions, the fairest and most sought-out belles invariably gave the swains from the Orient the preference."[14]

The achievements of the mission students were noted in the press, and New England's local papers often ran cheerful reports

Yale in the 1850s. The forces of modern scientific education were bubbling beneath the pastoral surface of the campus. *Courtesy of Yung Wing and CEM Students Research Academy, Zhuhai, China.*

Yung Wing as a student at Yale, circa 1850. *Courtesy of Yung Wing and CEM Students Research Academy, Zhuhai, China.*

Yung Wing, circa 1910. *Courtesy of Yung Wing and CEM Students Research Academy, Zhuhai, China.*

Liang Ju-hao (left) and Tong Shao-yi, shortly before leaving for the United States. *Courtesy of the Thomas La Fargue Collection, Washington State University.*

The first group of boys sent to America under the auspices of the Chinese Educational Mission, 1872. *Courtesy of Yung Wing and CEM Students Research Academy, Zhuhai, China.*

Illustrations from Li En Fu's book, *When I Was a Boy in China*, depicting the bandits who robbed the train carrying the Chinese Educational Mission from California to New England, and the buffalo the boys saw along the way. *Courtesy of Yung Wing and CEM Students Research Academy, Zhuhai, China.*

Yung Liang, aka By-jinks Johnnie, circa 1876. *Courtesy of the Thomas La Fargue Collection, Washington State University.*

Admiral Tsai Ting Kan. Even as an old man, his colleagues still referred to him as Fighting Chinee. *Courtesy of Yung Wing and CEM Students Research Academy, Zhuhai, China.*

Cao Shaoji as a student in America, circa 1878. Later in life, he would establish a prominent university in China, based on the American model. *Courtesy of Yung Wing and CEM Students Research Academy, Zhuhai, China.*

Self-portrait of Liang Dunyan, circa 1878. *Courtesy of Yung Wing and CEM Students Research Academy, Zhuhai, China.*

An American magazine illustration of a Confucian lesson at Hell House, the mission's headquarters in Hartford, Connecticut. *Courtesy of Yung Wing and CEM Students Research Academy, Zhuhai, China.*

The Orientals, the Chinese Educational Mission's baseball team, dressed for competition in front of Hell House in Hartford, Connecticut. Front row: Chen Juyong, Li Guipan, Liang Dunyan, Kuang Yongzhong. Back row: Cao Shaoji, Zhong Juncheng, Woo Chung Yen, Jeme Tien Yau, Huang Kaijia. *Courtesy of the Thomas La Fargue Collection, Washington State University.*

Chung Mun Yew, the Yale rowing team's coxswain, alone and with his teammates, circa 1879. Nicknamed Money, the timid Chung needed to be cajoled by his teammates into cursing. *Courtesy of Yung Wing and CEM Students Research Academy, Zhuhai, China.*

Former U.S. president Ulysses S. Grant with Li Hongzhang, China, 1879. Upon meeting President Grant, Li exclaimed, "You and I, General Grant, are the greatest men in the world." *Courtesy of Yung Wing and CEM Students Research Academy, Zhuhai, China.*

Zeng Guofan, Yung Wing's powerful patron. *Courtesy of Yung Wing and CEM Students Research Academy, Zhuhai, China.*

Yung Wing's wife, Mary Kellogg, on her wedding day. *Courtesy of the Thomas La Fargue Collection, Washington State University.*

Joseph Twichell, a close friend of Yung Wing's and the mission, with Mark Twain. *Courtesy of Beinecke Rare Book and Manuscript Library.*

of the boys' progress. The *Springfield Union*, for example, enthusiastically wrote that the boys

> are all fitting for our higher grades of schools, and will enter our scientific schools and colleges as soon as they are prepared to do so. Elijah [Zeng], the son of Mr. [Zeng Lensheng, the mission's translator] of this city, will enter the Sheffield Scientific School and Lemuel Lung the Troy Polytechnic this year. This is certainly a great achievement for boys who have only been in this country for two years. The American system of instruction has met with the undivided approval of the educated gentlemen in charge of the students, and they express themselves thoroughly satisfied with the progress of their protégés.[15]

To the relief of Yung Wing, Chen was recalled home in 1874 to be awarded another high-ranking position. His replacement was a Confucian scholar with an easygoing attitude, a man who respected the obligations of his tradition but took pains not to meddle with things he didn't quite understand, things like Western dress and baseball. With Chen thus replaced, Yung was convinced that he could go about the business of running the mission without having to appease a perpetually surly mandarin. His joy, however, was short-lived—the next year, Yung received a correspondence from Li Hongzhang, informing him that Chen was about to return to the United States as China's new envoy extraordinary and minister plenipotentiary in Washington. Yung understood Li's motives perfectly well. With the Burlingame Treaty in effect, the shrewd official wanted to do whatever he could to cement relations with the Americans, and placing a

high-ranking man in the capital was the best way to ensure that
the Qing court would be well represented in the United States.
That would be especially true if that man had some experience
with the natives. Li, Yung knew, had much sympathy for Chen;
even if he didn't share the strict Confucian's zeal for ritual and
protocol, Li considered Chen trustworthy and loyal, virtues that
trumped all others in the eyes of a committed bureaucrat.

Yung was distraught. Not only would Chen soon return to
his part of the world, but he would be in a position superior to
his own, one that would allow Chen to meddle with the boys'
education. With Chen the highest-ranking Chinese official in
America, the students might as well start packing their bags and
prepare to return home. Yung wrote Li respectful but angry
letters, urging him to reconsider the appointment. It was, Yung
realized, an uphill battle. Li had an incomplete grasp of the
mechanics of Western pedagogy. He would write to the mission
demanding that the boys not be taught by female teachers in
American public schools, and the idea of a three-month summer
vacation struck him as especially strange. In his letters to the
mandarin, Yung took special care to reemphasize the purpose
and value of the educational project. Sensing Yung's determination and unwillingness to yield to Chen's authority, Li realized he had no choice but to proceed with caution. He trusted
Chen, but he could not afford to alienate the well-connected
and wealthy Yung. Besides, he agreed with Yung's assessments
about Chen's designs and realized that the first thing on his
new emissary's agenda would be shutting down the mission he
perceived as corrupting and wicked. If the mission died less than
three years after its inception, Li himself would look foolish,

and all the benefits he had promised the imperial ministers—
educated men, Western technologies, weapons, closer ties with
America—would dissolve. Ever the master tactician, Li soon
found a solution. He wrote Yung, thanked him profusely for his
valuable input, and named him Chen's Hartford-based assistant.
Together the two rivals would thus be the official representatives of China in America, one in the nation's capital and one in
Connecticut, each balancing out the other's proclivities. With
this plan, Li would appease not only his subordinates but also his
innate Confucian desire for harmony. In America, as in China,
he would maintain his system in balance, free from chaos.

Pleased, Yung contemplated his next move. If he was to be an
emissary, and if he was to establish the mission as a permanent
fixture in the landscape, he had better erect a permanent headquarters for himself and his project. He purchased property on
Hartford's Collins Street and began planning the construction
of a house at a frantic pace. It was to be a three-story structure,
heated by piped-in steam and equipped with modern gas and
plumbing systems. And it would house all of the mission's official functions as well as the boys—many of whom now were
dispersed in schools throughout New England—when they came
into town for their mandatory Chinese education classes.

But Yung's greatest act of root setting had little to do with
bricks and mortar. After the maelstrom of the boys' arrival died
down, he had more free time to rekindle old friendships and
strike up new ones. Among those who commanded his attention
in particular was Mary L. Kellogg, an acquaintance of old college
friends of his. Ever since his first months back in China after
graduating from Yale, Yung had given the question of marriage

much thought. He could never, he realized, marry a Chinese woman, because any worthy daughter of China would necessarily adhere to the Confucian codes relegating her to subservience. Yung wanted an equal partner, strong willed and prepared to share the burdens of the world with her husband and family.

Sitting by the fireplace at the Reverend Twichell's house, Yung shared his concerns with his friend. There was no Chinese woman he would marry, he told his friend, and no American woman who would marry him. With a wry smile, Twichell responded that while the former point might be true, the latter certainly was not. Then he spoke glowingly of Mary Kellogg. The Twichell fireplace again worked its magic—it was around that very fireplace, after all, that Twichell's closest friend, Mark Twain, had met his wife—and Yung was soon engaged.

It was a risky move. Marrying a Christian woman, Yung knew, would not go over well with the suspicious officers of the Qing court. Still, as is often the case, the heart prevailed. On March 2, 1875, Yung Wing and Mary Kellogg were married.

This uncommon interracial union made national news. In an article headlined "Yung Wing Marries a Connecticut Lady," the *New York Times* reported,

Mr. Yung Wing, of Canton, China, chief of the Chinese Educational Commission now at Hartford, was married on Wednesday to Miss Mary L. Kellogg, at the residence of her father, B. S. Kellogg, in Avon, the ceremony being performed by Rev. J. H. Twichell, of the Asylum Hill Congregational Church in Hartford, a very particular friend of the bridegroom. The bride wore a dress of white crepe, imported expressly for this occasion from China, and elaborately trimmed with floss silk embroidery. Her brother and sister attended as groomsman and brides-maid. After the ceremony, a collation was served, in which Chinese delicacies were mingled with more substantial dishes of American style. Messrs. Yoh Shu Tung, manager, and Yung Yun Foo, teacher of the commission at Hartford, were present in national costume, but the groom, who long since adopted our style, appeared in full evening dress. The bridal presents were numerous and costly. Mr. and Mrs. Wing left on the evening train for [New York] on a short wedding trip.[16]

To the surprise of no one, Chen disapproved of the union.

While Yung was settling into the happy patterns of married life, however, the following month brought the sad and sudden news that one of his students, struck with scarlet fever, had died. Cao Jiajue was three months shy of his thirteenth birthday when he died. His funeral was held at the interim headquarters of the mission in Hartford on April 20. With Cao's family thousands of miles away, the task of providing a proper ceremony to honor his soul fell to the members of the mission and their supporters, men who saw to this solemn duty with dignity and grace. At one in the afternoon, mourners slowly passed beneath the black ribbons placed above the entryway of the building on Sumner Street and made their way to the front parlor. The deceased boy lay in repose for all to view in a casket with silver fittings. His body was dressed in a traditional silk robe, his head resting on a bed of white flowers. A wreath was placed on top of the coffin, inside of which were placed ritual Chinese objects. Baskets of floral arrangements sent from Hartford residents were placed around the room, a testament to the powerful bond between the city and its foreign guests. The Reverend Twichell, who just one month earlier had officiated at Yung's wedding, was now called upon to perform a funeral. Yung Wing translated the service into Chinese. Cao's fellow students carried the coffin of their friend to the waiting carriage, and the young boy was buried in Spring Grove cemetery.

In the short time they had been in the United States, the members of the Chinese Educational Mission had embraced their host country's cultures and customs, shared in the joys of sport and leisure, celebrated a marriage, and buried one of their own in American soil. Though they could never become fully Americanized, and despite Chen's misgivings and obstinate regulations, they were nevertheless acquiring fluency in the ways of the West. They were constantly reminded, by Yung and by their teachers, that they were to be the standard-bearers of a new China, bringing technology and order to a land riddled with contradictions and shackled by conservatism. All of this was in the future, though, and the boys could be forgiven for ignoring the hard work ahead of them as they prepared for a field trip down to Philadelphia, where they would be guests of honor at the much heralded Centennial Exhibition of 1876.

The Return

Philadelphia's Centennial Exhibition of 1876 was a celebration of ingenuity and creation in all of its forms.[1] Officially known as the International Exhibition of Arts, Manufactures and Products of the Soil and Mines, it was inaugurated in early May by President Ulysses S. Grant, who welcomed the world to a 285-acre parcel of Philadelphia's Fairmount Park to examine the diverse output of thirty-seven nations, from needlework to garden tools and steam engines to Turkish carpets. The centennial, the first world's fair to be held in the United States, was an acknowledgment of the country's rising prominence on the global stage and an affirmation of its great economic potential. In its hundred years of independence, the nation had birthed a culture in which technology and invention seemingly knew no limits: the 1870s alone saw the development of the telephone, the phonograph, and the lightbulb. Inside the centennial's temporary structures of glass and steel, Americans viewed with wonder the machines and tools that they hoped could build an industrious future for all mankind.

Over the course of the next six months, 9 million visitors descended on Philadelphia, an enormous turnout at a time when there were only 46 million people living in the United States.[2] The 60,000 exhibits were housed in the 250 buildings constructed for the event, with the participating countries represented through elaborate displays reflecting their cultures and histories. Great Britain built an Elizabethan, half-timbered pavilion on the fairgrounds, while Japanese carpenters impressed guests with the inimitable woodwork of an Asian "dwelling." The Egyptian government installed a grandiose model of an ancient pyramid in the centennial's Main building, and inscribed it with a cheery salutation: "the oldest people in the world sends its morning greetings to the youngest nation."[3]

A number of American states were represented at the centennial as well, and the delegation from Kansas stood out for its two-story replica of the capitol building made out of corn, triumphantly crowned with a statue of Pomona, the Roman goddess of plenty. On display elsewhere, in an atmosphere suffused with the heady, overbearing taste of the Gilded Age, were such varied goods as Liberian coffee, Krupp machine guns from Germany, a Canadian log house, Bedouin tents from Tunisia, Egyptian cotton, a 4,000-pound block of silver from Mexico, and Peruvian Inca relics. On the fairgrounds, people stood before the Statue of Liberty, which at the time consisted of only one hand, and tried to imagine the grandeur of its finished form. A narrow-gauge railroad was constructed in the park to allow visitors to take in the whole sweep of the exhibition, and the world's first monorail was engineered to link the halls of agriculture and horticulture. A filtered-water system separate from municipal sources was built specifically for the centennial, and an internal telegraph network was installed so that guests could instruct the drivers of their carriages to come for them when it was time to leave.

As a sober counterpoint to the excited air of the exhibition, the Catholic Total Abstinence Union of America built a 35-foot-high soft-drink fountain featuring a colossal statue of Moses for those who chose not to partake of the alcohol at any of the nine full-service restaurants on-site, while at the art gallery in Memorial Hall, the displays of modern sculpture, painting, engraving, and photography drew a steady stream of viewers. Especially popular were the European works that adhered to standards of decency different from those the puritanical American public was accustomed to, shocking and titillating viewers in equal measure with lush displays of passion and nudity. True to the modern spirit of the Philadelphia Centennial, even the erotica was automated: describing a mechanically operated wax sculpture of Cleopatra, a bemused William Dean Howells wrote, "A weary parrot on her finger opens and shuts its wings, and she rolls her head alluringly from side to side and faintly lifts her arm and lets it drop again—for twelve hours every day."[4]

The most popular attraction of all, though, was Machinery Hall. The latest industrial and mechanical inventions were gathered inside the building's fourteen acres, where visitors stood in awe of the motors and dynamos that would eventually propel the United States to a preeminent position among the world's economies. While the beauty of applied crafts and the detailed handiworks of other nations left their marks on visitors to the centennial, it was the technological wonders displayed at Machinery Hall that left the deepest impressions. In a place of honor within the hall stood the gigantic Corliss centennial steam engine, with its fifty-six-ton flywheel spinning without noise or vibration at thirty-six revolutions per minute. Powered by an external boiler, this enormous machine produced 1,400 horse-power and enough torque to drive a mile of shafting throughout the hall, providing free power to exhibitors like the Otis Brothers and Company, whose representatives were on hand to demon-strate the potential of their elevator hoisting device. George H. Corliss's steam engine was fired up twice a day for the eager crowds, resting on Sundays out of deference to its inventor's religious convictions. While Corliss's motor was piously observ-ing the Sabbath, though, the Hydraulic Annex was on hand to provide power from its massive system of water pumps, and guests could meanwhile consider the potential of the Brayton ready motor, an early ancestor of the internal combustion engine. Farther down the aisles were the Line-Wolf ammonia compres-sor, a refrigeration device; the Lightning rotary cylinder press; and the Wallace-Farmer electromagnetic generator. Alexander Graham Bell's telephonic telegraphic receiver was also pres-ent and ringing, delivering disembodied voices to a delighted public. Reflecting on the technological innovations on display at Machinery Hall, the *Times* of London wrote simply, "The American invents as the Greek sculpted and the Italian painted: it is genius."[5]

Yung Wing's boys, arriving at the Centennial Exhibition at the end of the summer, opted to first stop by the Chinese exhibit in the Main Building. There, amid all the bustle of the fair, an ornate entranceway mimicking that of an ancient pagoda proudly declared in Chinese calligraphy, "The great Qing Empire." Walking through the decorative gates, the students were greeted by Li Gui, a customs official sent to supervise the imperial pavilion. He was tasked with watching over the ivory carvings, porcelain vases, and silk screens sent to Philadelphia to showcase the arts of China. Li, who had taken in the full breadth of the centennial on his time off, wrote that it seemed to him that the rest of the world was one enormous factory. He was struck by the ability of the West to employ mechanical devices to improve its well-being, while the Qing had only fine and decorative objects to offer. "Since ancient times in China machine-making techniques were labeled as diabolical tricks which would only lead to wily scheming," Li wrote. "But how wily would it be if the scheming were applied to the benefit of the country and the people?"[6]

Meeting the young boys from Connecticut who came to visit him was a revelation to Li. He didn't know such intrepid Chinese existed. The students carried themselves with ease and familiarity among the Americans, "unrestrained in speech and movement."[7] Li peppered them with questions. What did they like best at the fair? Were they homesick? The students, finding themselves engaged by a Qing official who recognized the farsightedness of their mission in America, affably and at length "jabbered with the Pig-tails there," as the *Philadelphia Times* described their conversation.[8] The boys told Li that they loved seeing the printing presses and the ivories and that, even though they missed home, right now they needed to focus on their studies. As Li and the boys bid each other farewell, the imperial official, thoroughly convinced of the promise of the young students, noted, "The outcome of western education is beyond our estimation."[9]

Following a meal at the American-themed restaurant, the boys made their way to Machinery Hall, where they were captivated by the devices rattling away inside the clattering expanse of the massive building. Naturally enough, the students soon found themselves attracted to a set of marvels more enchanting than anything even the most advanced factory could produce. At the sewing machines and other exhibits that were staffed by female attendants, the boys stared in teenaged wonder at the pretty girls working the booths, each trying to use his nicely tailored flannel suit and exotic queue to its full advantage. Even more impressive than the girls, though, was the official meeting the mission's chaperones had arranged for the boys at the centennial. Through connections, the students were introduced to President Grant, who, after a quick round of introductions, spent a few moments shaking each boy's hand.

The students' English compositions and examination papers were put on display at the Connecticut exhibit, a great honor for the boys and one that proved to them that their achievements were the pride not only of their teachers and chaperones but of the entire state. In recognition of their general excellence, the boys were given an award by Sir Charles Reed of London, the head of the bureau of judges for educational exhibits. By any measure, the boys' trip to the centennial was a success, exposing them to famous men and inventors, foreign cultures and new technologies. There would certainly be no shortage of material to use for the paper they had been assigned on the topic "What

I saw at the exhibition," and, as they boarded the train that was to take them back to Connecticut, Yung Wing's students, having just experienced all that the modern world had to offer, could be forgiven for exuding confidence as they sailed into the coming academic year.

They would soon, the boys realized, be graduating from high school and moving on to college, entering Yale and the other colleges they had heard so much about. And college, the boys were sure, would be the place for them to shine. There, Tong Shao-yi's charms would grow brighter, Yung Leang's jokes more riotous, and Liang Dunyan's pitches more precise. High school had helped them become Americanized, but college would turn them into men.

For Yung, however, the autumn of 1876 presented a new set of problems, albeit of a familiar nature. The ever-meddling Chen, finding himself unable to manage the affairs of the students because of the obligations of his diplomatic position in Washington, had found just the man to stymie Yung Wing in his stead. Woo Tze Teng, a committed Confucian thoroughly opposed to all notions of reform, was seen by Chen as the perfect candidate to take his place as co-commissioner of the educational mission in Hartford, the ideal surrogate who could be trusted to keep an eye on the boys' slouch toward barbarism and Yung Wing's Americanizing ways. Chen appointed Woo to the post just as the students were settling into the fall semester, an unwelcome bit of news that Yung received with anger and dismay. He knew Woo from his Shanghai days in the 1850s and remembered him as a man who had never been able to find steady work in government service or achieve any sort of

meaningful office. Chen's elevation of Woo, a man without any
proven talent, to a position where he could determine the course
of the mission was deeply upsetting to Yung. He rightly saw in
Woo's appointment the work of the xenophobic elements of the
Qing court. Wasn't the spectacle of the Philadelphia exhibition
enough to prove to the mandarins that the world was advancing
and China was not? Yung would later write that Chen, through
this appointment, demonstrated his allegiance to the "reaction-
ary party with all its rigid and uncompromising conservatism
that gnashes its teeth against all and every attempt put forth to
reform the government or to improve the general condition of
things in China."[10] Chen had once again shown himself to be
just another tedious bureaucrat, stuck in the past and lacking
any sort of vision or imagination.

To be sure, Chen's dislike for America was clear from the
outset, but by working so tirelessly to undermine the success of the educational mission at every turn, even while in
Washington, he proved that his opposition to Yung's project
had less to do with a professional distaste for Western dress
and behavior and more to do with the entrenched despotism
of his personality. Reflecting on the tenacity of Chen's opposition, Yung came to understand that even the man's simple
mistrust of baseball games stemmed from the calcified thinking of the rigid Confucianism he held so dear. That was why
he was so upset to see the boys running between bases, their
cheeks ruddy and flushed, when they should have been reciting
the *Analects* or some other ancient text without even pausing
to reflect on the meanings of the words. Yung wrote that Chen
was a man who "all his life had been accustomed to see the

springs of life, energy and independence, candor, ingenuity, and open-heartedness all covered up and concealed, and in a great measure smothered and never allowed their full play."[11] Against Chen's mirthless existence stood the example of the boys, who were open to new fields of endeavor and took full advantage of the opportunities presented to them in America. "Now in New England," Yung wrote, "the heavy weight of repression and suppression was lifted from the minds of these young students; they exulted in their freedom and leaped for joy. No wonder they took to athletic sports with alacrity and delight!"[12] No wonder, too, that Chen felt he needed a man like Woo to keep an eye on things.

From the outset, Woo, like Chen before him, was wary of the students. They were far from the model of classical Chinese scholars. Here in Connecticut, the boys spoke their mind and were not afraid to question authority when they thought it appropriate. Yung Kwai, one of the students and another nephew of Yung Wing's, complained that Woo "was shocked at the behavior of the boys who dared to look him in the face and were not inclined to say yes to every word that came out of his mouth."[13] In response to this American impudence, Woo would address the boys in a lengthy tirade he had printed in the *Hartford Daily Courant*:

> It should be well understood that our government fosters men of talent, and regardless of heavy expenses sends you to the best institutions of learning. It is important that you should attend to your studies with diligence, but not neglect the rules of etiquette. If you do not closely apply

yourselves now, would not your inferiority be manifest when demands of life come upon you? If you deliberately neglect all the rules of politeness of your native country, on your return home, how can you live in sympathy with your fellow countrymen? . . . Let this letter of advice cause you to consider the past and present state of things, and make up your minds to this: since your stay here is brief, as compared to the time you have spent in China, foreign habits should not become so rooted as that you cannot change them. Chinese and English studies should be carried out together in order that you may attain to positions of usefulness, if not, of what use is your coming here?[14]

Woo would criticize the boys in public, but he scrupulously kept his reports about the mission a secret from Yung Wing. Whereas Chen would at least involve Yung in the endless debates over decorum and propriety in Connecticut, Woo preferred to address his scathing critiques directly to Beijing, bypassing the normal channels and working behind Yung's back. Woo packed his dispatches to Li Hongzhang with speculation and half-truths. The boys, he quietly reported, were becoming Christians and going to church. They were playing sports. They were neglecting their Chinese studies and had no appetite for Confucius. With language calculated to terrify the Qing officials, Woo declared that the students were forming secret societies and that they were destined to return to China as nothings, or worse than nothings. They were ignoring their studies, Woo wrote, and they were ignoring him.

When, many years later, Li Hongzhang asked Yung for an

official response to these and other accusations, Yung was shocked. He didn't even know that the complaints had been leveled in the first place. In all the time that he had been trying to work with Woo, Yung didn't suspect that his co-commissioner had been tirelessly vilifying the mission to the court. Instead of simply defending the mission on the merits of its accomplishments, as Yung might have done in cooler moments, he felt an urgent need to attack Woo and his secret memorials, calling them the "malicious fabrications of a man who was known to be a crank all his life . . . only attempting to destroy the work of [Zeng Guofan] who, by projecting and fathering the educational mission, had the highest interest of China at heart."[15] Yung, who had built his career by selecting innocuous phrases to gently nudge people toward his point of view, couldn't help hissing that Woo "should have been relegated to a cell in an insane asylum or to an institution for imbeciles."

Despite the bickering of his subordinates in America, Li, on whose word the mission lived and died, still supported Yung. More precisely, Li supported the elite cadre of fighting men and intrepid sailors that Yung's mission would eventually deliver to him. As long as the boys were advancing in their studies and performing well, Li reasoned, there was no reason to recall them to China just because they weren't listening to Woo's harangues about respecting their elders and memorizing the *Book of Changes*. All that mattered to Li was that the boys would one day return to China with degrees from West Point and the Naval Academy at Annapolis, armed with the knowledge of how to win battles against the Europeans and reclaim China's lost glory. Li imagined that the students would prove to the entire apparatus of the Qing dynasty that he, as their patron, was the most talented mandarin of them all.

As the school year progressed, Yung Wing lightened the acrimonious tone of the preceding months by celebrating the Chinese New Year with his neighbors in grand style. Unlike the raucous festivities held in San Francisco's Chinatown, where the ankle-deep ash of exploded fireworks littered the streets the next morning, the party given by the mission in Hartford was a restrained and elegant affair. In February 1877, Yung and his staff welcomed their friends, supporters, and the governor of Connecticut to the headquarters building. Aside from Yung, who wore his usual Western clothes, the officials of the mission were decked out in full, ceremonious Chinese attire. Awash in padded robes of quilted gray silk, the generous hosts dazzled their visitors, themselves wearing their finest evening dress, in rooms strung with smilax and hung with Chinese pictures and inscriptions. While the food was familiar to the locals—a spread of oysters, ice cream, *charlotte russe*, confectionary cakes, and fruit—the tea service, in traditional Chinese cups, took some getting used to. With no handles to protect their palms from the heat of the tea, the Americans gingerly carried their hot beverages around the rooms as they made their way through the party, hoping not to spill anything on one another as they mingled well into the night.

Of all the people in attendance that evening, perhaps none was as aloof and distant as Woo, who, despite the many social requirements of the mission and his professional interactions with Americans, was always awkward around the natives, ignorant of their manners and frequently confused by their customs. In June, even after he had been in the country for more than half a year, the tactless Woo indignantly refused to give up his seat to multiple women on one of the city's transit lines. In mocking, condescending language, the *Hartford Daily Times* recorded the bizarre behavior of this Chinese official, so different from those of the others, who were found to be unfailingly considerate and accommodating:

> One day last week, one of the Asylum Avenue cars was making its slow way outward, well filled with gentleman and ladies. The seats being all occupied, as lady after lady entered they were invited to sit by gentlemen, who in succession arose and politely gave their seats to the ladies until, finally, the only representative of the sterner sex who retained a seat was a portly Chinese commissioner. Soon the car stopped again, and the Oriental, who had been all along expressing by his looks a profound contempt for this silly chivalry of the Americans, felt the pressure of public opinion too strong to resist longer, and, rising, yielded his seat to a simpering school girl, who took it as if it belonged to her ladyship. The Celestial countenance grew darker, and its owner clung to the strap with a tightened grip until he reached his destination, the corner of Sumner Street, when, reaching the sidewalk, and meeting an acquaintance he exploded—"too muchee she!"[16]

Despite Woo's inability to settle into a comfortable and quiet American existence, and the mind-numbingly repetitive lessons in Chinese studies that he had instructed the boys to take at the mission headquarters—subsequently known as Hell House— the students themselves were having no problem racking up successes in their regular classes. Surprising no one, Jeme Tien-yau, the brilliant Jimmy, entered Yale in 1877. He was seventeen and had been in America for just five years, but his intellect transcended the boundaries of language and culture. In his first year in college, Jeme won his class's top prize in mathematics and was thrilled to study at Yale's school of engineering. The memory of the train ride from Sacramento to Springfield still fresh in his mind, he devoted himself to becoming a railway engineer.

By the spring of 1878, three other boys had sufficiently advanced through their studies and were given permission to graduate from Hartford High School in April.[17] The graduation ceremony was scheduled for the eighteenth, but on that morning it was clear that a severe storm would make it difficult for everyone to attend. Still, for their teachers and friends who braved the elements to share in the boys' accomplishment, Twichell and Northrop among them, the day was one of celebration and pride, filled with a sense of genuine accomplishment. From young children who had arrived in America ignorant of English, terrified of churches, and separated from their families by thousands of miles, the students had become well-adjusted young men, armed with practical knowledge and a sense of purpose and self-worth. As the audience proudly watched, the beaming students entered the room from the north aisle and walked toward a large central platform, where they took their seats to the tune of "Amaryllis," played by the school band of Hartford High. There, on the central dais, in a sea of girls in pastel dresses and boys in simple suits, sat the three representatives of the Chinese Educational Mission, wearing elaborate silk robes. One boy's outfit was embroidered with Chinese patterns, another accessorized with a pearl-gray sash, and the third coordinated with yellow satin leggings and a matching fan, topped off with a cap sporting the red button of a mandarin. On any other day, the boys strove to seem American, but on that day, their finest hour, they felt comfortable reminding their friends that they were Chinese and that they were proud. Through their hard work and dedication to their studies, the boys had earned this special indulgence. The three Chinese students—Cai Shaoji, Huang Kaijia, and Liang Dunyan—were scheduled to deliver graduation speeches on historical and current events, and while they waited for their turns, it must have been hard for them to ignore the fact that all eyes were on them.

When it was finally his turn to speak, Huang, known as Breezy Jack on account of his easy manner, rose and made his way to the stage. He presented an oration about the Frenchman Jean-Baptiste Colbert, the economic minister to Louis XIV whose thoughtful and wide-ranging reforms opened the way for France to become the preeminent Continental power. Huang liberally employed his hands to emphasize key points, winning applause and flowers from the audience when he was finished. While Huang's speech obliquely addressed the need for reforms in his homeland under the thin veil of French history, Cai Shaoji tackled China's plight directly. In his speech, entitled "The Opium Trade," Cai spoke from his personal experience about the devastating effects of the drug. At home in China, he explained, opium was for sale on every street in shops advertising "the magical soother" or "the priceless medicine." If people knew the truth, they would call it instead "the vile dirt." Cai told of fathers selling their children in order to support their habit and assured his listeners that using the drug was worse than murdering someone with a knife. He decried the disastrous Opium Wars and the humiliation of treaty ports, bemoaning the regrettable position China found itself in. As he finished, his voice reached a climax. "China is not dead," he said with passion, "only sleeping, and will eventually rise to the proud station in the world which God has destined her to fill." At this, the crowd, accustomed to the idea of manifest destinies, clapped loudly. But Liang Dunyan gave the best speech of the three. Long gone were the days in which his compositional skill sufficed only for cute ditties about kittens lapping milk. In the six years since his arrival, Liang, disciplined and bright, had become a master of logical argumentation and, despite his aversion to social interaction, an excellent public speaker. At a party, he would rather keep to himself; at the podium, he was in his element. He began speaking, having chosen another contemporary issue, the recent war between Russia and Turkey. Decrying the public's assumption that the Russians were innocent victims and the Turks bloodthirsty marauders, Liang insisted that Russia was "a thief in the uniform of a policeman," an aggressive nation seeking to steal the wealthy city of Constantinople from the Turks, a people whose greatest crime was being an Asian power in Europe. "Russia is a thief!" he repeated. Liang's heartfelt defense of "Asiatic" Turkey led the *Hartford Daily Times* to write that "no address received so much applause as this one, and no other was delivered with so much spirit, and with that off-hand sort of oration that marks the successful 'campaigner,' who carries [his] audience along with his positive and sweeping style." He was asked back to the stage when he had finished to take a second bow.

After a summer vacation mostly spent studying Chinese and reciting Confucian texts, the three graduates were off to Yale. The college, they soon realized, was no magical place. A few months into their freshman year, Liang, Cai, and Huang still felt much as they had before. Liang remained talented but reserved, doing well as a pitcher for Yale's baseball team but not inspiring the sort of camaraderie that makes college friendships last a lifetime. In his class's yearbook, Liang is mentioned matter-of-factly, with none of the enthusiasm and familiarity that marks most of his peers' entries. All three were excelling academically, and were admitted together to Kappa Sigma Epsilon, a secret society where they made new friends. But none was transformed.

Chung Mun Yew's story, however, was different. Entering Yale a year later, in 1879, the short and handsome boy, nicknamed Money because of his name's phonetic proximity to the English word, began to blossom. At Hartford High, he was a competent and well-liked student, even winning a five-dollar prize for declamation in his senior year. But he was no Liang Dunyan, no brilliant athlete and remarkable orator. In high school, Chung was just an affable chap, content with inhabiting the warm middle of his social crowd. College changed that. At Yale, he was recruited to the rowing team. It was clear that his diminutive size would make him a perfect coxswain, but it was also apparent that he lacked the requisite saltiness. The coxswain, Chung's friends explained to him, gave the crew its rhythm, and as such needed to employ colorful language. One of Chung's classmates recalled the boy's difficulty at adjusting to profanity:

He was told he must swear at the oarsmen to make them row their best; for he usually sat in his place in silence. Swearing did not come naturally to him, for he was grave and impassive; but finally, being told he must curse them, he would, at the most unexpected moments, and without any emphasis mechanically utter the monosyllable "damn!" whereat the crew became so helpless with laughter, they begged him desist.[18]

Chung's cleverness, however, more than made up for his timidity. A few days before competing in an important contest with Harvard in the fall of 1880, Chung set off on a secret mission. Returning shortly before the race, he explained to his teammates that he had gone to Cambridge to gather intelligence. They pressed him to explain himself further. Chung said that he had walked along the banks of the Charles River, observing the course that errant leaves took as they were pushed by the currents down the river. He measured the frequency and length of the Charles's ripples. Such data, he said, was extremely valuable: if he could calculate the precise nature of their rival's river, the Yalies could score an important victory. As his team won the race that year and the next, few doubted that Chung had much to do with the success.

Years later, dispatched to America as a Chinese diplomat, Chung attended a cocktail party and mentioned casually that he was once a coxswain at Yale. An incredulous man standing nearby sized up the elegantly dressed Chung. Interrupting the conversation, the man introduced himself as a graduate of Harvard and said that he very much doubted that Chung had ever even seen a university boat race. Calmly, Chung turned to face the man. "It is true that I had never seen a Harvard crew row," he said. "They were always behind me."[19]

Whether they were let down by their collegiate experience or transformed by it, the students who were enrolled in New England's colleges were deeply aware that their primary responsibility was to master the practical sciences that were needed in China. Almost to a man, they studied engineering or mining, took classes in mathematics and physics, and dreamed of the time when they would return home and put all of their knowledge to use.

Back in Beijing, however, Li was becoming increasingly impatient. He had just one goal in mind, to see the students enroll in America's prestigious military academies. Trains and mines were nice, but warships and infantry were what won battles. The boys' admission to West Point and the Naval Academy would require the approval of the American government, and Yung, who had been tasked with handling the students' applications through the State Department in Washington, held a more realistic appraisal of the students' chances of being accepted at either institution. A storm of anti-Chinese sentiment had been brewing in the United States, chilling America's relations with China despite the warm welcome shown to the mission in New England. On behalf of Li, Yung patiently waited for an answer from the State Department, hoping that the graduating students' hard work and excellent grades would be enough to persuade the American officials to accept the boys at the nation's military colleges and placate his superior back home.

Still, the strength of the anti-Chinese movement lingered in the back of Yung Wing's mind. This new wave of xenophobia, more vigorous than previous outbreaks, had its origins in an economic crisis out west. While Huang, Cai, Liang, and a number of other students enrolled in different high schools were preparing to graduate, a severe drought was taking its toll on the wheat fields of the American prairie just as the silver supply of Nevada's Comstock Lode dwindled to one-third of its prior levels. In San Francisco, where the boom-town mentality of the gold rush had bred an irrationally exuberant investment style that paid little heed to risk, the effects of these economic reversals and the ensuing havoc they wreaked on the stock markets were especially severe. Restless men, their fortunes evaporated, gathered in the vacant sandlots by the city hall, where they would listen with rapt attention to tirades given by speakers blaming the financial collapse on everything but their own shoddy gambles: it was the fault of the railroads, of the banks, and, most of all, of the Chinese.

Among the speakers, Dennis Kearny, an Irish sailor who had lost everything he owned when his mining stocks collapsed, drew the largest following. Each evening, in a sandlot illuminated by bonfires and raised torches, he urged the people of San Francisco to fight back against the powerful interests that were keeping them enslaved. "Before I starve in a country like this," Kearny swore, "I will cut a man's throat and take whatever he has got." He railed against the "lecherous bondholders, political thieves, and the railroad robbers," but reserved his strongest venom for the Chinese. Kearny spoke dramatically of sending balloons laden with dynamite over Chinatown and concluded the nightly tirades with his defiant coda, "The Chinese must go!"[20]

An observer described the ugly scene which unfolded frequently at the San Francisco docks, where incoming Chinese laborers were given a vicious welcome to America: "They follow the Chinaman through the streets, howling and screaming after him to frighten him. They catch hold of his cue [*sic*] and pull him from the wagon. They throw brickbats and missiles at him, and so, often these poor heathens, coming to this Christian land under sacred treaty stipulations, reach their quarter of this Christian city covered with wounds and bruises and blood."[21] Things were not much better for the immigrants once they settled in Chinatown. There, even when surrounded by their countrymen, the Chinese stayed indoors and secured the windows of their stores with thick wooden bars come nightfall as a precaution against the rampant and unprosecuted vandalism. Young men would call the Chinese "rats" and pelt them with rocks.

In July of 1877, the city erupted in an orgy of violence. As a crowd of ten thousand people gathered in the city to express support for a nationwide labor rebellion, an anti-immigrant organization seized the opportunity to channel the mob's anger toward the Chinese, urging the masses, "On to Chinatown!" Thus commanded, the crowd made its way through the Chinese section of the city, destroying laundries and setting fire to other local businesses. Chinese bystanders were shot dead in the streets as the mob pressed on to the dockyards of the Pacific Mail Steamship Company, which the crowd held responsible for bringing the despised Chinese immigrants to American shores. Firemen arriving on the scene to put out the flames were assaulted, the National Guard was unable to contain the violence, and it eventually took three days of street fighting and the arrival of the U.S. Navy to quell the unrest. Undeterred by their stalled insurrection, Kearny's followers switched their focus from hooliganism to political agitation and, by the end of the year, founded the Workingmen's Party of California. Led by Kearny, it was dedicated to anti-immigrant policies. Its platform of Chinese exclusion had a profound impact on American political discourse at the national level. Western congressmen, eager to ride the angry waves of popular resentment toward assured reelection, were quick to condemn the Chinese in the most lurid and ethnocentric terms imaginable.

The politics of race-baiting had already spread east by the time, in 1878, when Yung received word from the State Department. The terse reply was not a total surprise: there was no room for Chinese students in military academies. This was a decision, Yung bitterly noted, that smacked of Kearny-ism and sandlotism. The Americans disingenuously claimed that military colleges fell outside of the aegis of the Burlingame Treaty of 1868 and thus were not covered by the educational reciprocity guaranteed by that agreement. Although the boys were free to attend any private colleges that would have them—Tong Shao-yi, the mission's crown prince, had just begun his studies at Columbia, and a few other boys had entered the Massachusetts Institute of Technology—Yung knew that going forward the mission's worth would drop precipitously in the eyes of the Qing officials. The success of the Chinese graduates of Hartford High School enrolled in Yung Wing's alma mater and elsewhere wouldn't be enough to satisfy Li. It was professional soldiers, after all, whom Li Hongzhang was after, not Yale Bulldogs.

To make matters worse for Yung, by the end of 1880, the Americans, not content with simply ignoring the spirit of the Burlingame Treaty, had pushed the Qing court to allow them to modify the agreement with terms that authorized the U.S. government to "regulate, limit, or suspend" Chinese immigration. This diplomatic reversal, went the Qing's thinking, was rude and regrettable, but at least it wasn't accompanied by armed forces marching on the Forbidden City. In any case, the emperor, powerless to resist, agreed to the new, demeaning terms.

American politicians, eager to throw red meat at their constituents, were no longer bound by an international treaty to allow the Chinese to settle in the United States, and the era of the Chinese Exclusion Act was not long in coming. In 1881, a bill was put forth in the U.S. Senate to ban all Chinese immigration for the next twenty years. Senator John F. Miller, of California, who sponsored the proposed law, declared that the Chinese were "inhabitants of another planet," poisoning a country once "resonant with the sweet voices of flaxen-haired children" with the "gangrene of their oriental civilization."[22] His bill, enacted as law in 1882, marked the first time in American history that people were forbidden from entering the country on the basis of their nationality.

When the Burlingame Treaty was altered in 1880, Yung and Chen, united for once, lodged official protests in their capacities as diplomats, but without result. The headwinds were too strong. In December of that year, the situation had deteriorated to the point where Chen had to plead with the American government

to deploy the U.S. Army to protect the Chinese citizens living out west. Li, who had seen his hopes of a modern military
dashed by the refusal of the State Department to allow the boys
to study at West Point and Annapolis two years earlier, now
saw his position at stake as well. Ever attuned to the changing
favors of the imperial court, Li understood that the Americans,
once seen as the only Western power interested in dealing with
the Chinese on an equal footing, could be just as devious as the
rest. They broke their treaties with the same callous disregard
for Chinese rights as the Europeans and had little interest in
safeguarding the lives of the Chinese nationals on their soil.
America was no longer a favored nation at the court, and it
became increasingly obvious to Li that the educational mission
was a growing liability, which left him exposed to charges of
incompetence from the growing clique of Qing officials who
mistrusted American intentions. Never mind that the mission
was hugely expensive and had lately forced Li to take money
from his precious navy to pay for the boys' schooling. Ever the
politician, and eager to be on the winning side of any debate,
Li did the only thing he felt he could do to save his career: he
took steps to end the educational mission. He would toy with
a few possible ways of moving forward. Perhaps he could play a
rearguard action, he thought, defending the mission at the court
until the fifty students who would soon be studying at American
colleges received their degrees, while immediately recalling back
to China the boys who were still in high school. Not knowing
exactly what to do, Li wrote to Chen and Woo and asked for
their thoughts. Both advised terminating the mission. Yung,
unsurprisingly, was kept out of the loop.

There were domestic factors beyond the narrow confines of imperial politics that motivated Li's decision as well. From the outset, the entire educational project had been heralded by Zeng Guofan as a way to ensure that China would have a sturdy foundation upon which it could build a modern military complex, consisting of both capable soldiers and the factories required to keep them well armed. That, after all, was the reason why Zeng had sent Yung to Massachusetts to acquire the tools to build an arsenal during the 1860s. It had been more than twenty years since then, and the arsenal, which had launched China's first modern warship, *Tianqi*—"Auspicious"—in 1868, had grown in size and prominence and was eventually joined by a shipyard at Foochow, a mine at Taiping, a torpedo school at Dagu, and a naval college at Tianjin. Li knew that these local institutions offered him something that the mission to America could not: cover from the conservative critics at the court. There, as elsewhere in China's nascent defense industry, foreign experts taught the latest technology to Chinese workers and students, who were also exposed to a thoroughly Confucian education outside of their technical classes. Li could now see the outline of his eventual plan coming together. All the boys in America would be recalled and sent to assist and advise at these arsenals and shipbuilding yards in China. Li could have his weapons and be free from the taint of foreign influence at the same time.

When Yung Wing learned of Li's intentions, he was crushed. He believed that China needed not merely the martial trappings of modernity but also the mind-set that gave birth to the great innovations of the day, something Li's plan made no allowance for. Li was grasping for apples, while Yung was presenting him with the tree. At the Centennial Exhibition in Philadelphia, the boys had seen the latest in modern technology. More than that, they had felt a kinship to the culture that gave rise to elevators, Corliss steam engines, and telephones. China didn't need simply to build copies of Gatling guns and gunboats. It needed to understand the world through a fundamentally different perspective, an outlook framed by American schools. If Li gave up on the educational mission and sent the boys to the arsenals, Yung feared, China would be playing catch-up with the West forever, caught in its suffocating and stationary Confucian past, minting second-rate copies of Western weapons instead of nurturing inventors and great thinkers.

Sensing the coming fight, Yung had enlisted the support of Twichell in October 1880 to rally the prominent Americans with whom he was friendly to the mission's defense. Eager to assist a cause in which he believed so deeply, Twichell drafted a letter imploring the Chinese government to commit to the mission, laying out the reasons for keeping the boys in America. The letter was signed by the heads of many of the prominent colleges of New England and sent to the American representative in Beijing, who respectfully delivered it to Li. But even with a host of signatories standing behind Yung Wing and the boys, the plea failed to put a dent in Li's resolve. By December, Yung wrote to Twichell, "Woo's representations of the students together with the new treaty concerning Chinese immigration & the howl of the Pacific coast against Chinese all contributed to disgust Li & he has finally to my utter sorrow decided to give up the scheme."[23]

Since Twichell and Yung's appeal to Li's intellect had failed, it was time for them to appeal to his vanity. Li had always regarded himself as a steely soldier destined by fate and talent to build his nation. Yung searched for someone similarly eminent and powerful to convince Li of the mission's worth. Ulysses S. Grant came to mind as a natural candidate. Li, who referred to Grant as "the American Bismarck," had once met the former president in Tianjin, stepping forward to declare, "You and I, General Grant, are the greatest men in the world."[24] Yung had discovered that Grant was going to be in New York on December 17, and he asked Twichell to travel to the Fifth Avenue Hotel, where the ex-president was to stay, and intercede on the mission's behalf. Yung presented Twichell with twenty dollars in an envelope to cover the travel expenses. Twichell tried to think of a scenario in which he could accost Grant at the hotel long enough to make his case, but his imagination failed him. "I had served under Gen. Grant in the army," Twichell noted in his diary, "but was personally quite unknown to him. How could I dare?"[25]

In the end, Twichell solicited the help of a friend—Mark Twain. Twichell and the writer were extremely close, and Twain thought nothing of providing Twichell with an introduction to Grant, whose memoirs he would soon be publishing. Twain reported to Twichell that they were all to meet on the following Tuesday, December 21, in New York. At the hotel, Twichell was impressed by Grant: "[He] launched out in as free and flowing a talk as I ever heard, marked by broad, intelligent and benevolent views, on the subject of China, her wants, disadvantages, &c. Now and then he asked a question, but kept the lead of the conversation. At last he proposed of his own accord to write a letter to [Li], advising the continuance of the Mission, asking only that I prepare him some notes by giving him points to go by."[26]

Yung realized that this was the mission's last chance at survival. He had resigned himself to giving up on both the mission and China itself if this final gambit failed. In a letter thanking Twichell for all of his help, he ruefully added, "If the greatest general of the age, & the whole weight of American learning and Christian character are not heeded and their advice, then I say let China go to the dogs."[27]

In March, Yung learned that Grant's letter had in fact persuaded Li to keep the mission alive for the time being. In explaining this stay of execution, however, Li made it clear that by this point it was Woo, and not Yung, whom he wished to see in charge of the boys, writing that "Mr. Yung will find it impossible to be openly obdurate, and Mr. [Woo] will of course be cooperative."[28]

Li's change of heart had little to do with a newfound appreciation for the work of the students. Rather, he had seen in the recent outpouring of American support for the mission, as engineered by Yung and Twichell, an ominous signal that recalling the boys back to China would be considered a grave insult to the United States. He didn't want to have to take responsibility for a wrong move, or perhaps even cause a diplomatic incident. But neither did he want to appear too sympathetic to the Americans, or to clash with Woo and Chen. Ever the cautious politician, he sought a way to wash his hands of the mission. At the end of March—despite having informed Yung a few days earlier that the mission was, for the time being, safe—he wrote another letter, this time to his superiors in the court, admitting that the majority of students in America had been corrupted by Western influence and that the mission was costing China a great deal of money. He requested official instruction on how to proceed, but left no question as to where he stood personally on the matter.

On June 8, Li's superiors sent their own memorial to the emperor: because the boys "went abroad at an age susceptible to foreign influences, gradually they adopted the local customs and became culturally displaced and remodeled. Before they could have acquired the advanced technology of the west, they all plunged themselves into the American culture. The government is sincerely disheartened. Since all bureaus are in an urgent need of talented people, they should be recalled immediately."[29]

The emperor agreed the next day. The mission was finished.

On July 9, Twichell wrote in his journal, "Another dispatch from China received yesterday removes all doubt. The Mission is doomed. After all that has been done to save it, it must die ultimately and all its glorious promise fail. Alas. Alas. The disappointment of all its friends is extreme. Poor Wing, it is heaviest of all upon him. God sustain him. It is apparently, or in my judgment, the result of his separation from it. That gave the opposition a chance which has been abundantly improved. Surely 'tis a strange Providence."[30]

At the time of the mission's closure, over sixty of the students were enrolled in American institutions of higher education. Of that number, twenty-two were at Yale, eight at the Massachusetts Institute of Technology, three at Columbia, one at Harvard, and the rest at disparate colleges and technical

schools throughout the Northeast. Another five years in the
United States would have been enough for all of the mission's
students to graduate according to Yung's original plan. Only two
students—Ouyang King and the brilliant Jeme Tien-yau—had
had a chance to graduate, receiving their degrees a few months
before the mission was recalled.

By the time the emperor's decision made its way to Yung
Wing, the students, having only recently wrapped up the year's
classes, were enjoying a well-deserved summer vacation together
at Bantam Lake, Connecticut. Yung solemnly arrived at the lake
to tell them the sorry news. The boys, who had been preparing
a celebratory picnic, were stunned. They walked slowly back to
their tents and packed up their belongings.

Some students of the mission, however, had a year earlier
resolved never to return to China. Tan Yew Fun and Yung Kwai,
the student who had dared to question Woo's authority, had
both converted to Christianity while living in America and had
been ordered by an incensed Woo to return home in the fall
of 1880. As they passed through Springfield, Massachusetts,
on their way to the Pacific coast, where a ship would be waiting to deliver them to the certain punishment they would face
from Qing officials, both boys decided to take their chances
and jump off the train, eventually making their way back to
Hartford. There, Twichell wrote, they "went into concealment,
and remained behind."[31]

Yung Kwai, although continuing to be comfortably supported
in America by his uncle Yung Wing, nevertheless retained bitter
memories about the management of the mission during his years
of study. He still reviled Woo, who fought with him at every

turn and instituted policies designed to stifle any sort of original thought. Writing of his uncle's co-commissioner, Yung Kwai rhetorically asked, "What else could have been expected from a man brought up to shut his eyes to everything not Chinese for fear that his relish for the dry husks of Confucian classics might be spoiled thereby?"[32] He explained his decision to stay in the United States with a simple metaphor: "A bird born in captivity cannot appreciate the sweet odor of the woods, but let it once have free space to exercise its wings, off it flies to where natural instinct leads."[33] After he jumped off the train and found refuge, his natural instinct—and intellect—led him to Yale and then toward a graduate degree in mining from Columbia.

Tan Yew Fun, meanwhile, made his way back to his host family, the Carringtons of Colebrook, Connecticut. There, he was welcomed as a full-fledged member of the household, which included doing chores around the house and barn. Mrs. Carrington, who had lost a son in the Civil War, lavished on Tan all of the affection and concern she showed to her natural-born children. On Tuesday, August 24, 1880, she simply noted in her diary that "Tan had his queue cut."[34] In so doing, he severed his last link to imperial China. Three years later, Tan died of pneumonia and was buried as a Carrington in the family's plot in Colebrook.

In the summer of 1881, the boys preparing to leave America bid farewell to their friends and acquaintances. One student, who had grown accustomed to spending every Saturday shooting with an American friend, solemnly gifted the gun he had carried on their outings together to his partner "as a pledge of eternal friendship."[35] Another boy, Liang Cheng—who had been the captain of the baseball team at Phillips Academy—visited with Henry Fearing, a Massachusetts businessman and strong supporter of the mission. Liang assured Fearing that their separation was only temporary and that one day he would return to Amherst as the Chinese ambassador.

He made good on his promise. In 1903, Sir Liang Cheng, as China's minister plenipotentiary to the United States, Cuba, Mexico, and Peru, reunited with his old friend. He was accompanied by seven Chinese boys whom he had brought to be enrolled in local schools. They presented Fearing with a silver loving cup, bearing the image of an uneducated Chinese boy timidly alighting from a carriage on one side and an image of the same youth, thoroughly schooled, standing proudly on the other.

In 1905, Fearing welcomed a group of forty Chinese students who were then studying in America to his home, which was draped with the yellow dragon flag of the Qing empire for the occasion. There, at a reception for these spiritual descendants of Yung Wing's educational mission, Sir Liang spoke to the assembled boys about his own experiences as a student in America more than two decades earlier. Not in attendance, but prominently noted on the evening's program, was Yung Kwai, who had by that time lost the restlessness of his youth and settled into a comfortable and prestigious career as the secretary-interpreter of the Chinese legation in Washington.

In August of 1881, however, more than a hundred of Yung Wing's students were still in America, awaiting their ultimate departure for China. The families of Twichell's Asylum Hill Congregational Church held a farewell service for the remaining boys at the Bartlett home. Woo Yangzeng, one of the students at the event, was presented with a letter addressed to his mother from Mrs. Bartlett, under whose roof he had lived for so many years in America. She wrote,

> *Dear Mrs. Woo,*
> *You will, I am sure, be glad to see your little boy grown into a man and feel proud of him. He has been with us during his whole stay in America, and we have become very much attached to him. He has pursued an upright, steadfast course in his studies as well as in his general character. And we feel that he will be a useful man and serve his country with honor to himself and to his parents. We shall miss him and the others who leave us tomorrow, and hope for his success in whatever he may undertake. I hope that we may see him sometime in the future, but if we do not we shall never cease to wish the best things for him. With sincere respect and sincere wishes,*
> *Margaret L Bartlett*
> *Hartford 1881*[36]

On August 8, an auspicious date in the Chinese calendar, forty pieces of luggage were arranged in a pile outside of the Asylum Street depot in Hartford. On the sides of the black leather trunks and boxes were the words "Chinese Commission" in English and various characters and addresses in Chinese. The first group of twenty-two boys to make the long trip home stood in the summer heat in their Western dress while they waited for the train, wondering what the future had in store for them. A procession of

saddened supporters of the mission came by to see their friends
off, including old colleagues and classmates who tried to assure
them that the separation was only temporary. Woo, the paranoid
architect of this sad scene, was by now thoroughly despised by
all. Fearing for his life as he was about to accompany the boys on
the voyage back to China, he made sure that they were searched
for weapons before being allowed to board the train. As the
ladies waved their handkerchiefs and the proud puritan men of
New England tried their best to remain stoic, the train pulled
away, carrying the students toward Niagara Falls and then on to
San Francisco. On September 27, the last detachment of boys
undertook this same rail journey west, wearing bows of black-
and-white silk in the buttonholes of their jackets, mourning the
death of the Chinese Educational Mission.

Assembled in San Francisco, the city that had so awed them
as fresh arrivals to the United States, the boys, who had once
known nothing of American culture and pastimes, challenged
the members of a local baseball team to a quick game. In front
of a gathering crowd of spectators accustomed to racist invective
and anti-Chinese legislation, the Orientals took to the field for
one last hurrah. Liang Dunyan stepped to the mound, cradled
the ball in his left hand, and soon, "with the most surprising con-
tortions of the body, while his queue was describing a series of
mathematical curves in the air," launched a sequence of pitches
that bewildered the American batters.[37] The Orientals won
their final game, and, with their spirits raised somewhat, Yung
Wing's students boarded the ship that was to bring them home
to China.

Part III

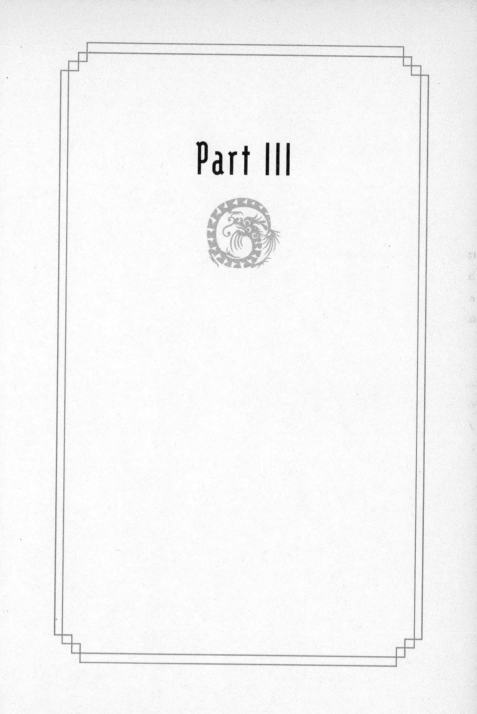

The Prisoners

As the ship carrying them home made its way from the San Francisco Bay and into the Pacific Ocean in the fall of 1881, the boys stood on the deck and stared at the city's slowly disappearing skyline on one side and the open waves and empty horizon on the other. Finally, when distance and dusk clouded their vision, they retired to their quarters and to sleep.

Still anxious about what their future would be, with some of the boys thinking about uncompleted degrees and others about severed relationships, they began to entertain a soothing thought. At the very least, the boys told one another, they were returning to China as the very embodiment of the type of men their country needed most, clever young mandarins eager and ready to take their place at the nation's helm. "I take comfort," one of the boys wrote to his American headmaster in Massachusetts, "in knowing that back home I'll no longer be a child but a Man, with respect and with dignity."[1]

But even that hope lost its ability to steady the boys after a few days in rough waters. Another thought, far less optimistic, came in its place. Once a cohesive group with a common endeavor and a shared destiny, the boys were gradually realizing that as soon as they disembarked in Shanghai, the Chinese Educational Mission would cease to exist. They might gain power and influence. China might welcome them back with open arms. But no matter what course their futures took, they would never again congregate monthly as they did in Hartford to play ball, chat, and reassure one another—with a pat on the back, a warm word, or a smile—that whatever happened, they were all in it together.

Some found that thought more troubling than others. Strolling on the deck, Yung Leang had reason to be pessimistic. Whereas in Connecticut, true to his nickname of By-jinks Johnnie, Yung was rowdy and impulsive, rarely finding time to think about his future, here on the ship he had plenty of opportunity to reflect on what life in China would hold for him. He, like Yung Kwai, was a nephew of Yung Wing's, and he had heard his uncle's stories many times and knew all about the older man's efforts to relearn Chinese after returning home from New Haven thirty years earlier. Yung Leang also knew about Yung Wing's humiliation at the hands of Hong Kong's British barristers and the years he spent struggling to find steady employment. While his uncle was a Yale graduate, Yung Leang had only begun his studies at the college before being yanked out and shipped back home by imperial decree. All the preparation, the years of learning English, and the time spent studying were for nothing. What would he do back home without a college degree? If only he had had the chance to graduate from Yale, like his friend Jeme

Tien-yau, he could reasonably expect to find a lucrative position in Shanghai or Hong Kong. Jeme was already an engineer and spoke with calm certainty of the foreign companies he believed would vie for his services once home. Yung Leang had only a high school diploma, which would have sufficed had he been born into a wealthy and well-respected family, like his friend Tong Shao-yi. Had that been the case, he could probably have counted on some comfortable arrangement to materialize, some measure of employment that would stimulate his wallet if not his mind. Aside from his prosperous uncle, Yung Leang came from a family of modest means; like Yung Wing before him, he knew he would have to make his own way.

On deck, at least, he could lose himself in nostalgic reflection. In Hartford, he was known to everyone as the life of any party. Still, he kept up with his schoolwork. At his high school graduation, he delivered the winning speech in the prestigious rhetoric competition, winning a bouquet of flowers and the praise of his peers, Chinese and American alike. His friends came to see him as a trusted source for a quick joke or a harmless prank. While on the ship, then, he was still By-jinks Johnnie and as such obliged to provide merriment. Passing the time in conversation, he assumed his place at the center of the group's attention.

The ship stopped in Yokohama, Japan. A few days later, someone shouted that Shanghai was visible in the distance. Yung Leang rushed to the deck. Seeing China—the homeland he left as a young boy and where his parents and siblings now must be waiting his return—he forgot his grim thoughts for a moment. He would show his family how educated and responsible he was, how mature. The other students were running from their berths to the deck. For the first time since they were children, the boys were home.

As the ship cut through the shallow waters of the port, their laughter dissipated. It became clear that they were being welcomed not by their families but by a phalanx of police officers. After disembarking, the students were ordered to hurry up and grab their trunks. The boys had taken no more than ten or twenty steps on Chinese soil before a small squad of imperial gendarmes encircled them. The captain of this cheerless homecoming party informed them quietly and curtly that they were all to march in an orderly fashion to a nearby location, which he referred to as the Knowledge Wishing Institution.

This institution was, in fact, the local police station, a compound made up of narrow, white, and poorly lit buildings laid out in such a way that each edifice appeared to serve no other purpose than stunting the growth of the one immediately adjacent to it. The building, the boys later learned, had been shut down for ten years, and the seaside smell of rot and decay stung their nostrils. The captain instructed his men to divide the guests— the term suggested they were not prisoners—into small groups, each occupying its own modest-sized cell.

Stunned silent, the boys obeyed the orders. Although they had practiced their Chinese during the monthly language sessions, few spoke their native tongue with sufficient confidence and skill to reason with the guards. One or two tried, but soon realized that after nearly a decade in New England, even a grammatically correct sentence in Chinese came out sounding foreign, stilted, wrong. Instead, they conferred with one another in whispered English, nervous and confused, trying to ascertain the cause of their incarceration. Yung Leang became self-conscious at the sound of his voice. He noticed, as he later wrote in his journal, that he pronounced English words with the weathered and pitted texture so common in the voices of his American friends and teachers at Yale, drawing out syllable after syllable, prolonging and soundlessly rolling his *r*'s. There was more talk of prison, more speculation. A few hours later, conversation dwindled. As night began to fall, the boys grew silent with exhaustion and tried to sleep, not an easy task, given that their beds were made of wooden boards laid on top of rickety stools.

The next morning, their second day in China, Yung Leang and his friends were awakened by shouting guards who rattled their clubs on the cells' bars and ordered the boys to get ready for interrogation. In groups of three and four, they were let out of their cells and led to a small, mildewed office, where the captain and a few other officers began asking them questions. What, the officials demanded, were they doing in the United States for so long? Why hadn't they returned earlier? Were they still loyal subjects of the emperor?

Shocked, the boys repeated, nearly in unison, the same explanation. They were, as each told their dour inquisitors, sent on an official mission to study the ways of the West so as to apply foreign knowledge for the benefit of China. Their supervisors had been the Qing court's official emissaries to America. Growing increasingly frustrated, the boys repeatedly pledged their loyalty to no other ruler but the emperor. Yet no matter what they said, none of the boys seemed to get through to the officers—not even Yung Leang. A skilled orator, he imagined he was debating with his Hartford high school friends and delivered a brief but eloquent plea, doing his best to sound reasonable and reverential all at once. He, too, was brusquely interrupted, told to sit down, and presented again with the same set of senseless questions.

Cooperative and accommodating as they tried to be, Yung Leang and his friends could not summon the elegant Chinese that men in their position were expected to command. Instead, they stuttered and paused for words and often, frustrated by their inability to communicate, blurted out entire sentences in English, a language none of their interrogators understood. Aware that their replies failed to produce the desired effect, the students became immensely disheartened. The whole experience, Yung later wrote in a letter to an American friend, was "upsetting and baffling, a humiliation I did not expect and did not know how to respond to."[2]

As the officials kept pounding away with their questions, the boys grew increasingly irate. With tempers flaring, it didn't take long for Yung Leang to slip into his familiar role of By-jinks Johnnie. Speaking almost entirely in English, he no longer bothered to try to make sense to his captors. Watching him with amazement, Yung's interrogators must have thought him mad or rebellious, or both, staring at him blankly, no longer bothering to repeat their questions. The man in front of them, they probably concluded, was a simpleton, too feebleminded to accept any responsibility for his otherwise incendiary behavior. A short while later, the officers thanked Yung brusquely and ordered the guards to accompany him back to his cell.

Confused, angered, and frightened, several of the boys found comfort in writing long letters to the friends they'd left behind in America. "The prison," wrote the student known as Breezy

Jack to his host family in Connecticut, "was infested with the filth and fifty-seven different kinds of foul smells. . . . Your western imagination is too sublime to conceive a place as vile as this so-called institution; you may have read [about] Turkish prisons or Andersonville horrors, but compared with this, they must have been enviable places."[3]

Yung Leang was immediately struck by the corruption at the prison. Writing to his American friends, he complained bitterly: "The food we got was simply awful, hardly fit for a pig, so we got hold of the man who had charge of feeding us, because we were told he had taken a rake-off of 50 percent from our food allowance, and the cook 50 percent of the balance, so that in reality we got only 25 per cent, or 5 cents a day for food and fuel included for the cooking."[4] All the boys could do was close their eyes and think of the rich food in Connecticut. One student glumly wrote, "We have not ceased to be homesick and to pine for America."[5]

When these letters and others made their way back to the students' friends in New England, the cause of the boys' mistreatment was soon taken up by the press, which was happy to run the most overblown accounts. On January 9, 1882, for example, the *Hartford Evening Post* ran an article claiming that Zhou Chanjian, a graduate of the Hopkins Grammar School, had kept in touch with Mary Sherman, his Connecticut sweetheart, a crime for which he was beheaded in Hong Kong. That Hong Kong was ruled by the British and that the supposed execution was highly implausible meant little to the excitable press.[6]

After a few more days of futile interrogations, the boys were finally let go, but not before the captain who had led them into the Knowledge Wishing Institution emerged and, flanked by his gendarmes, escorted them to the court of a local mandarin, where they were made to genuflect and pledge their allegiance to the Qing dynasty. When that short and humiliating ceremony was over, the officers ordered each boy home. After nearly a decade of constant, close companionship, the group was forced to disband. Under the guards' impatient watch, they hadn't the time for proper farewells and just looked on as their once cohesive group splintered into separate individuals, each bowing his head, each headed back to his own village. "Alas!" wrote Breezy Jack to an American friend, "friends whom I had associated with for so long were separated from me without the chance of saying goodbye and we know not when we shall see them again."[7]

More than the humiliation at the port, more than the torments at the police station or the prostration at the viceroy's palace, it was this sudden separation that most plagued Yung Leang. As he watched his friends walk their separate ways, he felt devoid of energy or hope. His diary entry for that day reads simply, "Alone."

When he finally arrived home, Yung was received by dozens of excited relatives, who peppered him with questions about his time abroad, focusing on the mundane machinations of everyday life. What, asked a relative, do Americans eat? When, inquired another, do they wake up in the morning? And why do they wear such strange clothes? Yung patiently answered all their questions, diving into tale after tale of life in Connecticut and never shying away from any embellishment or exaggeration he thought might serve his story well or amaze his listeners. Americans, he reported, were voracious eaters. A meal was not considered complete until a few pints of ice cream and a dozen or so pies were consumed, washed down with delicious amber-colored ale that made the stomach sing and the mind swoon. All that food, of course, needed time to be properly digested, and so Americans slept a lot, sometimes failing to wake up before midday. That, he concluded, explained their clothes, for who had time to arrange long silk robes and delicate slippers when one had to rush out of bed and out to the field, the factory, or the office? Yung's relatives gasped and applauded, plying him with tea and treats.

His homecoming lasted a few more days. Then his relatives gradually returned to their homes, his parents to their work, his younger siblings to school, leaving him alone and without direction. In a few days, Yung knew, he would receive official word from the local mandarin, informing him of his new career and giving him further instructions. He sat outside, day after day, waiting for the letter to arrive.

When it finally did, Yung was crushed. He was ordered to report at once to the naval academy in Foochow, where he was to begin training as a sailor. Yung was crestfallen. In the navy, he would hear nothing but clipped orders barked at him by impatient superiors in Chinese that he could barely understand. Worst of all, he was By-jinks Johnnie, the flouter of authority and ill equipped for the disciplined business of war.

Doing his best to disguise his disappointment, he broke the news to his parents that evening. The next morning, he set out for Foochow. Yung felt ill-suited for life in China. In this, he was not alone. Years later, a fellow student, referring to himself in the third person, recalled that: "One day the writer was passing a country village dressed correctly in Chinese costume and had spoken to no one. He soon noticed that he was being followed by a number of boys who stared at him and sang out 'Fan Kwai' (foreigner). Greatly puzzled, he afterwards asked a friend the reason why. The friend laughingly answered: 'It was your manly bearing and the style of your walk which made you appear so different from others.'"[8]

When Yung arrived at the naval academy, he found it as horrible as he had feared it would be: endless rows of flat buildings, vast and empty expanses of muddy, run-down training grounds, and short, stout brick watchtowers, gnawed by the wind and overcome by moss. It was nothing like Yale.

At first, Yung hated his new surroundings. The academy, he wrote in his journal, was "dark and dull." Whenever he spoke Chinese, he couldn't help thinking that it came out sounding mangled and metallic, and he largely kept to himself, a stranger among the other enlisted men. Then, however, one by one, fellow graduates of the mission showed up at Foochow: Kwong Wing-chung, Sit Yau-fu, Yang Sew-nan, and the rotund Wong Kwei-liang. Together, the five young men used their free time to re-create in Foochow some semblance of Hartford. On a remote field, far away from the eyes of officials and guards, they built an ersatz baseball field, tying together pieces of bamboo to create makeshift bases. They cut down a rotting plank board, whittled it into a shape roughly resembling a baseball bat, and fastened heavy ropes tightly together—the closest the boys could get to actual baseballs. Shirtless, barefoot, and giddy, the five passed their hours pitching, slugging, and sprinting, chatting noisily in English and referring to one another exclusively by their

American nicknames. When times were rough, the boys of the mission would comfort one another with an English phrase they had themselves crafted in more pleasant times: "That's alright, old boy, take it easy!"

Still, being at a naval academy, they had to spend a few hours of each day on maritime exercises, consisting mainly of climbing aboard the eleven ships that made up the local naval detachment and sailing about peacefully. To their chagrin, the mission's graduates were each assigned to a different ship. They had already attracted the suspicion of their superiors, who viewed their foreign habits and strange conversations with mistrust and thought it best to break up their little nucleus. Still, Yung didn't mind too much. Unlike the large, commercial liner that he took back to China, the wooden vessel on which he now served was small and intimate, and he loved climbing on deck and spending hours looking at the Foochow coastline in the early morning light. The view was lovely: the small ragtag fleet, harbored at a spot known as Pagoda Anchorage, faced a steep, terraced hill, on which stood a few rubber trees. At the base of the hill was a large two-story building made of stone, the Foochow arsenal, built decades earlier by a French engineer eager to convince the local viceroy of his nation's good intentions in southern China.

Sharing the waters with the Chinese, a detachment of eight French warships had been docked at Foochow for months. Yung's colleagues gawked at the heavily armored European vessels, strange steely serpents that were at once thoroughly fortified and fantastically fast. In the same time it took the Chinese junks to complete one tour across the bay, the French completed three.

The sight of the French ships breezing by unnerved Yung. It was true, he wrote in his journal, that the French had never before made any attempt to attack the Chinese fleet at Foochow, and that had they wanted to do so they probably would have found a suitable opportunity long ago. Still, the sight of the French cannons was a terrible omen. Disheartened, he looked away.

On the morning of August 23, 1884, Yung found himself loading ammunition on the *Chien Sheng*. As a small ship, it had its charms; it was light and nimble and could easily weave through the bay's various inlets, treating its crew to some spectacular scenery. Armed only with the rifles of its sailors for defense, it was one of the dimmer stars in Foochow's naval constellation, and as such it and its twin ship, the *Fu Sheng*, were never dispatched too far from base. Their sailors often watched as the crews of the other vessels sailed out to sea on long and grueling patrols. The staff on the other ships were considered more capable and trustworthy, while the crew members of the *Fu Sheng* and *Chien Sheng* were largely regarded as slow and incompetent, barely deserving of their uniforms. Still, Yung didn't care. At Hartford, he had often been concerned with being perceived as an empty-headed, fun-loving clown. In Foochow, he realized, less prestige translated into an easy, uneventful life. While never imagining a serious future for himself in the navy, he was more than happy with his lot for now. "The water soothes me," he wrote an American friend, "and, without much to do, I am content."

It was eight or so in the morning when the ship sailed out to sea, and Yung thought about spending another afternoon running the bases with his friends on their makeshift baseball field. He had been mindlessly going through his chores below deck for less than an hour when a loud explosion tore through the ship and threw him to the floor.

Jumping back to his feet, Yung ran upstairs and bounded onto the deck. From across the bay, the eight ships of the French detachment were closing in quickly. In the distance, the *Yang Wu* and *Fu Hsing*, the fleet's only two armored ships, were in flames, their hulls torn apart by cannon fire, their crews perched on the edge of their vessels, too far from land, forced to make a grim decision between the flaming ship and the sea.

Not knowing what else to do, Yung began to shout. "We're under attack!" he screamed as loud as he could. "We're under attack!"

The *Fu Po*, sailing abreast of the *Chien Sheng*, was the next casualty. A French barrage tore it apart and set it ablaze. Watching the other ship through the smoke and haze, Yung could make out the unmistakable, rotund figure of Wong Kwei-liang, his old school friend, his back and hair on fire, desperately trying to put out the flames. Yung tried to shout, but couldn't muster a sound. Wong writhed for a few moments more before summoning the strength to jump into the water. Yung still couldn't speak. He ran to the rail of his ship, forgetting the battle around him. His eyes combed the small patch of sea between the two ships, waiting to see his friend resurface. There was nothing. Wong was gone.

Yung let out a terrible howl. He ran below deck and grabbed a rifle. Leaning his weapon against the rail, he fired impotent shots at the French ships, the foreign interlopers who had left

the cracked shells of the inferior Chinese vessels bobbing help-
lessly in the water. Yung was in a trance. The image of Wong's
tortured last moments, distant and anguished, recurred in his
mind. He wanted to cry or vomit. But more than anything, he
recalled in an essay written decades later, he wanted revenge.

An errant shell now hit his ship's magazine, a few feet away
from his usual station, where he had been going about his duties
several minutes before. A blast erupted from the belly of the
ship, sending burned wood and charred flesh high in all directions. Mortally wounded, the *Chien Sheng* began to sink.

Yung looked around. He steadied himself among the shifting slivers of his vessel, clutched his rifle once more, and fired
angrily in the direction of the imperious French, fired until the
boards beneath his feet were entirely submerged in water and an
explosion sent a wave surging toward him, washing away his gun.
Yung's lungs filled with saltwater. He waved his arms about and
kicked in the water, coughing violently, doing his best to keep
afloat. The explosions continued, and a rain of debris peppered
the sea's surface. Around Yung were burning planks, shredded
barrels, and singed canvas, not to mention men in various stages
of dismemberment, all of which had been catapulted through
the air and thrown in the water, covering the sea's surface with
a gruesome patchwork of broken ships and lifeless sailors. Yung
noticed he was bleeding, although in his fury he had no recol-
lection of having been wounded. If he did not make it to shore
soon, he would die.

He swam as hard as he could. He could now see that Foochow
did not fare much better than the ships entrusted with its protection: where the arsenal had stood, there was rubble. The

rubber trees on the side of the hill burned slowly, each releasing a slim pillar of bilious black smoke. Farther inland, as far as he could see, Foochow was in flames.

Yung made it to shore nearly fifteen minutes later. As soon as he did, he rolled onto his back, the cool mud soothing his wounds. He gave himself a quick once-over and discovered lacerations crisscrossing his entire body, from his feet to his shoulders. The sight made Yung nauseous, and he closed his eyes, pressing them firmly shut and taking long breaths. It wasn't that bad, he told himself. He wasn't dead. Not like Wong. He'd made it to shore, and all he had to do was just lie there in the mud and wait for it all to be over.

Soon, however, two shots whizzed above his head, shattering a rock ten or fifteen feet to his right. Sharp pebbles came down like hail from the sky, a few lodging themselves in his right arm, one nipping at his cheek. Another explosion covered Yung in a thick veil of mud. He needed to move again, and fast.

But moving was not easy. He was barefoot, and the ground was covered with jagged rocks and debris. He tried to run, but with every step came a deep cut. He walked as fast as he could, but his head soon began to spin. Looking down at his left foot, he noticed a large gash. He was losing a lot of blood. In the distance, he spotted a hut, which he recognized as part of the naval academy, used mainly to allow the guards short rests in between their patrols. Hobbling, he expended the rest of his strength and made it to the small, empty building. He tore off a piece of his shirt, tying it as tightly as he could around his left foot. Then, with no more fight left in him, he collapsed into a deep sleep.

He would revisit the events of that day in interviews

throughout his life. The next morning, he was awakened by hunger—short stabs in his lower abdomen. Sitting up slowly, he was still in much pain, but the bleeding seemed to have stopped, and he could find no other life-threatening wounds. He spat into his palms and rubbed them against his face, removing layers of caked dirt, soot, and blood. Using a piece of wood lying on the ground as a crutch, he slowly stood up, breathing hard and muttering curses. His first priority was to find some food.

Yung left the hut, and started walking slowly along the banks of the Min River. He was struck by a burning stench that caused him to wretch, an odor more foul than anything he had smelled the day before. The dead were lying everywhere, baking in the summer sun, and fires were still devouring everything they could find. At the foot of a nearby tree—miraculously untouched by the flames—he spotted three soldiers cooking rice over a makeshift fire. He walked over to the small group and, without asking for permission, dug his filthy fingers into their pot, grabbed a fistful of scalding, half-cooked rice, and put it in his mouth, slurping it down noisily. Then, he collapsed.

When he regained his senses, it was dark. The soldiers were gone, as was the rice. He was propped up against the tree. His body was sore, his head throbbing. Once again, he lost consciousness.

The next morning, with the sun nearly at its zenith, he woke up covered in sweat but otherwise feeling much better than he had the day before. Able to stand up on his own, he found walking a much more agreeable task. Continuing on his path up the river, he spotted a large group of men in uniform a quarter of a mile down the road and hurried to see what they were doing.

The group, he quickly realized, was a rescue mission sent from the city to collect the last remaining survivors of the Pagoda Anchorage attack. A boy helped him onto a sampan moored nearby, and he lay down on the boat's flat bottom, surrounded by other wounded men, all of them telling one another where they were when the French struck and what they knew about what had happened since.

On the boat, many things became clear. A robust man who was the vessel's captain told Yung and the others that the attack was a retaliatory measure by Admiral Courbet, the commander of the French forces in China for a minor scuffle a few days earlier between French and Chinese troops in Vietnam. All of the Chinese ships at Foochow, the captain said, hanging his head low as he spoke, were destroyed, 796 Chinese sailors were lost, hundreds more wounded. The French, on the other hand, suffered only a dozen casualties and lost no vessels.

Again, Yung felt overcome with rage, the same anger that seized him as he watched Wong's painful death. But if he wanted to avenge his friend, he would need a concrete and actionable plan. All of the misgivings he had felt upon learning that he was assigned to the naval academy were forgotten, all thought of other pursuits washed away. Yung wanted revenge. As the sampan sailed around the bay and toward town, he began plotting. He would stop at the naval headquarters, collect the salary he was owed, replenish his supplies, and then return to the academy and rejoin the battle. He would no longer spend his days playing baseball and joking around but instead devote his every hour to training and hoping for an opportunity to come face-to-face with the invaders.

When the boat docked at Foochow's civilian harbor, and the wounded men on board grudgingly limped ashore, Yung found the townspeople both confused and panicked. Faced with defeat, the local officials, terrified of the Qing court's wrath, had fled town. Yung could sense uncertainty and fear in the faces of the men tending the stores and the women working in the fields. It was like nothing he had ever seen, and the depressing spectacle of resignation and failure made him deeply ashamed.

Although he did his best to avoid comparisons—trying instead to focus his wrath on the French—it wasn't hard to imagine what his American friends and colleagues would do if Hartford or New Haven were somehow dealt a similar blow. His professors had told stories of the Civil War and of battles that devastated entire towns but failed to break the spirit of their inhabitants. Why couldn't the people of Foochow be the same way? Why couldn't they show resolve, determination, pride? Yet the fact remained that those people were victims of a murderous attack, and nothing was quite so pointless as engaging in futile, hypothetical assertions about how they might or might not compare with anyone else under the same trying conditions. Besides, as Yung walked through the door of the naval command center, he knew that he was Chinese, not American, and his loyalty lay with his own nation and his own people.

Chaos was more in evidence inside the naval headquarters than out on the street. Some officers sat at their desks looking stunned, while others darted up and down the corridor, bellowing orders to no one in particular. The floor was filthy, and a few maps lay crumpled in the wastebasket in the corner of the building's main hall. Making his way through the pandemonium,

Yung arrived at a small desk occupied by two men, the bursars entrusted with the Foochow navy's finances. Taking a deferential tone, Yung softly apologized for bringing up an issue as mundane as money at a time such as this, but added that he had not eaten in days and that all his belongings had probably been destroyed in the attack and the ensuing fires that had devastated most of the barracks. He was owed, he concluded, three months' back pay, a total of thirty-three dollars.

"We," said one of the bursars, pausing and sighing before finishing his sentence, "have no money."

Yung's temper flared up. He stood there, furious, staring at the bursar. The man stared back. Then he reached into a drawer and retrieved a few crumpled bills, the equivalent of three dollars, gently pushing the money toward Yung.

"All we can afford right now," the bursar whispered almost inaudibly.

The man's demure demeanor struck Yung forcefully. The clerk was not, Yung realized, another corrupt official pocketing public funds, but a helpless bureaucrat looking with horror at a crisis he could not control. The three dollars, Yung understood, was truly all that the coffers of this once powerful naval center could spare. He took the money and walked out to the street, destitute.

Without money, he realized, he would have to return to his base, or whatever was left of it, as early as possible, for he knew no one in Foochow and had no way of supporting himself for more than a few days. He should spend the three dollars, he thought, buying food, tea, and other essentials before reporting back to the naval academy. On his way to the small general store, however, a tailor's shop caught his eye. Yung walked in. For the first time since his return to China, he knew what he had to do.

A bit later, he emerged in a fresh blue suit, very much like the one he had worn when he entered Yale as a freshman. The tailor also sold him a pair of cheap brown leather shoes, a shirt, and a tie. This new wardrobe cost him all except fifteen cents of his pay, but as he returned to the street he felt strong and defiant, like the soldiers in the stories his professors liked to tell about the unbending American spirit and its grace under fire. It was something of this same spirit, perhaps, that had once led China's legendary emperors to outwit their enemies and claim glory. Now, as Yung walked back toward the naval headquarters, in his suit and armed with the industriousness he had learned in America, he felt ready to fight once more. A man with such assets, Yung thought, could never be stopped.

Armed with this nearly transcendental confidence, he entered the building and sought out the most senior officer he could find. He was, he told the man, a survivor of the battle of Foochow, and he would like to return to his base and assume command. The officer shrugged his shoulders. So many men had died in the attack, he told Yung, that anyone crazy enough to show such conviction was worthy of trust. With a few unceremonious words, he promoted Yung to the rank of captain, and drily told him to return to the academy and assume command over his new outfit, consisting mainly of other survivors and recruits too recent to have been taken to sea when the French guns began to blast.

By nightfall, Yung was back at the academy. He paid little mind to its disrepair. Instead, he asked his men, twenty or thirty tired, hungry, and anxious sailors, to join him at the one place where he felt most comfortable, the makeshift baseball field. There, he gave a speech. He spoke of pride and duty, of honor and country, of man and his responsibilities to himself and to others. The future of China, he told this small group, depended on their ability to protect its waters and show the Western nations that any attempt at invasion or subjugation would meet a similarly fiery fate. And if they had any hope of victory, they had to abandon their old habits, their fear, their passivity, and their antiquated tactics. They had to fight like modern men.

"One Vast Jellyfish"

ad he been around to witness his friend transform himself from the playful By-jinks Johnnie to the determined naval commander Captain Yung Leang, Tong Shao-yi would have likely laughed. Back in Hartford, the two had been inseparable, the king and the jester, spending as much of their time together as their schedules allowed. They were both energetic, and both subscribed fully to the American ideal that nowhere was identity more meaningfully forged than on the playing field of one sport or another. In addition to baseball, Tong and Yung Leang, eager to prove themselves as men, would box together, ride horses through nearby fields, and fire their rifles at bottles and trees. But whereas Yung could now put all of that practice to use in his career as a military man, Tong's fate had guided him toward distinctly different endeavors.

After the mission had been recalled, Tong Shao-yi found himself back at home, restless and bored, the putative prince of a future he now realized would probably never materialize. Worse,

A destroyed Chinese vessel in the aftermath of the Foochow naval disaster, 1884. *Courtesy of Yung Wing and CEM Students Research Academy, Zhuhai, China.*

"Sino-Japanese War: The Fierce Battle on the Floating Bridge at Jiuliancheng," by Kobayashi Toshimitsu, October 1894. *Courtsey of Sharf Collection, Museum of Fine Arts, Boston.*

Tong Shao Yi in Korea. Together with Yuan Shikai, he spent his free time riding and shooting. *Courtesy of Yung Wing and CEM Students Research Academy, Zhuhai, China.*

Yuan Shikai. An early champion of the mission graduates' rise to power, he would ultimately disappoint them with his imperial ambitions. *Courtesy of Yung Wing and CEM Students Research Academy, Zhuhai, China.*

Empress Dowager Cixi and her attendants. *Courtesy of Yung Wing and CEM Students Research Academy, Zhuhai, China.*

The Guangxu Emperor. His voice, one American contemporary observed, was "light and thin like a mosquito." *Courtesy of Yung Wing and CEM Students Research Academy, Zhuhai, China.*

A political cartoon celebrating the Boxer Indemnity Fund. Alone
among foreign powers, the United States used its portion of the
Chinese compensation to support the education of Chinese students.
Courtesy of Yung Wing and CEM Students Research Academy, Zhuhai, China.

Li Hongzhang at the opening ceremony of the extension of the Kaiping Railway, engineered by Jeme Tien Yau. *Courtesy of Yung Wing and CEM Students Research Academy, Zhuhai, China.*

Liang Dunyan on an official mission to the United States, circa 1910. *Courtesy of Yung Wing and CEM Students Research Academy, Zhuhai, China.*

The students of the Chinese Educational Mission shortly before leaving America for China, San Francisco, 1881. Front row: Liang Dunyan, Ouyang King, Chung Mun Yew, two unidentified students. Back row: Chen Juyong, Sung Mon Wai, Jeme Tien Yau (wearing hat), two unidentified students, Huang Kaijia. *Courtesy of Yung Wing and CEM Students Research Academy, Zhuhai, China.*

Graduates of the mission meet in Tianjin for the first reunion since their return to China. Despite having been back for nearly a decade, they still made a point of observing Christmas. Front row: Liang Pao Chew, unidentified graduate, Kwong King Yang, two unidentified graduates. Middle row: Won Wai Shing, unidentified graduate, Kin Ta Ting, Liang Pao Shi, Lok Sik Kwai, Liu Yu Lin. Back row: Jeme Tien Yau, Chung Mun Yew, Kwong Young Kong, Willy Tseng. *Courtesy of Yung Wing and CEM Students Research Academy, Zhuhai, China.*

In 1919, now men of prominence, Yung Wing's boys met at the Shanghai school where they had once prepared for their voyage to America. Front row: Shen Teh Yew, Chung Mun Yew, Lok Teh Chang, Low Kwok Sui, Ting Sung Kih, Woo Huan Yung, Woo Kee Tsao. Middle row: Ching Ta Hee, Tsai Ting Kan, Chu Pao Fay, Tao Ting King, Woo Ying Fo, Tong Yuen Chan. Back row: Chow Wan Pung, Tong Shao-Yi, Yung Liang, Wong Yew Chong. *Courtesy of Yung Wing and CEM Students Research Academy, Zhuhai, China.*

The final reunion of the Chinese Educational Mission, Shanghai, 1936. Front row: Chung Mun Yew, Wen Bingzhong, Ding Chongji, Tong Shao-Yi, Zhou Shouchen, Woo Chung Yen. Back row: Zhou Chuanjian, Yung Liang, Kuang Bingguang, Su Rhuizao, Tao Tinggeng. *Courtesy of Yung Wing and CEM Students Research Academy, Zhuhai, China.*

Following negotiations by mission graduate Liang Dunyan, a new group of students were sent to American universities in 1911, their tuitions covered by the Boxer Indemnity Fund. *Courtesy of Yung Wing and CEM Students Research Academy, Zhuhai, China.*

whereas in Connecticut he could spend time with any number of entertaining friends, now he had only his cousin Liang Ju-hao, the sour Cold Fish Chalie, to keep him company. Unlike most of their peers, the two boys were spared the humiliation of being relegated to menial positions thanks to their wealthy family. Biding their time, they spent their days in listless comfort at their paternal homes, waiting for further instructions from the imperial court.

Realizing that the conservative Qing would not be especially tolerant of the boys' American ways, the Tong clan wasted no time in reacquainting Tong Shao-yi and Liang Ju-hao with Chinese customs. If the boys, so went the logic, could not be the Western-educated reformers they were trained to be, let them accept the traditions of Confucianism. Within months of his return home, Tong Shao-yi was married off to the daughter of a neighboring clan. Shortly afterward, he and Liang were dispatched to Seoul, a proving ground for China's emerging cadre of professional diplomats.

Seoul, at the time, figured prominently in the ongoing dispute between China and Japan. Although the Chinese had for centuries considered Korea as almost a part of their empire—a view not always shared by the Koreans, but largely uncontested by them throughout the reign of the earlier Ming dynasty—the two countries had begun to drift apart after the Qing, reviled by Seoul as "barbarian Manchus," claimed the Mandate of Heaven. Korea, declared its emperor, would proceed on its own. It became the Hermit Kingdom, closed off to all foreign schemers. A few unfriendly visits from Western gunboats, however, persuaded the Koreans to reconsider their policies and reluctantly appeal to China for protection. This delighted the Qing's mandarins: battered on its own shores and forced into one territorial concession after another, China could nevertheless claim Korea as a haven of Chinese might and influence, a peninsula where China was still the uninterrupted sovereign of the East. In addition, a show of strength in Korea would allow the Chinese to send a powerful signal to Japan. A common sentiment among the Chinese was hatred of the Japanese—they were referred to as *wojen*, or dwarves. The Chinese saw Korea as the likely battlefield on which their empire would once and for all defeat the *wojen*. Li Hongzhang himself captured the emotions that governed China's policies in Korea. "With scarcely a tribute that was worth while in all these hundreds of years," he wrote in his journal, "Korea has ever been independent and even resentful of our influence or interest; but just as soon as trouble looms up on the horizon, from causes having their source either within or without the kingdom, she comes begging for help. And help has never been denied, for the people of the country are our people, and they share with us the everlasting dislike for the pygmy Nipponese, with their strutting ways and ignorant presumptions."[1]

As Tong ambled around the ship carrying him to Korea and to his new life as a Qing official, a rustle from beneath a nearby tarp interrupted his thoughts. With a swift motion, he pulled back the canvas and uncovered a ragged young stowaway. The frightened man, his hiding place revealed, pleaded with Tong: I can see by your dress, he said, that you are a mandarin, and I beg you to help me board any ship headed to America. The stowaway took a breath and intended to continue his plea. Before he could, though, Tong interrupted the man and extended his hand in friendship; even in tramp's clothing, Tong still recognized his fellow Chinese Educational Mission graduate Jang Ting Shan.

It took Jang a moment to comprehend just who this officious-looking man greeting him so warmly really was. Once he recognized Tong, with whom he had shared a passion for tennis back in New England, he beamed with delight. He told Tong that he was hoping to sail to Sumatra and from there, somehow, to find his way to Hartford. He had been assigned to a naval school and could no longer endure a position as a torpedo operator. All he could think about was Yale, which he had been about to enter before the mission was recalled. He had to go back, he told Tong, no matter what. While Tong had committed himself to serving the imperial court, he could not fault a fellow student for wishing to return to the liberal and comfortable world of Connecticut. Sympathetic, Tong promised to help. As soon as the ship docked in Seoul, he arranged for his friend's passage to America, sending him off with wishes for success. Whether Tong was tempted to join Jang on his journey back to Connecticut, he did not say.

Tong, Liang, and several of their colleagues were confronted in Korea with yet another foreign set of customs. In the United States, they had met numerous men of merit, from Ulysses S. Grant to Joseph Twichell. Men like these shared the determination to excel in their fields, work hard, and cultivate their considerable abilities. In Seoul, however, the boys met the products of a radically different value system. From their first day in the Korean capital, Tong and his friends observed the Qing bureaucracy and wondered what sort of man it produced. In

Seoul, as in China, determination, hard work, and ability were all subjected to calcified rules, shackled to protocol, and stifled by ceremony. Their superiors, even the seemingly intelligent and capable ones, were constantly memorializing the throne in Beijing and keeping a worried eye on each other, accustomed to the backstabbing that came with life shadowed by a capricious court. In America, the boys had chatted with the president. In Seoul, they were forced to show pious reverence toward even the pettiest officials.

To take their minds off their new circumstances, the boys spent much of their free time with one another. Cai Shaoji—the orator who had impressed the crowd with his high school graduation speech about the opium trade—was also a member of the small group of the educational mission's graduates in Seoul, as was Woo Chung Yen, nicknamed Big Nose for obvious reasons. Back in Connecticut, both Woo and Cai had been active members of the Orientals baseball team; here, they were instructed to wait in palace antechambers and bow before their superiors.

In Korea, Tong's cousin Liang Ju-hao found himself unable to adjust. Still the same ornery boy he had been in school, he was restless in this new, stifling environment. Writing to the Gardners, the family he had lived with in Hartford, he vented his frustrations:

> For every high official we call upon, kneeling down as respect is required . . . The returning students are now men earning their rice by the sweat of their brows, compelled to work under atomical salaries by the tyrannical mandates of their superiors. . . . [W]hat is worse, the officials are

not conscious of the oppressions the returned students are undergoing and still adhere to the idea that they are well off compared to the students who have always stayed in China. That may be correct, but remember how much more advanced is their knowledge compared with that of the other students. Well, those officials will not stand arguments, are too blockheaded to listen to rationality, and too obstinate to yield to justice. . . . When one goes to Hades, another equally obstinate conservative is reinstated, and at the moment of his ascending to petty office, arrogates to himself the legal authority over the affairs of people.[2]

Within months of arriving in Korea, Liang was deeply depressed. The personality traits that had once earned him the name Cold Fish Chalie came again into high relief. He craved efficiency and professionalism and had never outgrown his zealous insistence on justice and fairness, lashing out anytime someone appeared to be giving or receiving a smidgeon of preferential treatment. This behavior, naturally, placed him squarely outside the circle of the popular and charismatic boys, but nonetheless gained him the respect of some teachers and adult guardians, who were amazed to see someone so young approach life with such seriousness.

In Seoul, Liang was appointed to the city's customs office, where graft was a time-honored ritual. Like Yung Wing decades before him, Liang refused his colleagues' demands that he join them in the solicitation of bribes. But unlike his teacher, who had the calm and the wisdom to march into the supervisor's office and remove himself from the scene, Liang didn't want to escape his inconvenient circumstances. He wanted to stay and complain. He did little to hide his contempt for his colleagues. And he spent most of his hours writing feverishly to the Gardners—his sole connection, he now felt, to a civilized world of promise and possibilities.

It disgusted him, he wrote, to be "surrounded on every side by people who have no regard for morality." Particularly offensive was the tradition that allowed wealthy and ambitious mandarins to purchase promotions from their superiors. To Liang, nothing more aptly represented the degradation of the Qing system of governance than this foul way of doing business.

By this time in the mid-1880s, as China suffered one defeat after another, others in the imperial system were beginning to feel as Liang did. Although he had no way of knowing it, his views were shared by the emperor. The Son of Heaven had come to see the full extent of the corruption that handicapped China and kept its ranks in Korea and elsewhere swelled with incompetent officials. Since the birth of the self-strengthening movement two decades earlier, quiet conversations on the topic of reform had been whispered within the walls of the Forbidden City. Yet modernization had been hobbled at every step by political intrigue, which stymied the court and prevented any meaningful reforms until the 1890s. By that time, the myriad challenges buffeting the Qing dynasty had grown in both number and scope.

During the 1860s, the modernizers of the self-strengthening movement had identified critical problems in the way the imperial government operated. Among those who wished to enact changes, none held a higher status in the Qing court than Prince

Gong. The prince was an uncle of the six-year-old emperor Tongzhi and a confidant of the boy's mother, the empress dowager Cixi, who, since her son ascended to the throne in 1861, had ruled the empire in the child's stead. With Prince Gong's lofty connections and imperial lineage, he had unexpectedly chosen to serve his country in a position unthinkable in the China of old. He became the de facto head of the Zongli Yamen, the Office for the Management of the Business of All Foreign Countries. For the first time, a member of the imperial household was working to standardize and expedite commerce with the outside world in a manner far removed from the traditional, ceremonial exchanges of bowing and fealty. Established in 1861, the Zongli Yamen was China's first true office of foreign affairs, and there Prince Gong eagerly dealt with such matters as translating tomes of international law into Chinese and designing the flag that was to fly from all Qing vessels: a serpentine dragon on a yellow ground, with a red sun in one corner. Although a strong proponent of antiforeign policies in his youth, Prince Gong now wished to lead the empire into a position where it could engage properly with the rest of the world. With the prince at the helm, China would no longer be negotiating with the foreigners through the hodgepodge of local warlords and the Ministry of Rituals, and it was taking its first steps toward centralized diplomatic practices. Thus, when word spread that Cixi's son Emperor Tongzhi had died at the age of eighteen, foreign diplomats and businessmen were excited by the prospect of Prince Gong's son assuming power in accordance with Chinese custom, an event that would mark the ascension of the proreform party to the highest level of imperial governance.

The empress dowager had other plans. She would not allow any person, either emperor or regent, to take her place at the helm. She began to move against all of those members of her family who were looking to seize control of the empire. The greatest threat was Prince Gong: his eye trained on the throne, the prince had spent the past decade plotting his ascent. To undermine Cixi, he formed an alliance with like-minded nobles and used the codex of rigid rituals governing life in the Forbidden City to assail Cixi's loyalists. After her favorite eunuch, for example, failed to observe a negligible point of court etiquette, Gong had him executed. But brinksmanship was a game at which few could outplay Cixi: when Prince Gong himself eventually committed a minor infraction against protocol, Cixi convinced her vast network of sycophants at the court to strip the prince of all authority, allowing him to keep his title but rendering him and his family powerless.

With Gong removed, Cixi turned to the next big threat, her own daughter-in-law. The young woman hailed from an important clan and was pregnant by the late emperor. If that child proved to be a boy, he would be the most logical choice to succeed his father as monarch. If that happened, Cixi's own role would be greatly diminished—her daughter-in-law would become empress dowager in Cixi's place, relegating the old woman to the Summer Palace and a life of luxury but no real influence. By spring, both the young woman and her unborn child were dead. Some at court suspected that she was forced to commit suicide—killed, they whispered, by the empress dowager herself.

By the time Cixi's campaign was over, only one Manchurian

candidate was left standing: Guangxu, the four-year-old cousin of the deceased emperor, who once again would require the services of the empress dowager, his aunt, to govern in his name until he reached adulthood. With the boy's parents—Cixi's sister and her husband—fully subservient to the empress dowager, the grand dame of Chinese politics found herself once more in charge. Cixi, the woman whose wardrobe was kept in three thousand camphor chests, the accomplished painter and student of literature, the monarch who sat behind a screen for propriety's sake while she listened to the reports of her male ministers, would continue to guide China as the only female ruler in Qing history.

The installation of Guangxu as emperor in 1875 was received with near-universal opprobrium. Westerners regarded the boy emperor's family with trepidation, highlighting his father's staunch antiforeigner views. Confucian zealots at the Qing court were deeply troubled by the appointment as well, although for very different reasons. According to ancient imperial protocol, one of the emperor's most sacred duties was to show filial piety to the former emperor. This meant that even if the incoming emperor wasn't the preceding monarch's son, he at least needed to belong to the next generation of royals. That wasn't the case with Guangxu; he was a cousin of the late emperor, considerably younger but nonetheless a member of the same generation, which meant that he couldn't properly conduct the rituals of ancestor worship. This was an insult to tradition many in the Forbidden City couldn't bear. Protesting the boy's enthronement, one mandarin set himself on fire outside the hall where the ceremony took place, and several Manchu princes paid Muslim horsemen from the western provinces to ride menacingly through Beijing's streets, an intimation that a civil war was in the offing. From behind her ornate screens, Cixi calculated her next move.

Calling on powerful friends to put an end to the brewing insurrection, Cixi trusted one man in particular to come to her defense. Admiring the empress dowager's ambition and her penchant for political survival—so akin to his own—Li Hongzhang was a close ally, and to counter the Islamic horsemen hired by Cixi's detractors, he sent four thousand well-trained men to defend the palace. Order was soon restored, and the Guangxu emperor remained on the throne.

As the boy emperor grew into a man, he proved to be a far cry from his debauched predecessor, who had spent much of his time at the imperial brothels in the company of both men and women. Under the tutelage of Weng Tonghe, a loyal and capable scholar, Guangxu became a serious and curious youth, increasingly impatient with his position's empty, ceremonious gestures. As he neared his seventeenth birthday, and with it his independence from Cixi's regency, he was contemplating his own ideas about government and reform. In 1889, Guangxu came of age, married, and prepared to replace his aunt. A party was thrown in honor of the departing empress dowager, who had no choice but to accept her fate in the nearby Summer Palace. There, in the Hall of Happiness in Longevity, where over one hundred different dishes were cooked for each of her two daily meals, Cixi plotted her return to power.

With his domineering aunt at some distance, Guangxu began his reign in earnest. But he was not fit for the pressures of governing. As a toddler, he was seen more as a pawn in a game of imperial power and influence than as a real child in need of warmth and love, and was largely abandoned by both his biological mother and his aunt. Having been committed to the care of envious eunuchs who mistreated him and left him frail in body and tortured in mind, he did not present well. Meeting the young emperor shortly before his coronation, the American minister Charles Denby was unimpressed. Guangxu, he wrote, was "a delicate youth . . . small and thin and gives no promise of possessing physical strength." The emperor, the minister observed, had large, black eyes, a smooth and hairless face, and a voice "light and thin like a mosquito."[3]

His shortcomings aside, Guangxu vowed to wean China off its worst habits. As he was preparing to marry, he wrote an edict to China's provincial governors, threatening them with the "direst penalties" if they imposed taxes on their people to help pay for lavish wedding gifts.[4] He ordered his own household budget cut by one-third, although he wisely stopped short of censuring his aunt's lavish lifestyle. But, most importantly, he sought an account of his nation's progress not from the mouths of sycophants and duplicitous mandarins but in French and English books and newspaper accounts.

What he learned there shocked him: news of rebellions and bandits, floods and droughts, one disaster after another plaguing China and no one willing or able to take responsibility and act decisively to stop the collapse. He hadn't realized how isolated he was from his country. Angry and distraught, the emperor wanted to take immediate action. He didn't, however, know where to begin. Pondering his problem for a while, he settled on the very same issue that had bothered Liang Ju-hao in Seoul, the tradition that allowed officials to purchase their promotions at a premium. The emperor realized that it was not merely a symptom of a sick system; it was, instead, the disease. It sponsored the advancement of unqualified candidates and contributed to the nation's slow demise. Official circles, the emperor wrote in an edict, were "over-crowded by men of mediocre ability and often of low standing to the detriment of the public services." To that end, Guangxu ordered the Board of Revenue, the court's treasury, to stop selling official titles and positions at once. Furthermore, he wanted his ministers to thin out the lower ranks of the hierarchy by "frequent denunciations of incompetent and avaricious prefects, sub-prefects, department and district magistrates."[5]

Such an ordinance, one could assume, would have appealed to Liang, Tong, and the other graduates of the educational mission serving in Korea, addressing their sense of justice and desire for order. The imperial edict, however, never made its way to Seoul. It did not, according to all available accounts, make much of an impression even at home in China. Desperate for cash, and unable to think of alternative sources of revenue, Guangxu's ministers found it easier to ignore their sovereign than to give up the money they earned from selling titles, particularly since abolishing the ancient tradition of bribery would infuriate a substantial number of the nation's wealthiest and most influential citizens.

In Korea, then, Liang, was left to sulk. With an encyclopedist's obsession, he meticulously cataloged China's ills. "We have no courts and every affair has to be referred to the district magistrates," he wrote his friends in America. "Living near my humble village is a man who was said to be worth $1.5 million, the father of one of our students. . . . [E]very cent of that immense sum was spent in a lawsuit, and moreover, his life too, for he had to commit suicide to escape punishment, after finding that his opponent was still favored by the district magistrate."[6]

Liang's cousin Tong Shao-yi, on the other hand, was taking a less gloomy approach to life. Unlike Liang, Tong had nothing of the cold fish about him. He had always been a good student, a great athlete, and a natural leader, and in Korea, too, he thrust himself into the very heart of things. Appointed to the service of Paul Georg von Möllendorff—a Prussian nobleman whom Li Hongzhang had rewarded with the plum position of overseeing the empire's interests in Korea for having supplied him with German weapons—Tong enjoyed a life of luxury, respected by his superiors and peers, and entrusted with the delicate work of setting up Korea's foreign service.

But Möllendorff's loyalties, it was soon apparent, lay not with Li but with the principles of justice and progress. In Korea, Li had expected Möllendorff to crush any flowerings of local independence. If, went one example of Li's logic, Korea established its own customs service, it would soon fall prey to Western traders seeking to plunder it as they'd plundered China, which, in turn, would mean the end of Chinese influence. Li, then, expected his Prussian underling to keep Korea's trade policies closely tethered to those of China. But Möllendorff—a graduate of the University of Halle, one of the centers of the German Enlightenment— firmly believed in each nation's right to self-determination, and viewed Li's dictates with increasing unease. Seeking support for his principled stand, he grew closer to Korea's King Gojong and was soon converted to the cause of Korean nationalism, giving himself the Korean name Mok In-Dok.

Exasperated, Li ordered Möllendorff back to China. Obedient by nature, the Prussian returned to the mainland, settled in the southern port city of Ningbo, and spent the rest of his years working in the Chinese customs office and writing on Chinese history. His departure, however, did little to improve China's position in Korea: Japan was drumming up its commercial pursuits in the peninsula and had negotiated, in 1882, for a small military presence to protect its interests. China, the suzerain, was uneasy with Japan's setting up camp right inside its sphere of influence; it needed a strong man to make sure Korea remained squarely under Beijing's thumb. Searching the imperial rolls for someone to replace Möllendorff, Li came across the name of Yuan Shikai.

Yuan's biography leaves little doubt that he was destined to be a celebrated soldier. When he was a small boy, his family moved away from its village in the Henan province to a military-like compound in the hills, which they named Yuanzhai, or the fortified village of the Yuan family. At Yuanzhai, learning was secondary, and days were spent riding horses, boxing, and entertaining friends. Such pursuits, of course, were considered lowly by the well-groomed scholars and moneyed merchants of the upper echelons, and Yuan soon discovered that life outside the compound held little promise or pleasure for him. He failed the imperial examinations twice and, ruminating on his future, realized that the only sensible path for him to pursue was a life in uniform. The military, he quickly learned, wasn't much different from Yuanzhai, and he excelled without effort. Although Yuan was only in his midtwenties at the time, Li Hongzhang chose him to curb the Japanese influence in Korea, where the young warrior quickly proved his worth.

In 1884, Yuan, heading a small army of fifteen hundred men, easily extinguished a Japanese-backed coup d'état, burned down the Japanese legation's building in Seoul and killed forty Japanese soldiers. Yuan could not have hoped to show his skill and power better than he did. William Elliot Griffis, an American minister who knew Yuan at the time, captured the general admiration for the fierce Chinese general: "Lofty was his air," Griffis wrote, "impressive were his mien and his bearing and high-handed were his actions."[7]

Tong Shao-yi was equally awestruck: he had never before seen a Chinese official with such military prowess and conviction. Back in Connecticut, the representatives of the Qing were men like the obese Woo or the obtuse Chen, guarded in speech and movement and paling in comparison with the robust Americans. But Yuan, he could tell, was a different breed, someone who, like Tong himself, would feel right at home on the football fields of New England. Even more impressively, Tong, accustomed to being the incomparable Ajax, felt an unusual sense of deference to Yuan. Although the military commander was only three years older than he, Tong nevertheless came to see Yuan as a father figure and offered him his friendship, loyalty, and skill. Yuan, for his part, decided that he and Tong made an excellent team. Tong was smooth where Yuan was rough. Tong was eloquent, while Yuan was comfortable only with the clipped cadence of military orders. Tong was loved by everyone, Yuan feared by all. But what most impressed Yuan was that Tong, unlike so many of the cowering, effete members of his class, was calm under pressure, eager to fight, and as handy with his fists as with his words. Writing to Li, Yuan recommended that Tong be appointed to the position of consul and requested that Tong serve as his chief adviser for as long as Yuan was posted in Seoul.

Unable to refuse the hero of Korea, Li agreed, and Tong received his first promotion and first position of real influence and power. For ten years, Tong served under Yuan, entrusted with checking Japan's ambitions and furthering China's interests in Korea. He composed elegant memorials to the throne for Yuan to sign, gained the trust and sympathy of Chinese and Korean mandarins alike, and spent as much time as he could horseback riding, often accompanying Yuan in the field. Eventually, he also rescued his dour cousin Liang from the dreariness of the customs office, placing him in Yuan's service as well. The appointment did little to assuage Liang's boredom: the people of Korea, he wrote his friends in Connecticut, were hostile to foreigners and prone to "laziness" and "procrastination."[8]

Yet the Koreans weren't the biggest problem. Across the sea, Japan was gearing up for war. After the attempted coup in Korea was foiled by Yuan, the Japanese demanded compensation for the damage Yuan had inflicted. Looking to avoid any provocations, the Qing court agreed to discussions and dispatched Li Hongzhang to negotiate.

On the other side of the negotiating table Li met Ito Hirobumi. The son of modest farmers, Ito began his political career in Japan as an adherent of the neo-Confucian Sonno jōi movement, which translates as "Revere the Emperor, Expel the Barbarians." In 1863, however, he was chosen as one of five students dispatched by the

Japanese emperor to study at University College in London; like Li and Zeng Guofan a decade later, Japan's highest officers realized that the only way to meet the challenges presented by the arrival of foreigners was to learn their ways. Upon his return, Ito no longer believed the foreigners to be barbarians, but considered them a clever race with much to teach the introverted Japanese. His beliefs and experiences placed him at the very center of the Meiji Restoration, a radical period of transformation that propelled the small island nation from a reclusive kingdom to a global power within the short span of fifty years. Eager to reform his nation as fast as he could, and operating with the blessing of his superiors, Ito traveled to the United States to learn about Western currency systems; he also spent more than eighteen months in Europe, surveying the Continent's constitutions in order to provide Japan with a founding document of its own. In December of 1885, he would become his nation's first prime minister; eight months before that, however, he traveled to Tianjin to meet with Li.

The agreement was simple. Both China and Japan would pull their expeditionary forces out of Korea within four months. The Korean king would be permitted to retain military advisers from a third nation, and neither empire would send forces to Korea without first notifying the other. Despite the respect that Ito and Li had for each other, both men knew that the agreement they signed was worthless. War would break out sooner or later. The only question was when.

The answer came soon enough. Determined to secure China's primacy in Korea, Li gave Yuan free rein to run things as he saw fit. Often against the advice of his reform-minded deputy

Tong, Yuan governed the kingdom as if it were Yuanzhai, his boyhood compound. In 1894, he had ample opportunities to flex his military muscles in suppressing the Donghak, a millenarian sect that was rapidly drawing followers. In need of additional men, Yuan wrote the mandarins in Beijing for backup, and they, in turn, adhered to protocol and reported the dispatch of forces to Tokyo. Shortly thereafter, a young Korean reformer with ties to Japan was murdered in a Japanese-run youth hostel in Shanghai's international legation. The two events were unconnected, but for the higher-ups in the Japanese emperor's court they presented a golden opportunity: the murder, they claimed, was a deliberate assassination, probably arranged by Li Hongzhang, the very same Li Hongzhang who was now sending troops to Seoul. China, the Japanese propaganda continued, was getting ready to take over Korea by force.

Again, the Donghak presented a perfect excuse. Three months after having been subdued by Yuan and his men, the group revolted again. The Korean government, weakened and split between nationalists, Chinese loyalists, and supporters of Japan, turned to Tokyo for help. Only too glad to oblige, Japan sent its own troops to Korea, effortlessly crushed the revolt, and then contacted the Qing with a compromise: a mutual Sino-Japanese declaration in support of Korean reforms.

It was a compromise China would never accept. If Korea erected its own modern governmental structure, financial system, and military, the era of Chinese influence would end. And yet, by refusing the Japanese proposal, China had opened itself up to claims of obstinacy and belligerence. On July 12, 1894, Japan, eager for a chance to put its European-bought ships and guns to the test, instructed its minister in Seoul to "use any pre-text available" to justify a conflict.[9] Eleven days later, Japanese troops marched into Seoul, seized King Gojong, and established a puppet government, which immediately announced the abro-gation of all treaties with China. In Beijing, the Qing court issued a declaration of war: "Korea has been our tributary for the last two hundred odd years," it read. "She has given us tribute all this time, which is a matter known to the world . . . but the *wojen*, without any cause whatever, sent their troops to Korea and entered Seoul. . . ." It was time, the statement concluded, "to root the dwarves out of their lairs."[10]

In theory, this was China's war to lose. The Qing had nearly a million soldiers at the ready, a vast advantage over Japan's 270,000 men. But in the field, the Chinese troops owed their loyalty to an eclectic assortment of warlords and commanders, while Japan's army was well run, its objectives perfectly under-stood, and its orders clearly communicated. And the Japanese, largely trained by Western advisers, were well armed and pre-pared for modern warfare; on the Chinese side, many soldiers still grasped bows and arrows as they rushed into combat. It didn't take long for these discrepancies to play out.

In Seoul, Tong, Liang, Cai, and Woo were bracing for battle. They were young and energetic, they disliked the Japanese, and they had come of age listening to Americans telling them inspir-ing stories of the Civil War and the brave men who gave their all for the future of their nation. Most reassuringly, however, the graduates of the educational mission had Yuan; the general, they were all certain, would soon ride into battle and teach the Japanese a bitter lesson.

But as war broke out, Yuan vanished. Some claimed that he was ill and in need of treatment, others that he had been recalled to Beijing for consultations. Tong didn't know why he was absent. It didn't matter. When he most needed his hero, Yuan wasn't there. In the absence of clear directions from the court, Tong did his best to remain calm. It didn't take long for him to understand that without the illustrious general to lead them, China's armies in Korea were in great peril. Since Tong was not a soldier but a civil servant, he decided that the front line was no place for him and his colleagues. Along with his cousin and his friends, he beat a hasty retreat to the mainland.

He left at just the right moment. On the night of September 14, 1894, early in the war, Chinese troops, encamped in the northern Korean city of Pyongyang, received faulty intelligence that the Japanese troops were not expected for at least a week. Careless and unworried, they engaged in a traditional feast, eating and drinking through the night. Lurking in the surrounding mountains, the Japanese waited patiently, and as the Qing's men stumbled into bed, they emerged and attacked. "Our comrades," wrote one Chinese soldier who survived the battle, "fell like mown grass."[11] Within a few hours, more than 2,000 Chinese troops were dead and 6,000 imprisoned. The Japanese lost only 189 men.

Things were not much better at sea. Here, too, China had a theoretical advantage, equipped, as it was, with a modern navy that Li had purchased from Germany several decades back, staffed by the graduates of the schools at Foochow and elsewhere. But, once again, the Japanese were better organized and more fluent in the ways of modern combat. The Chinese, possessing capable ships, still lacked a fundamental understanding of how to employ them properly in battle. To cite a popular anecdote, one of the most advanced vessels in the Qing fleet, the *Kuang Chia*—under the command of the Chinese Educational Mission graduate Woo King Yung—is believed to have spent the days prior to the war's outbreak not preparing for the coming fight but instead on a mission delivering fresh lychees to the empress dowager. On September 17, at the battle of the Yalu River, on the border between China and Korea, Japan destroyed five of China's ships and killed more than eight hundred of its men. With no one to stop them, Japanese forces then stormed through Korea to Manchuria and into the strategic town of Port Arthur. Seeing some of their slain comrades there—their ears and noses cut off by their captors—the Japanese executed their revenge. They stabbed soldiers and civilians alike in the stomach and severed their heads. They did not differentiate between the sexes, driving both men and women into the lake to drown, tying them together and shooting them on the spot, spearing them on bayonets, and gouging out their eyes. Nowhere was mercy in evidence.

"The defenseless and unarmed inhabitants were butchered in their houses and their bodies unspeakably mutilated," wrote the American correspondent of the *New York World* newspaper. "There was an unrestrained reign of murder which continued for three days. The whole town was plundered with appalling atrocities." Reacting to the reports, the Japanese calmly responded that while it was not their interest to harm noncombatants, its soldiers were nonetheless "transported with rage at the mutilation of their comrades by the enemy" and therefore motivated "to inflict vengeance without discrimination."[12]

As 1895 dawned, a Japanese victory seemed inevitable. On
January 20, with the temperature dropping to minus fourteen
degrees Fahrenheit, the opposing armies met at the Shangdong
town of Weihaiwei. Out at sea, Commander Tsai Ting Kan
was providing support, leading a squadron of torpedo boats.
Commander Tsai was the very same Fighting Chinee who,
more than two decades earlier, had been assigned to work in a
New England machine shop after having been deemed by his
American teachers unfit for any serious position because of his
unruliness. The teachers, however, had it wrong: even though
Tsai could not, like his more settled friends, spend endless hours
reading and writing at his desk, he did have both talent and
discipline. All he needed was a way to channel his energies and
his penchant for conflict toward a constructive end. The navy
gave him just that; unlike his friend By-jinks Johnnie, Tsai took
to life on the sea from the very first, and by 1884, just three
years after returning home to China, had already been promoted
to lieutenant. The torpedo boats, in particular, suited his temperament; like Tsai himself, torpedo boats were unassuming but
capable of taking down much larger vessels. Braving the cold,
Tsai braced for battle.

Leading China's naval forces that day was Admiral Ting
Ju-cha'ng, while Admiral Ito commanded the Japanese fleet.
Certain of his victory, Ito was nevertheless not looking forward
to the fight: his Chinese counterpart was an old friend. In an
emotional letter to Ting, Ito expressed his regrets that the two
had to meet again under such trying circumstances, and then
went on to appeal to his old friend's reason. The Qing's policies,
he wrote, were retrograde and indefensible. In the long term,

China would have to recognize its errors and change its ways. There was no need for bloodshed, Ito wrote; if Ting surrendered, the Japanese would treat him and his men with kindness, escorting them to Japan, where they would stay as honored guests until the end of the war. But Ting, of course, had to refuse. He could not resettle his entire fleet in a foreign country.

Looking on at the brewing battle was Yung Leang. Now a veteran captain in command of his own vessel, By-jinks Johnnie was as distraught as the rest of his colleagues at the notion of the imminent defeat. With trepidation, he watched Ting's every move. The old admiral drafted a document of surrender, demanding that all Chinese forces be allowed to retreat unharmed. Then Ting set down his reply to Ito's letter. "I am thankful for the admiral's friendship," he wrote, "but I cannot forsake my duties to the state. The only thing now remaining for me to do is to die."[13] With that, he called six carpenters to his quarters and ordered them to build him a coffin. It was ready the next morning, and Ting climbed inside, rolling around to make sure it fit his frame. Then he tipped each of the craftsmen two dollars, bade farewell to Yung and the other officers under his command, and retreated to his chamber to drink a fatal dose of poison.[14] Yung and Tsai, along with Ting's other men, did not know how to respond. On the one hand, the admiral's death, in all of its old-fashioned, ritualistic glory, was inspiring. On the other, it was counterproductive, a futile grasp at dignity where a more levelheaded attempt at strategy might have better served the cause. Still, the result was the same: the war was lost. Admiral Ito seized all of the Chinese vessels, but allowed his defeated enemies to keep one small junk with which to transport

Ting's body back to Beijing. As the boat sailed by, Ito ordered his men to salute their fallen enemy.[15]

At first, Beijing tried to play down the extent of its failure, even claiming victory at the early stages of the fighting. Soon enough, however, the Qing had no choice but to admit defeat. True to their tradition of deflecting blame away from the emperor, a scapegoat had to be identified. No man was better suited to this sorry role than Li Hongzhang, the mandarin whose vision and coffers had brought the now vanquished navy to life. Stripped of all his titles, dismissed from all his posts, he was reviled in one memorial after another. "His name," wrote one fellow mandarin, "stinks in the nostrils of his countrymen."[16]

But as the Japanese captured one strategic outpost after another, the Qing, perhaps recalling Li's Taiping-era heroics, reinstated the disgraced mandarin and ordered him to negotiate an end to the war. It was, in the convoluted logic that governed China at the time, a perfect solution: if the humiliated statesman succeeded in bringing an end to the conflict, the emperor would be praised for having the wisdom and the insight to forgive Li his sins; if Li failed, however, the failure would be his alone.

Again, Li traveled to meet Ito Hirobumi, this time in Tokyo. Ito spoke in English. Li used a translator. Doing his best to save face, the Chinese official proposed a joint Sino-Japanese alliance against the West. Ito refused. Li proposed an armistice. Before the Japanese had the chance to reply, however, a deranged youth burst into the room, pulled out a revolver, and shot Li. With a bullet lodged beneath his nose, the elderly Chinese leader collapsed. Embarrassed, the Japanese emperor apologized for the violent attack, sending his personal physician to tend to the wounded Li, who would survive this attack. The old mandarin being too weak to continue the negotiations, Li's son took his father's place at the table. On April 1, 1895, China accepted the Japanese terms and ended the war.

Peace, however, brought with it little joy. The Qing paid dearly for the armistice: they agreed to keep out of Korea, relinquish the Liaodong Peninsula and the Penghu Islands, cede Taiwan to Japan, and pay an indemnity equal to the annual imperial budget. More than its treasury or its territory, however, it was China's pride that suffered the greatest blow. Emperor Guangxu released an official letter explaining his nation's defeat: "How deeply we pondered the settlement no tongue can tell," he wrote. "Heaven has not withheld its augury. The sea over-flowed the coast and camps were submerged. Tormented by alternate schemes of offense and defense, we trembled at night and labored and grieved by day. After careful consideration we determined upon our course. The officials and people of the empire must make allowance for our difficulties." Delivering the monarch's words in full, the *New York Times* titled its report "A Pathetic Proclamation."[17]

The graduates of the Chinese Educational Mission who had fought in the war couldn't have agreed more. Yung Leang quit his position as captain. He was on track to advance and become an admiral himself, but the faltering navy wasn't able to provide much in the way of a proud future. After the French attack on Foochow, he had been consumed with a patriotic fervor. Now, after this disaster, he felt nothing of the sort. Peddling his skills as a fluent English speaker, he took a job working as a translator at the American consulate in Canton and then accepted a more lucrative position teaching English at a school for girls.

Meanwhile, Tsai Ting Kan had been taken prisoner by the Japanese along with his entire squadron, not returning home to China until a year after the war had ended. There, he faced allegations that his captivity was a hoax and that he had surrendered of his own accord, selling his skill and vessels to the enemy. Tsai was found guilty of inappropriate behavior—there was not sufficient evidence to suggest treason—and was demoted. True to his American nickname, he swore to fight on until his rank and reputation were both restored.

Even worse, perhaps, than China's defeat was Japan's triumph. Though Japan was forced by international pressure to return some of its gains—the Russians, in particular, were concerned about Japan's meteoric rise and looked to limit its expansion— the land of the Rising Sun was hailed the world over as an emerging power. China, on the other hand, was described by the British newspaper in Shanghai as nothing more than "one vast jellyfish."[18]

Such words stung Tong Shao-yi. Back home, with no official position and no powerful patron, his health took a turn for the worse. Sick and bitter, he turned to drugs. Having dabbled with opium before, he now smoked it with increasing regularity.

But whereas the defeat had deflated By-jinks Johnnie and the once gallant Ajax, it invigorated the formerly sullen Cold Fish Chalie. In peacetime, Liang Ju-hao had seen China only through the lens of incompetence and corruption. But the war had given him a renewed sense of pride, spurring him on to serve his empire wholeheartedly. He won an appointment as the director of railway transport in the northeastern regions. While mostly a ceremonious position—the northeastern regions, like the rest of China, had almost no railway infrastructure at the time—Liang found himself uncharacteristically eager to serve. Before being recalled to China, he had studied for one year at the Stevens School of Technology in Hartford. There, his journey on the transcontinental railroad still fresh in his mind, he took as many engineering classes as he could and devoted himself to the study of trains. It took more than a decade, but Liang was beginning to feel that the future he had imagined as a boy—that of an innovator putting Western technology to use for the benefit of China—might come to pass after all.

Returning to Tianjin, Liang conducted his affairs with a verve rarely before on display. When a French company, hoping to lure the court into a lucrative contract, sent the Forbidden City a gift of six railway cars—magnificently upholstered with yellow, green, and blue satin and fitted with all of the latest luxuries—it was Liang who was sent to meet the representative of the generous French company at the docks. Upon arriving at the pier, though, Liang noticed that the Frenchman sent to organize the delivery of the trains was at his wit's end. Tianjin, the Frenchman could plainly see, had none of the heavy cranes necessary to unload the precious cargo from the ships. There was no way, he told Liang, to get the trains onto the barge that would carry them to their destination in Beijing. Before the war, Liang would probably have agreed with the Frenchman and then written his friends in Hartford a long letter about the inefficiency of China's ports or the inanity of its customs

officials. But standing on the dock at Tianjin was a reborn Liang,
who was determined to effect change in any way he could. He
smiled. There were no cranes, he admitted, but a handful of
Chinese workers, with the right foreman and the right spirit,
would do the trick. The Frenchman, disbelieving him, replied
that men could not feasibly carry trains. Liang was reassuring;
come be my guest at my home, he told the engineer, and in the
morning all will be well.

The next morning, the Frenchman was amazed to see the
railway cars, neatly lined up, standing atop the barge, awaiting
their chaperone. The Frenchman and Liang set off to shepherd
the trains to their destination. When the terrain proved too
difficult for passage, Liang, despite having been taught more
modern techniques at his American college, employed a solution straight out of the playbook of Chinese antiquity, ordering
his men to place a series of long poles on the ground, creating
a series of makeshift rollers. The workers hauled the cars to
Beijing with ease, by means of a tried-and-true method of imperial engineering.

This Frenchman's generosity in sending the trains to the
court, however, was not indicative of Europe's attitudes toward
China in the wake of its devastating loss to Japan. Witnessing
the Qing court at its weakest, the Western powers that had
hitherto been hovering over China now swooped in, hungry
for concessions. If the Son of Heaven wasn't stealthy enough to
swat off the Japanese, went the logic, he hadn't a chance facing
England, France, Germany, or Russia. Making resistance even
more futile was China's heavy debt to Western nations: burdened by its immense indemnity and other soaring expenses, the

court borrowed 350 million yuan from foreign banks between 1894 and 1896 alone.

In his working quarters at the Hall of Complete Harmony, Emperor Guangxu refused to succumb. In July of 1895, he issued an edict intended as a call to arms. "In the past," he wrote in his red imperial pencil,

> the path to good government has always involved *yin shi zhi yi*, or measures appropriate to the times. How much more so at this time of national difficulties. What is most needed is that persons high and low all be of one mind, to plan for self-strengthening and to remove the hidden sources of our troubles. Your sovereign has worked tirelessly from dawn till dusk, learning from past mistakes to avoid future ones, seeking only to alleviate oppressive government and chronic ailments, and energetically to institute practical measures as soon as possible.[19]

A list of practical measures followed: currency reform; railway construction; training programs for soldiers, postmen, and miners; reorganization of the navy; and establishment of modern schools. In Beijing, fifty scholars from the prestigious Hanlin Academy opened a book depot so large that it occupied a forty-room complex, sponsoring a journal of ideas, translating Western books, and holding lectures on international affairs. Similar establishments sprang up across China.[20] First on everyone's list of priorities, however, was still the military, for it was weapons, not books, that China needed if it was ever to stand up to its enemies.

Untainted by the colossal military debacle he had avoided by feigning illness, Yuan Shikai resurfaced, supporting the cause of self-strengthening and telling a British baron that unless China "undertook some measure for her own preservation, nothing could save her falling to pieces." Yuan's fearsome façade worked its magic: "If all the Chinese generals were like General Yuan Shi Kai," wrote the admiring baron, failing to mention Yuan's convenient disappearance from Seoul, "the armies and their financial arrangements would not be in the condition they are now."[21]

Genuine and robust as the spirit of reform was, it failed to produce any immediate results. China was still China, its bureaucracy lumbering, its traditions observed, its suspicions perennially in bloom. The fits and starts of modernity weren't enough for the emperor. He wanted immediate transformation. He wanted China to follow the example of the Japanese and erect a new system of government, a new civic culture, and a new economy almost overnight. What he needed, in other words, wasn't a reformation; it was a revolution.

The Hundred Days

he stifling summer of 1898 found Tong Shao-yi living comfortably. After the disastrous war against the Japanese, with Korea lost, the Qing court sought to install a capable official as its representative in Seoul, someone who could monitor developments and gauge the chances of a Chinese resurgence in the region. Tong was an ideal choice. He was intimately acquainted with the politics of the kingdom and was generally liked among Seoul's elite. Serving under Yuan Shikai, he was perceived by many as the sensible, civil Chinese, the one to address when the haughty general behaved imperiously, the one who could get things done. Now free of Yuan's shadow, Tong's return to the Korean capital was an amicable one. Although the role of Qing representative in Korea no longer carried the prestige and prominence it had before the war—Korea had declared itself an empire and now sought protection from Russia, despite Japan's recurring efforts to exert its influence—Tong spent his days doing what he loved best. Keeping a stable of fine horses, he rode for hours

each day, and added to his burgeoning collections of porcelain
and firearms.

Meanwhile, Tong's old friends, the boys who had admired
him in Connecticut and served with him in Korea, were themselves entering an august maturity. His cousin Liang was thriving as a railway director, constantly planning the expansion and
improvement of the limited tracks under his control, invigorated
by the work and the responsibility. And Woo Chung Yen, nicknamed Big Nose, who in the 1880s had been little more than a
junior customs official in Korea, was beginning to attract attention. After the war, Yuan Shikai, entrusted with rehabilitating
China's crushed army, drafted Woo, whom he had known and
liked in Korea, to be his new chief of munitions. From there,
Woo rose to become Yuan's foreign relations officer, a position
that offered the former Yalie power and respect.

Equally impressive was the ascent of Cai Shaoji. A brilliant orator and an excellent athlete, he arrived in Korea with
Tong, Liang, and Woo, and he, too, was immediately noticed
by Yuan. After a brief period in the general's service, he had
been awarded the rank of magistrate, allowing him to amass
a small fortune through a number of lucrative trade and mining contracts. Although Cai proved to be a masterful business
administrator, his true passion was education. He had spent
two years at Yale, been inducted into the Kappa Sigma Epsilon,
and always felt that a college education was the foundation of
a fruitful, meaningful life. After fleeing Korea following the
Japanese invasion, he worked on the mainland to raise funds
to establish an American-style college in China, an effort that
won the attention and patronage of Sheng Xuanhuai, a senior

mandarin. Sheng had been a believer in the self-strengthening movement all those years ago: having witnessed the might of Western weapons during the Opium Wars, he became a believer in Western technology, and followed the fate of the educational mission with interest. He was a perfect ally for Cai, who pitched Sheng the idea of establishing an American-style university in China. Sheng used his rank and influence at the court to win support for Cai's plan, and together the men waged a successful campaign that culminated in the founding of Peiyang University in Tianjin in 1895. Theirs was the first modern university in China.

Selecting a motto for this new institution, all Cai had to do was look back at his days in New Haven: whereas Yale's motto was "Light and Truth," Peiyang's was "Truth in Facts." These words were inscribed on a crest, featuring three fortresses and looking every bit like the logo of an American college. The curriculum, too, took more than a page from New England's finest schools; Cai set up academic departments teaching law, civil engineering, mechanics, mining, and metallurgical engineering in Tianjin, supplying each with textbooks and lab equipment ordered from America.

As the nineteenth century drew to a close, mission graduates were sprinkled throughout the empire. Liang Dunyan, the Orientals' pitcher, ever standoffish and bright, had found his way into the service of Zhang Zhidong, a member of the court's Grand Council and one of the most influential officials in China. Liang's reserved demeanor and conservative outlook suited the mandarin's temperament, and Liang was gradually promoted through the ranks. By the end of the war in Korea,

Liang had secured a reputation as a competent and loyal young man and had attracted the attention of Empress Dowager Cixi, who showered him with motherly compliments and gifts.

To Woo and Cai, Liang and Tong, as well as to their fellow mission graduates now mostly secure in midlevel positions throughout the Qing's dense hierarchy, life must have seemed as if it was finally, belatedly, beginning in earnest. It was sixteen years since the boys had landed back in China and been escorted to the Knowledge Wishing Institution and four years since the war had thrown many of their careers into a tailspin. With graduates of the mission serving in the government, navy, mines, and railroads, the summer of 1898 seemed to suggest that perhaps the mission's goals would be met after all, that American-educated boys would slowly and diligently guide their nation toward progress.

They seemed to have a natural ally in the emperor. Impatient with the gradual pace of change, Guangxu strove for more immediate results. Like a man possessed, he began issuing decree after decree—a total of forty in three months—informing his subjects that reforms were coming. His edicts were nothing less than shocking. They portrayed many of the prevailing traditions as useless and disparaged many of the mandarins as feckless artifacts. "It has been the habit of one-half of our officers to observe only the technicalities of old and obsolete usages," went one typical imperial missive, "and we have tried once before to lay bare the utter uselessness of such practices in the government of the empire in the present crisis. . . . The bane of the country has been the deeply rooted system of inertness and a clinging to obsolete customs."[1] Here, in his own handwriting, was the Son of

Heaven, renouncing the very system he was born to uphold and embody. The imperial examination system, he wrote, with its focus on Confucian learning, was "hollow, useless and unpractical"; it was to be dramatically overhauled.[2] Instead of ancient texts, he decreed, students would now be required to write essays on pertinent modern topics. The art of calligraphy, once so highly valued, was declared "an empty accomplishment."[3] A university would be erected in the heart of Beijing; whatever it could not teach, Chinese students would learn abroad. Members of the court, too, would be sent abroad for long periods of time, to observe the ways of the West. Temples were to be converted to schools. There would be no exceptions. "Now," read one communication, "after this decree, let no one say that he has not been given fair warning."[4]

The mandarins, reeling from those edicts criticizing everything they had studied and aspired to be, were dumbfounded. Unsure of what to do, they resorted to the one activity that was at the center of their being: they memorialized the throne, asking for clarifications. Between mid-August and mid-September, court secretaries were forced to transcribe 660 memorials by hand.[5] Stalling for time, some officials claimed that the emperor's edicts, some of which were mechanically tapped out across the newly strung telegraph wires, were not in themselves binding, because only orders in the emperor's own vermilion pencil, delivered by imperial runners, were authentic. Infuriated, Guangxu demanded obedience.

He realized that a revolution on such a grand scale was too much to undertake single-handedly. In need of confidants, the emperor welcomed two new advisers into his circle, Kang Youwei

and Liang Qichao, both scholars and writers who blended traditional Confucianism with radical egalitarian ideals. Kang, for
example, was interested in extending the spirit of reform to
the nuclear family itself, replacing the institution of marriage
with renewable one-year contracts between men and women and
entrusting the upbringing of children to a communal collective
rather than to their parents. While the extent of Kang's and
Liang's influence over the emperor remains unclear—competing
historical accounts offer vastly different versions—those close to
China's young monarch could tell that his campaign to thrust
China into the modern era was just the beginning.

For the most part, the people surrounding Emperor Guangxu,
Cixi among them, were content to observe the reforms from
the sidelines. Acting on the same cautious instincts that had
preserved their class for centuries, these mandarins waited to
see what became of the emperor's edicts before choosing sides.
But by September of 1898, a single imperial action may have
alienated them for good: desperate for sound advice, Guangxu
made the fatal decision to call on Ito Hirobumi.

The victorious Japanese leader, visiting China to survey the
concessions his nation had gained at war, was admittedly the
best man to turn to for any talk of reform. More than most of
Japan's politicians, he was the emblem of the Meiji Restoration,
living proof that, with diligence and skill, one could travel to
the West and import the best of its virtues and ideals to Asia.
Abandoning whatever residue of pride or resentment he might
have had, the emperor invited Hirobumi to the Forbidden City,
where he quizzed him about the mechanics of modern government. Around the same time, Kang suggested a Sino-Japanese

alliance, and another of the emperor's close confidants met with Japanese military officials.

Such respectful—some said groveling—measures toward the Japanese were more than most high officials could bear. Whereas before the emperor had seemed misguided and naive, he now appeared mad or, worse, traitorous. He wasn't about to reform China, went the whispers in the court's highest echelons; he was about to destroy it.

Guangxu himself was not oblivious of such intimations. With each day, he and his fellow reformers grew more distrustful and alarmed. The emperor was scheduled to visit Tianjin with his aunt; paranoid, his advisers became convinced that Cixi would seize the occasion to detain her nephew and put an end to his reign. The only way to safeguard the monarch's well-being, they argued, was to equip him with a private army of his own, a task for which no man in China was better fitted than Yuan Shikai. Now based in Tianjin, the thirty-nine-year-old general was at his prime, collecting wealth and encomia, waiting for his opportunity to march back onto the stage. Yuan was summoned to Beijing and, after being judged sufficiently deferential to the emperor and his vision, was appointed vice president of the nation's war board. He would soon, he was told, receive further instructions.

In the meantime, official concern over Guangxu's actions reached a feverish peak. A delegation of officials, including Li Hongzhang, visited Cixi in the Summer Palace and argued that her nephew and his counselors were all part of a vast Japanese conspiracy to subdue China. As tensions rose, both sides let their suspicions run rampant.

Determined to strike first, the emperor's advisers devised a plan. Knowing that Guangxu was deferential to his aunt and would never take any measure against her or her circle, they decided to act on their own. Tan Sitong, one of Guangxu's closest allies, secretly called on Yuan and presented the general with a plan that he claimed had the emperor's approval. Yuan's orders, Tan stated, were to kill Jung-lu—a powerful military commander as well as a former lover and current confidant of Cixi's—and imprison the empress dowager in the Summer Palace.

Yuan doubted the veracity of the documents before him, which were written not in the emperor's familiar vermillion pencil but in black ink. He told Tan that he would not be a traitor, and after a curt salute he quickly traveled to Tianjin. There, he sought out Jung-lu and told him about the plot brewing against him in Beijing. Jung-lu, in turn, informed Cixi.

At dawn on September 21, the empress dowager left the Summer Palace and rode to the Forbidden City. In a huge hall lit by flickering lanterns, she confronted her nephew. She accused him of betrayal. The Manchu princes, she told him, had decreed that the emperor was no longer fit to rule. Cixi herself would resume her regency.

Despite his zeal for reform, Guangxu was still a Confucian, still firmly committed to the virtues of filial piety. He prostrated himself before his aunt. "Punish me according to the law!" he is reported to have wept. "I deserve it. I am not fit to rule."[6] Cixi barked out some orders, and Jung-lu and Yuan Shikai were both escorted into the hall, the latter unable to look Guangxu in the eyes. Eunuchs were summoned to carry in writing implements. Guangxu sat down to write as Cixi dictated an edict. He had asked the empress dowager to return and advise him, Guangxi wrote, and she consented. "We have repeatedly besought Her Majesty to condescend once more to administer the Government. Now she has graciously honoured us by granting our prayer, a blessing indeed for all our subjects."[7]

Thus came to an end a brief and brilliant period, known as the Hundred Days' Reform. "Friends of China," mourned one Connecticut newspaper, "as well as friends of human progress, may lament the fall of the reforming emperor."[8] With Cixi in power, the emperor moved into the Summer Palace, where he spent his days in idle pursuits. His associates, Kang Youwei and Liang Qichao in particular, were now wanted men. Seeking to flee the country, they needed sympathetic supporters with whom to stay until their escape could be arranged. In Beijing, they were told, there now lived an old man who was a great friend of reformers everywhere. Decades before, went the rumor, he had been a student in America and devoted his life to a failed attempt to educate young Chinese boys in American colleges. That man would not refuse to help them. Find Yung Wing, they were told.

After the mission was recalled to China, Yung had followed his boys back home. By now, he had two young sons of his own, but he had left them behind in the United States with their mother. His first and greatest love was the mission, and he felt compelled to petition the officials who had ended it. Even if he wouldn't change their minds, he would at least make sure that the mission, his lifework, was remembered as a moderate success.

Once back in China following the cancellation of the

educational mission, Yung called on Li Hongzhang and was
shocked when Li casually asked why he had let the project fall
apart. Trying his best not to lose his temper, Yung replied that
an imperial decree—orchestrated by Woo Tze Teng, Chen Lan
Pin, and Li himself—demanded that the mission be dismantled
and the boys returned to China. "If I had stood out alone against
carrying out the imperial mandate," Yung asked Li, "would not I
have been regarded as a rebel, guilty of treason, and lose my head
for it?" Casually, Li dismissed Yung's claim; at heart, he claimed,
he was always in favor of allowing the boys to remain in America
and complete their studies. Seething, Yung asked how he "could
have been supposed to read [Li's] heart at a distance of 45,000
lis"? And why, he persisted, hadn't Li written him privately and
encouraged Yung to fight the orders from Beijing? Li, an expert
at eluding blame, replied that Woo was at fault.[9] A few days
later, Yung, acting out of sheer politeness, accepted Woo's invitation and called on his old nemesis; taking the same tone as Li,
Woo claimed that he was not to blame for the mission's demise
and that he himself had suffered great opprobrium since returning to China. Leaving China in disgust, Yung returned home to
Hartford, only to find his wife, Mary, suffering from an acute
liver failure that had taken a toll on her health. In 1886, she
succumbed to her illness and died. Yung endeavored to console
himself by returning to China and pursuing further reforms. He
tried to set up a national bank and to promote a national railroad
system. But everywhere he turned, he saw the same dawdling
bureaucrats, the same culture of obsequiousness, the same rigid
adherence to rules and traditions. His passion for the motherland
had grown so faint that when the war with Japan broke out in

1894, he later wrote, his "sympathies were enlisted on the side of China, not because [he was] a Chinese, but because China had the right on her side."[10]

The Hundred Days' Reform gave Yung new hope; when it died, so did his faith in the future of China. When Kang and Liang knocked on his door, he recognized kindred spirits and arranged for them to sneak into Japan. Aware that his act constituted treason, he had to flee as well, first to foreign friends in Beijing and later to British-run Hong Kong.

But while the court continued to prosecute—and, often, execute—members of Emperor Guangxu's inner circle, Cixi and her minions were well aware that China could not afford to abandon altogether its efforts at reform. Cautiously, several industries, such as the navy, the telegraph, and the railway, were deemed a national priority. More than anything else, Beijing needed qualified men who were not infected with the emperor's revolutionary zeal, men who possessed knowledge of Western technology and reverence for Eastern philosophy in equal measure. Very often, the American-educated students were a perfect fit: by 1898, they were largely unaffiliated with any one political movement or idea, without followers of their own, and were seen as loyal and hardworking.

First among them, unsurprisingly, was Tong Shao-yi. After serving as consul general in Korea for nearly three years, he was recalled back to Beijing and reunited with his former patron and fallen idol Yuan Shikai. Whether he was thrilled to see Yuan once more or still smarting from the general's decision to abandon him in Korea, Tong did not say or write. Instead, he greeted Yuan respectfully and once again took his place by Yuan's side.

With the general's role not clearly defined—he was officially entrusted with overhauling the nation's army, but his reputation and natural inclination propelled him to meddle in all realms of civic life—neither was Tong's. One of his several portfolios was director of the Northern Railways, in charge of six hundred miles of tracks, a far bigger operation than the one awarded to his cousin Liang Ju-hao. Prestigious as the appointment was, the position was not yet of any real importance. China's attempts at constructing a large-scale railway system, dating back to the middle of the nineteenth century, had been hesitant and largely fruitless affairs. In 1875, for example, foreign merchants in Shanghai attempted to build a railway between the bustling metropolis and Woosung, a small village at the mouth of the Yangtze River. It was to be a practical demonstration: twelve densely populated miles separated Woosung from Shanghai, and the Westerners hoped that as soon as the locals glimpsed the wonders of modern transportation, they would clamor for more. The locals, however, were horrified. Laying tracks on the ground disturbed the feng shui of the village, and upset the delicate equilibrium of heaven and earth. In a bid to stop the project, Woosung's landowners asked for an exorbitantly high price for each patch of land, but the wealthy foreigners were willing to pay. Finally, after months of legal entanglements, the railway was built. This project, so difficult to complete, was short-lived: several months after launching its operation, a locomotive of the Shanghai–Woosung line hit an oblivious Chinese peasant strolling down the tracks. The man died, sending the local villagers into an uproar. Stepping in, the authorities paid the foreign investors for their losses, dismantled the tracks, and sent them, as well as the engines and the cars, to a buyer in Formosa. The train station was turned into a Confucian temple.

Somewhat more successful was the attempt to connect the Kaiping mines with the nearby town of Beitang, at the mouth of the Hai River. Despite the protestation of the mining company's Chinese shareholders, a local British engineer, C. W. Kinder, was determined to build a railway. With bits of scrap metal and assorted materials found lying around the mines, he fabricated a small engine, which he christened Rocket of China. When the Qing court found out that a railroad had been built without its approval, it reacted vehemently. It prohibited Kinder from any further experimentation. But following an appeal backed by Li Hongzhang, Kinder was allowed to continue. Before long, his line connected Beijing, Tianjin, and Shanhaiguan on the Manchurian border, becoming, in the process, China's first true railway.

News of the metal beasts roaming the rural landscape spread quickly. Most of China's mandarins reacted unfavorably. A governor of Shaanxi Province neatly captured the prevailing spirit of resistance when he told an American visitor of his dislike for trains. "They bring in foreigners, whom I do not like," said the governor, "and they throw men out of work."[11]

Keenly aware that the Chinese looked on railways with mistrust, Western companies did their best to soothe the mandarins. Regarding, perhaps, the inhabitants of the Forbidden City as curious children who could easily be impressed with trinkets, company after company sent all manner of toys to Beijing. In 1885, for example, an American company sent the empress dowager a complete miniature model of a working railway. It consisted of one thousand feet of tracks with switches, a turntable, a passenger locomotive, mail and baggage cars, freight cars, a Pullman parlor, and sleeping cars, each five feet long and complete with tiny seats and berths. The model, an exact replica of an American train, amused Cixi, but did not persuade her to crisscross her country with foreign tracks.

When Tong stepped into his new position as a railroad official, he thus quickly realized that if he wanted to succeed, he had to tread lightly. Instead of pushing for far-reaching, ambitious projects, he spoke in measured tones and called for cautious endeavors. He focused on running those tracks currently under his supervision as efficiently as he could, without making too much of an effort to convince the court that additional railways were necessary.

What Tong's position lacked in authority, it more than made up for in opportunity to mingle with the most prestigious foreign firms operating in China at the time. At this, he was a natural. With his American manners and impeccable English, Tong came off as the quintessential Westerner. The foreigners, incensed with the obtuse mandarins and their inscrutable ways, welcomed Tong as a much needed breath of modernity in the otherwise stale atmosphere of Chinese commerce.

One foreigner in particular took to Tong, a young American engineer dispatched to northern China by a Sino-European mining company. His name was Herbert Hoover. Not long after taking up his office, Hoover realized with dismay that the Chinese had their own way of doing business: Chang Yen-mao, the viceroy in whose district Hoover had hoped to work, was only interested in mining for gold, which he believed would greatly enrich him. He had no room for Hoover's practical concerns and exhortations that a growing economy needed, more than anything, coal, iron, and other industrial minerals. Chang was insistent: he wanted gold. Exasperated, the future president of the United States had no choice but to dig for precious metals. At a train station, Hoover made the acquaintance of Tong, who invited the American to ride in his private car.

"Tong courteously invited us to ride with him," Hoover later wrote in his memoirs, "and there began a firm friendship which was to have many curious developments in after years. He was . . . a man of great abilities, fine integrity, and high ideals for the future of China. Tong soon exploded in his antagonism to Chang Yen-mao . . . explaining him as a palace creation who had risen from a groom by well-applied corruption."[12]

With men like Hoover by his side, Tong found his job enjoyable. The American-educated mandarin and his Western colleagues talked sports, rode horses, and spent hours discussing China and its future, a future that would soon take a bloody and unexpected turn.

The spasm known to history as the Boxer Rebellion began with a few peasants and youths harboring empty stomachs and dim futures and looking for someone to blame for China's troubles. The foreigners presented an easy target, whether they wore the missionary's cross or the trader's coat or the mercenary's boots. There was much about the foreign intruders for the impoverished Chinese to dislike. They had strange customs; they stole swaths of land; they talked incessantly of their demonic religion —"a widely disseminated pamphlet," the historian Jonathan Fenby notes, "said that Christians worshipped a Chief Devil who had been so wicked that he had been executed."[13] The foreigners showed little respect for the Chinese way of life. Worst of all, their arrival signified the beginning of China's woes. With no national newspapers to inform them, few academies to educate them, and no civic institutions to represent their concerns, most of China's citizens were ignorant of the underlying causes of their nation's decline. Lacking other means of channeling their helplessness and rage, they turned against the Occidentals.

At first, anti-Western attacks were too sporadic to be considered a cohesive response. Across the country, local tracts were published, inciting the already agitated peasants against the foreigners, missionaries in particular. "No rain comes from Heaven," read one popular wall poster, "The earth is parched and dry. / And all because the churches / Have bottled up the sky."[14] Shandong Province alone saw an estimated one thousand antiforeign protests. Soon, these disparate demonstrators learned to speak in one voice and espouse a single slogan: "Support the Qing, destroy the Foreign."

It was the slogan's pledge of imperial loyalty that most pleased the court. Unlike the Taiping half a century earlier, the disgruntled peasants were not casting the blame for their misery on the court. Instead, they blamed the British, the French, the Germans, and the other Westerners. After some initial, feeble attempts at curbing the antiforeign riots—the viceroy of Zhili executed one hundred of his subjects for staging an attack on a British missionary, calling the perpetrators "robbers and malcontents"—the court came to see the demonstrators as a tremendous untapped resource. Ever the mistress of political calculations, Cixi observed the rising rebellion with enthusiasm. Many of the demonstrators belonged to a group called the Righteous Harmony Society, which the foreigners, noticing the protesters' obsession with martial arts, dubbed the Boxers. They preached rigid adherence to the strictest moral codes and performed magic rituals that they believed would render them invulnerable. These disciplined, strong, and zealous men, Cixi imagined, might very well be the force she needed to finally remove the yoke of foreign occupation from her empire. While the Boxers are widely revered in China today, and considered by many contemporary historians to be an admirable, if somewhat misguided, anticolonialist movement, most graduates of the Chinese Educational Mission saw them as a menace. To Yung Wing's boys, the Boxers were a primitive and potentially disastrous cabal, representing all the values that had been stifling China's growth for centuries. Their sheer numbers and deep commitment, however, were hard to ignore.

With this in mind, Cixi did what the imperial court did best, which was to refrain from action and observe events as they unfolded. And unfold they did, at a dazzling pace. Sweeping north toward Beijing, Boxers, most of them illiterate peasants, murdered Westerners, pulled down telegraph lines, and incited the local population to join with them in their violence. They tore up railroad tracks and assassinated a Japanese diplomat. Cathedrals were set ablaze, and Chinese who had converted to Christianity were attacked in the capital.

Even faced with such violence, the court maintained a serene face. The Boxers, one mandarin told the British consul in Tianjin, were merely "good citizens on bad terms with the Christians."[15] Incensed, the resident representatives of Europe's nations demanded that the uprising be curbed at once. The

foreigners backed their words with deeds; the same British consul in Tianjin, livid at the local official's inability to deal with
the rioting peasants, sent for a military force to protect Her
Majesty's subjects and interests in the city. Catching wind of
the request, the Forbidden City sent its magistrate in Tianjin an
edict, directing him to resist the foreigners by force. With the
incendiary passion of true revolutionaries, the Boxers attacked
the British forces, killing sixty-two men.

The attacks in Tianjin and elsewhere only served to steady the
West's resolve. Europe's nations demanded that the court put an
immediate end to the Boxers' violence. On June 16, 1900, Cixi
convened her closest advisers to discuss the matter. One sound
voice dismissed the Boxers as charlatans whose claims of magical powers were a hoax; the empress dowager, however, would
hear none of it. "Perhaps their magic is not to be relied on," Cixi
said; "but can not we rely on the hearts and minds of the people?
Today China is extremely weak. We have only the people's hearts
and minds to depend upon. If we cast them aside and lose the
people's hearts, what can we use to sustain the country?"[16]

The meeting ended without any resolution, and the mandarins in attendance agreed to meet again the following day. When
they did, Prince Tuan, the president of the Zongli Yamen, the
court's foreign ministry, produced a document that he promised
would change everything. Taking it from Tuan's hands, Cixi read
it aloud. It was, she said, an ultimatum composed by the nations
of the West. They demanded that the emperor be relocated to
a designated residence, that China's revenues be collected by
the foreign powers, and that China's military affairs be con-
signed to foreign control. That these crude demands were a clear

forgery—they were, in fact, the work of Prince Tuan—did not seem to bother anyone. Such words of Western insolence were all Cixi and her men needed to see. The empress dowager stood up to speak.

"Today," she declared, "they have opened hostilities, and the extinction of the nation is before us. If we fold our arms and yield to them, I will have no face before my ancestors when I die. Rather than waiting for death, is it not better to die fighting?"[17]

Meekly, one mandarin protested that, in the past, China had failed to defeat any single European power and instead was humiliated by England, France, and even Japan. The chances of successfully waging war against not one but all of the West's nations, he said, were not good. His colleagues ignored him. They had no choice. Speaking of the situation in terms of honor and filial piety, Cixi had made conflict inevitable. On June 20, China declared war.

Unsure what to make of China's strange bout of belligerence, European emissaries swore that they knew nothing of Prince Tuan's supposed ultimatum. When they saw that their words carried no weight with the Qing court, they prepared for battle. Those who had devoted their entire lives to infusing China with the spirit of the West bitterly protested Cixi's decision. So enfeebled by old age that his servants had to carry him to his desk, Li Hongzhang did his best to stop the madness. Writing to his old friend the empress dowager, he allowed himself such candor as he hadn't dared display his entire life. For the first time, Li spoke his mind openly and plainly: "My blood runs cold at the thought of events to come," he wrote presciently. "Under any enlightened sovereign these Boxers, with their ridiculous claims of supernatural powers, would most assuredly have been condemned to death long since . . . your Majesties . . . are still in the hands of traitors, regarding these Boxers as your dutiful subjects, with the result that unrest is spreading and alarm universal."[18] He was ignored.

Back in Tianjin, Tong was equally alarmed. Although he was an official of the court, he represented an industry—the railroad—perceived by the Boxers as emblematic of all Western evils. He was also American-educated, spoke English most of the time, and spent his days interacting with the city's foreign residents. Concerned for the safety of his family, he turned to his friend Herbert Hoover, who arranged for Tong and his family to take refuge in the compound of the city's international legation.

Luckily for Tong, Hoover wasn't just a good friend but a crafty engineer as well. Sensing an imminent attack even before Cixi declared war on the Westerners, he designed a system of defensive positions across a five-mile perimeter. Using huge sacks of grain he found in nearby warehouses, Hoover put up barricades and dug trenches in key strategic points, proving himself to be an expert tactician. The women and children were gathered in the basement of municipal hall. The men of the international legation, 2,400 in total, prepared for battle.

On June 17, a force of ten thousand Boxers and imperial troops, armed with at least sixty pieces of artillery, swarmed the city, shouting "Sha, sha," or kill, kill, and setting fire to every foreign building in sight. With the telegraph wires cut, the international legation's defenders had no way to call for help. Risking their lives, an Englishman and three Russian Cossacks rode on horseback through the artillery to inform the nearest headquarters of the allied Western armies of their distress. In the meantime, positioned behind Hoover's sacks of grain, the defenders fought back as best they could.

Six days later, the battle was over. The allied forces, recognizing the potential of Tianjin as a strategic location en route to the capital and responding to the urgent request of the emissaries, sent a detachment of nearly eight thousand men that arrived a few days after the fighting started. With their superior arms and training, these soldiers had no difficulty overwhelming the Boxers and their allies. The city was soon free, its foreign residents elated. Tong, however, could not share in the festivities. Rushing to find his family, he learned that his wife and daughter had both been killed.

Devastated, Tong fell into a deep depression. He was deeply in love with his wife and mourned her loss intensely. As Tong grieved, Tianjin's defenders joined with the other allied forces in marching on Beijing. Hungry for revenge, the pillars of troops making their way to the Forbidden City set fire to every village they passed. Along the way, the troops passed Liang Dunyan. While his graduation speech at Hartford High School, the masterful oration about the Russian bear, was a criticism of the West's tendency to mistrust Asian nations, he was now deeply sympathetic to the European allies. The Boxers, he realized, were a disaster, an illogical and harmful movement. Even though he had grown close to the empress dowager and respected her political prowess, he saw Cixi's declaration of war as a grave mistake. As he greeted the troops, he summoned his old rhetorical skills and made sure no acts of violence or vandalism occurred in the area under his control.

But such restraint was only temporary. Soon enough, the foreigners would reach Beijing and then seek revenge. As they had done once before, Cixi and her minions prepared to flee the palace, burying whatever treasures they couldn't take with them in anticipation of their eventual return. A concubine who argued that it was beneath the emperor's dignity to flee was seized by two eunuchs and tossed down a well. Even though she disguised herself in simple clothes, and exchanged her hundred-course meals for simple suppers of noodles and eggs, the empress dowager still stood out. Somewhere along the way, a disgruntled Chinese soldier shot at her. He missed, and was immediately captured and beheaded, but the old woman was shocked at such betrayal. "Before," she later reflected, "I was just like a piece of pure jade, but [now] the jade has a flaw in it . . . and it will remain there to the end of my life."[19]

Cixi's mind was further burdened by what she had seen in the course of her escape. Usually sheltered from China's daily strife by the tall walls of her palace, she now witnessed the horrors wrought by her regime. Francis H. Nichols, an American writer who was traveling through the same regions at approximately the same time as the empress dowager, painted a grim picture of the famine-stricken cities and villages that Cixi was now seeing for the first time:

The famine sufferers were compelled to live in fields in the suburbs. For shelter they dug caves in the clay banks by the side of the road, and they made their death lingering by eating coarse grass and weeds. All around Sian when I visited it were these grim, blackened caves. They were nearly all empty. The men, women, and children who had lived in them were all dead. According to native statistics 130,000 perished from hunger in one suburb. . . .

And all the time food was becoming scarcer. By-and-by human flesh began to be sold in the suburbs of Sian. At first the traffic was carried on clandestinely, but after a time a horrible kind of meat ball, made from the bodies of human beings who had died of hunger, became a staple article of food, that was sold for the equivalent of about four American cents a pound.[20]

Weary, startled, and at a loss, the empress dowager wanted the war she had just recently started to end. Like so many times in the past, the court needed a trustworthy man to negotiate the terms of surrender. This time, however, trustworthy men were harder to find: because so many of the Qing's upper echelons had gleefully supported Cixi's ill-fated declaration of war, few remained who could skillfully and honestly broker peace. Not knowing whom else to turn to, Cixi once more turned to Li Hongzhang.

Although the frail septuagenarian—weakened by the attempt on his life a decade before in Japan—could barely walk, he couldn't refuse his sovereign. With great difficulty, he met with Western representatives and negotiated the Boxer protocol, signed on September 7, 1901. It was, by far, the most punishing treaty China had ever been forced to accept. Beside a stratospheric indemnity—450 million taels of silver, a sum so immense that the protocol allowed China a period of thirty-nine years to pay it—Li had to agree to a litany of humiliating terms.

Defending his friend and monarch, he insisted that Cixi's name
be removed from the list of war criminals, but had to concede
instead to a demand that she immediately abandon all affairs
of state and end her life as a private, if exalted, citizen. Foreign
nations would be allowed to place troops in Beijing. The list of
territorial concessions continued to grow.

Unsure how to restore its credibility and regain the nation's
trust, the Qing court resorted to a time-tested tradition and
began promptly to execute, exile, or force suicide on any mandarin deemed responsible for the shameful defeat. With the
hard-liners gone, it was time to consider the future. An imperial
decree sent a clear sign that the spirit of reform was once again
alive in China.

"Unless we cultivate talents," it read, "we cannot expect them
to exist. Unless we promote education, we cannot cultivate talents. Unless we reform civil and military examination, we cannot promote education. Unless we study abroad, we cannot make
up deficiencies education at home."[21] Since America had closed
its doors to the Chinese with the Chinese Exclusion Act of 1882,
and since dispatching students to Europe was too costly, the
court directed its energies and its resources inward, setting up
more than 100,000 modern schools and educating more than 2.9
million students. Cai Shaoji's Peiyang University was the obvious
model to emulate; having graduated its first class just before the
Boxer Rebellion, the institution was being increasingly referred
to by reform-minded mandarins as a sterling example the rest
of China should follow. Cai was flattered. The rebellion had left
him impoverished; his passion for education was therefore the
primary force propelling him forward. Shortly after the war, he

was appointed the university's president, a position from which he gladly dispensed advice to other officials entrusted with setting up similar schools. And his advice was sorely needed: desperate for rapid change, the court issued edict after edict in an effort to overhaul the nation's educational system. First, Beijing announced that the imperial exams would be reformed; shortly thereafter, it clarified that they would be altogether eliminated. A 1,300-year-old pillar of China's imperial system was abolished with a stroke of the vermilion pencil.

These ambitious plans, however, would go nowhere without capable custodians. Finally, the students of the Chinese Educational Mission rose to lead their country.

Liang Ju-hao, in Tianjin with his cousin Tong Shao-yi, was promoted and entrusted with running the all-important Beijing–Shanhaikuan railway line. Seized by the allied forces during the Boxer uprising, they suddenly and without warning placed it back into China's hands in the fall of 1902. The line, Liang was told, was a costly business, having been subsidized to the tune of $1.5 million Mexican dollars per year. Drawing on the sort of economic ingenuity he had admired in Hartford, Liang realized that smooth management was only the beginning. If he wanted the company to thrive, he needed to increase revenue and expand the customer base. Coolies, he knew, were an untapped market. To China's traditional higher classes, those wretched laborers were service providers, not very different from oxen or cows. To Liang, they were potential patrons, a large population with needs and means. Knowing that about 400,000 workers embarked on a monthlong journey from northern China to Manchuria every year for the annual harvest, Liang offered them a deeply discounted ticket costing a dollar and a half. Since going by rail saved them a month's worth of lost work, many gladly paid the fare. They increased the coffers of the railway and at the same time were able to boost agricultural production. In less than two years, Liang's line was turning a profit, earning more than $300,000 annually.

Impressed with Liang's ability to turn the railway from a financial liability into a moneymaker, the court awarded the young manager an exorbitant salary of $2,000 Mexican per month; in comparison, the town's magistrate made only $140. Wealthy, celebrated, and powerful, Liang could now afford to take greater risks. Few things pleased him more than laying down tracks. It meant more to him than just the opportunity to win customers and make money. The lessons of his boyhood train journeys on America's transcontinental railroad were clear, and it was apparent that China would never become a thriving, modern nation unless it could follow America's lead and construct miles and miles of tracks to rush passengers and goods to all corners of the empire.

It didn't take much contemplation for Liang to find an obvious direction in which to expand the railroads. Approximately twenty-seven miles to the west of the Forbidden City lay the imperial ancestral burial grounds. Each year, the entire court would embark on a pilgrimage to the graves of their forebears to perform the ritualistic duties of filial piety. Liang memorialized the court, suggesting that the already established Beijing-Tianjin line be extended westward to the burial grounds. Almost immediately, his proposal was approved.

There was, however, one snag. Liang proposed the extension

late in the fall of 1906. The annual pilgrimage was the following March, leaving whichever engineer took on the project less than six months to complete the new railway. Liang made a few inquiries with foreign firms, all of which refused him on the spot. None, it seemed, wanted to be responsible for an embarrassing failure to finish the project on time. That bothered Liang little; he knew just the man for the job.

Jeme Tien-yau, the mission's most brilliant student, the erstwhile "Jimmy" who had left America with a degree from Yale, had learned from the earliest days of his return to China that his intellect was not as well regarded at home as it had been in Connecticut. He had been drafted into the navy and spent most of his career in near anonymity. He taught engineering at a host of naval schools, only in 1888 convincing his superiors that his American education in railroads made him suitable to the burgeoning world of China's trains. Still, even as a junior railway engineer in the service of the court, Jeme, modest and kind, failed to stand out. He seemed to be forever relegated to menial, secretarial tasks. When his old colleague Liang wrote and offered him the project, he was thrilled. At his current position, Jeme stood under the shadow of foreign engineers, whom the mandarins respected and preferred. But now Liang was a mandarin, and Jeme had his chance. He took the job.

As talented at managing his workers as at designing elegant and efficient railroads, and displaying a level of attention to detail and gift for precision uncommon even among Europe's finest engineering firms, Jeme completed the railway in time for the imperial pilgrimage. Liang was impressed, but not surprised. Having spent many years with Jeme, he knew the true worth of his brilliant childhood friend. Soon, the ambitious railway manager dreamed up a bigger, bolder task—a railway connecting Beijing with the Inner Mongolian town of Kalgan, approximately a hundred miles to the northeast. A strategic frontier town, Kalgan was notoriously difficult to reach because it was surrounded by steep and impenetrable mountains. Still, Liang decided to try.

Almost immediately after word of the project spread, British representatives wrote to the court and argued that since British loans had paid for many of China's previous railway lines, this one, too, ought to be built by Her Majesty's engineers. Every project within the confines of the Great Wall, they argued, was Britain's to refuse. Incensed, Russian diplomats came forth to protest. The proposed railway, they argued, may originate in Beijing, but its terminus, Kalgan, lay outside of the Great Wall and close to Russia's sphere of interests. It therefore followed that Russian engineers had to build the line. This, in turn, infuriated Japan: having dealt Russia a military blow in the Russo-Japanese War of 1904–05, the Japanese argued that whatever rights Russia might have had in the area were now theirs. As the three powers fought among themselves, the Chinese court suggested a compromise. Jeme Tien-yau, they proposed, would survey the terrain and do with it whatever he could. If he failed to lay the tracks, the issue of who had the rights to the line would once again be debated.

Regarding Jeme as an unqualified novice, Japan, Russia, and Britain agreed at once. Let the Chinese engineer try, went the logic, and when he failed there would be no other obstacles the Qing could erect. But Jeme, pioneering several techniques and inventing devices designed to make the work more efficient, succeeded. Within months a railway line, a marvel of modern engineering, snaked its way through the dangerous peaks and into Kalgan. The Westerners were impressed, and the Chinese were ecstatic. Even those who had previously reviled trains as a devilish creation now saw Jeme's achievement as a source of great pride. Here, after all, was the first railway built, entirely without foreign aid, by a crafty and ingenious son of China, a sign of a promising future for the country.

Jeme became a national hero, but the glory wasn't his alone. Throughout China, mandarins were rapidly realizing that the graduates of the Chinese Educational Mission were men of a different caliber, enterprising and skillful and free of the fetters that bound most of their peers to lives lacking daring. On board warships and in the belly of mines, in train stations and diplomatic offices, the returned students were entrusted with responsibility and overwhelmed with praise when they succeeded. The handful of men at the group's social center—Tong Shao-yi, Liang Dunyan, Liang Ju-hao, Cai Shaoji, Jeme Tien-yau, and a few others—came to be known by their colleagues and superiors as the Cantonese Clique and were regarded as heirs apparent to the highest positions in the empire's mandarinate. And whenever one graduate advanced in the ranks, he nearly always promoted his boyhood friends, with whom he would still talk in English and whom he would still address by the same nicknames given out in the schoolyards of New England more than three decades earlier. In the halls of imperial power, where previous generations of mandarins would solemnly recite passages from the sacred *Analects*, the men would greet one another with their favorite phrase, "That's alright, old boy, take it easy!"

The affinities between the mission's graduates ran deeper than mere friendship. It was not uncommon for them to marry into each other's families. Both Jeme and Chung Mun Yew, Yale's famed coxswain, for example, married the sisters of Tan Yew Fun, their friend who had chosen to stay behind in Connecticut and died in Colebrook of tuberculosis. And when the graduates' children came of marriageable age, their fathers would often marry them off within the group: among others, Liang Ju-hao's son Pete married Tong Shao-yi's daughter Mabel, and Liang Dunyan's daughter married Jeme Tien-yau's son.

With the Cantonese Clique at its heart, the small group of graduates soon had its men helming every major industry in the nation. Together, they were working to make China a modern nation. And once again, they had a patron in Yuan Shikai.

11

Sunset

The first decade of the twentieth century was kind to Yuan Shikai. He emerged from the turmoil and humiliation of the Boxer Rebellion with his reputation intact and enjoyed near-universal admiration among the Chinese. His soldiers, most mandarins were convinced, were the nation's best trained, heirs apparent to Li Hongzhang's Ever Victorious Army, the mighty and turbaned warriors who had defeated the Taiping. Comparisons to Li were inevitable: both men brimmed with confidence, both were master tacticians, and both were driven by oversized ambitions. When Li died in November 1901 at the age of seventy-eight—the indomitable leader was so infirm that he had to be carried from his chair to his bed, unable to utter any sound louder than a whisper—Yuan was appointed to Li's role as the viceroy of Zhili Province, with responsibility for the imperial capital of Beijing.

The viceroy who oversaw Beijing, naturally, was first among his peers, and the position was historically awarded to men of

great merit. Stepping into his new position, Yuan wasted little
time in once again assembling the graduates of the educational
mission at his side, inviting the men who had served under him
in Korea and elsewhere to return to his employ. Summoned
first was Tong Shao-yi, the protégé whom Yuan showered with
numerous appointments, including head of customs in Tianjin,
superintendent at Peiyang University, and special commissioner
for foreign affairs. Next, Yuan recalled Cai Shaoji from the presidency at Peiyang and appointed him chief adviser for foreign
affairs. To replace Cai at the ever important university, Yuan
tapped Liang Dunyan, who was also given portfolios in the maritime customs office at Tianjin and entrusted with running the
Beijing–Fengtien railway. Even Yung Leang, who had quit public
life following the defeat of the Chinese fleet more than a decade
earlier, was called to assist the empire. When the letter from
Yuan Shikai requesting his service arrived, By-jinks Johnnie was
only too willing to quit his position as an English teacher at a
girls' school and report for duty as the traffic manager on Liang
Dunyan's railway.

Yuan, of course, was a soldier first and foremost, and as such
he needed a military attaché to keep his army ready and disciplined. Yuan asked Tong whether he knew of anyone who possessed the skill, spirit, intelligence, and experience necessary for
such a vital position. Tong replied that he knew the right man:
Tsai Ting Kan, whose childhood friends knew him as Fighting
Chinee. Yuan summoned Tsai to an interview and, sensing the
man's worth, engaged him on the spot.

It is not difficult to see what attracted the general—raised in
the fortified compound of the Yuan family—to the Cantonese

Clique and their fellow educational mission alumni, men who
had come of age in the austere world of Puritan New England.
The graduates of the mission were well educated and athletic,
and they recognized the value of personal responsibility. Perhaps
more importantly, Yuan saw that they understood the foreigners.

And the foreigners, in the aftermath of the Boxer Rebellion
and the disastrous war that followed, were posing a mortal threat
to China. Weakened by seven decades of military defeats, China
entered the twentieth century ill equipped to resist foreign
threats and incursions. The British were eying Tibet, the French
ramped up their presence in Hainan, and Japan and Russia were
both inching toward Manchuria. If all those attempts at annexa-
tion went unchecked, Yuan realized, the Chinese empire would
be pulled apart. He made it clear that he expected his men to
strive toward one goal: putting checks on the foreigners.

In 1904, Tong Shao-yi had been assigned to tackle the British.
Yuan instructed Tong that Britain must not be allowed to colo-
nize Tibet as it had India. The British, fearing a Russian invasion
of the Himalayan kingdom, had invaded Tibet earlier that year
and sought to establish a protectorate there. Beijing viewed this
move as a grave violation of China's de facto sovereignty over
Tibet. After all, the Qing officials argued, the British had negotiated four treaties with China in the nineteenth century; in each,
they acknowledged that all questions of access to Tibet had first
to be cleared with the Forbidden City. To remind the British of
this precedent in light of the recent developments, a Chinese
delegation led by Tong was sent to Lhasa, the capital of Tibet,
to negotiate with the invaders.

Meeting the British officials, Tong immediately disliked Lord

Curzon, the viceroy of India, who treated the Chinese with dis-
dain and refused to compromise. Most of Tong's colleagues at the
delegation considered the case hopeless in the face of Curzon's
intransigence, but Tong saw the situation differently. In America,
he had learned that in democracies even the most imperious men
were still subject to the will of the people. He knew that Britain's
invasion of Tibet was deeply unpopular with British voters.
Time, he told his friends, was on China's side. Besides, Tong had
learned that a senior member of the British delegation to Lhasa,
Lord Kitchener, the commander of the British armed forces in
India, second only to Curzon in the colonial hierarchy, had been
deeply opposed to the invasion and preferred that Tibet remain
under Chinese control. In his American English, Tong took the
opportunity to introduce himself to Kitchener, who soon took
a liking to the cosmopolitan Chinese official. Both men were
riding enthusiasts and shared a passion for Chinese porcelain.
Back home, Tong had by this time amassed an impressive collection of antique vases, and, after discussing the artistic merits
of the various dynasties with Kitchener, he arranged to have a
few choice items delivered to his new acquaintance.

The domestic pressures in Great Britain and Kitchener's
continuing opposition to the invasion eventually wore Curzon
down. In 1906, Britain and China signed an agreement that
amounted to Britain's acceptance of China's suzerainty over
Tibet. It was a rare victory for Chinese nationalism, and Tong
returned home to an enthusiastic welcome from Yuan. Tong's
achievements, the general noted with pleasure, were proof that
if China could be tough, smart, and resolute, it could stand up
to even the most powerful of Western powers.

But not all of these newfound expressions of national dignity were played out on such a large scale. Some of the mission's graduates, like Liang Dunyan, fought against foreign subjugation with more subtle strokes. While other Chinese officials unhesitatingly performed the kowtow before the Europeans and yielded to any foreign demands, Liang was strict and unyielding. When the sons of powerful British officials were suspected of smuggling explosives by train that were bound for local revolutionaries, Liang, in his capacity as the railway's manager, immediately arrested them at the train station and took them into custody. The British consul protested, Liang's superiors apologized profusely, and the young men were eventually released, but the statement had been made: no more smuggling attempts occurred in Liang's district.

Yuan was impressed by Liang. Here, after all, was a tough-minded man who knew how to deal with foreigners. He summoned Liang and gave him the position of China's de facto minister of foreign affairs. To Yuan's amazement, Liang refused.

He informed Yuan that he was too introverted for the job and that he wasn't suited to handshaking and backslapping. Besides, he found China's domestic troubles far more pressing than its diplomatic concerns. If Yuan truly valued his talent, he should appoint him as a provincial minister and let him implement reforms at home.

But Yuan wasn't one to accept refusals. Curtly, he informed Liang that the position was his whether he wanted it or not. Liang was frustrated, but not for long. Shortly after taking office, he stumbled upon an international issue that suited his sensibility for local development. Since returning home to China two decades earlier, Liang had never stopped thinking about his time in Hartford, considering his years in America to be the most joyful and formative of his life. He was convinced that he owed his talents, skills, and drive to the time he spent in New England. Like Yung Wing before him, he believed that China needed to send more of its sons abroad, to American schools in particular. In Liang's previous position as an official in charge of mines, he could do little to further his educational aspirations, but here, at the foreign ministry, he perhaps could initiate some useful programs.

Liang found willing partners in the American diplomats stationed in China. They were open to the idea of using a portion of their Boxer indemnity—the reparations China was obligated to pay the United States—to send a group of Chinese students to American colleges. Sketching the outline of this new educational mission, Liang suggested that a preparatory school be built in Beijing that would teach English to the next generation of Chinese students before they set out across the ocean, sparing them the embarrassment and laughter he and the rest of Yung Wing's boys first experienced in New England when they mispronounced words or forgot the names of the foods they were being served. In time, Liang's new school would evolve into Tsinghua University—today considered to be China's most prestigious educational institution. At its inception, the school's first director was another of Yung Wing's boys, Tong Kwo On.

Liang's negotiations with the Americans were progressing smoothly, and he prepared to travel to Xiamen on behalf of the empire to greet President Theodore Roosevelt's Great White Fleet, the American naval detachment sent to circumnavigate the globe and herald the maritime might of the United States. Before Liang left, though, he stopped by the Forbidden City to pay a visit to the empress dowager, with whom he still maintained a close relationship. Cixi, especially fond of the serious and capable Liang, asked him what he planned to do after he met with the fleet. He dutifully replied that he would return to Guangdong and sweep the tombs of his ancestors, a yearly ritual of filial piety, and pay a visit to his elderly mother. "How old," asked Cixi, "is your mother?" Liang, days short of his fiftieth birthday, replied that she was seventy-three. The empress dowager smiled and said, "Same as me!" In a tender gesture, the woman who had coldly dispatched so many members of her own family removed her jade hairpin and handed it to Liang. "Give this to her from me," she said. Liang, deeply moved, bowed and left the room. Before setting off on his mission, he still had to do one more thing. A reverent creature of tradition despite his modern affectations, Liang consulted the *Book of Changes*, the ancient Chinese system of divination. The result, *lingua*—meaning "you will return to an empty nest"—startled him, and he struggled with its implications while on his journey.[1]

While Liang was busy conducting his official business, Emperor Guangxu unexpectedly died. He was two years shy of his fortieth birthday. The court hastily declared that the emperor had died of a prolonged illness, and a doctor determined that the cause of death was natural. But the mandarins, keenly attuned to conspiracies and immersed in the suspicions of the empire, advanced other theories. Some said that Guangxu was poisoned by Cixi; the empress dowager, they argued, was old, and feared that if she died before her nephew, nobody would be able to oppose his reforms in her absence. Others held that Guangxu was killed by Yuan Shikai: the general, went the thinking, realized that Cixi would not live much longer, and, if neither she nor Guangxu were in the picture, Yuan would be the empire's most powerful man and its logical ruler. A century later, in 2008, Chinese scientists examined hair taken from Guangxu's body and found arsenic levels in the emperor's blood that were two thousand times higher than ordinary.[2] It is now clear that Guangxu was assassinated—by whom, we may never know.

As dawn broke over Beijing the next day, Cixi presided at a meeting of the Grand Council to discuss who should take Guangxu's place on the throne. As the deceased emperor had no sons of his own, Cixi culled candidates from the highest-ranking Manchu families at the court. She settled on a toddler, the grandson of her former lover Jung-lu. The child, two months short of his third birthday, was given the name Puyi. The boy's father would serve as regent, and Cixi would retain a largely ceremonial position as the empress grand dowager. Pleased that the imperial nomination process had gone so smoothly, Cixi enjoyed a lunch of pears and fainted. When she regained consciousness, she announced that she was "seized of a mortal sickness and without hope of recovery." She issued a decree summing up her illustrious career, one rife with "calamities from within and aggression from without [that] have come upon us in relentless succession."[3]

Drawing her last breath, Cixi made a final pronouncement: "Never again allow any woman to hold the supreme power in the state."[4] She turned to face west and died.

Liang Dunyan received the news of Cixi's passing with sadness, but he wasn't surprised. The *Book of Changes* had been right: he would be returning to an empty nest after all.

While the empire was mourning the deaths of both Guangxu and Cixi, Tong Shao-yi was aboard a ship headed for America. With the successful negotiations in Tibet to his credit, Tong was once more assigned an important diplomatic mission, this one considerably closer to his heart. As China struggled to contain Russian and Japanese aggression in Manchuria—both nations were increasing their presence in the region—Yuan had ordered Tong to go to Washington. Officially, the purpose of his visit was to thank the Americans for their generosity in allowing the monies from the Boxer indemnity to be used to further the cause of Chinese education. But the real goal of Tong's mission was to persuade the Americans to sign a declaration supporting Chinese sovereignty in Manchuria and to invest in the region's development. Yuan hoped that an active American influence in the area would prevent other powers from meddling in the ancestral Qing homeland.

Tong headed back to the United States with high hopes. He was slated to meet with President Roosevelt and his secretary of state, Elihu Root. More than that, though, Tong was looking forward to seeing the familiar American landscapes of his boyhood. His would be a triumphal visit: the dutiful student returning to the United States as a proud and accomplished son of China.

Bad news, however, met him at the docks when he arrived. That same morning, he learned, Root had signed an agreement with the Japanese ambassador, Takahira Kogoro, affirming

Japan's right to govern large areas of land in southern Manchuria. Tong was distraught. He rushed to see Root, who tried to sugar-coat Tong's negative assessment of the Manchurian concessions. Root insisted that the agreement specifically affirmed China's sovereignty over its territories. That was true, Tong replied, but its language also seemed to suggest that Japan was free to pursue its interests in Manchuria. The meeting failed to produce an understanding, and Tong had the feeling that the Americans had sacrificed China in order to appease Japan. Disappointed, Tong cut his visit short. He was no longer in the mood for friendly rem-iniscences. He boarded the ship home, and was further dismayed when a stop in Germany—where he had hoped to elicit support from the kaiser—also failed to live up to his expectations.

Tong arrived home to find China a changed nation. With the empress dowager and Guangxu both gone, the court's highest-ranking noblemen stalked the halls of the palace, planning their next moves. Puyi and his father were powerless and lacked pro-tectors. The door was wide open for a strong individual to usurp control of the empire. Many feared that person would be Yuan Shikai. Guangxu's supporters at the court did not trust Yuan. He was, after all, the reason the Hundred Days' Reform had failed. If only the general had sided with the emperor rather than with the empress dowager, China could have avoided much of the misery that befell it in the preceding decade. To Cixi's loyalists, Yuan was too ambitious and crude, just the sort of man who would poison an emperor who stood in his way. Collectively, the mandarins, who were uniformly divided on everything else, agreed that Yuan was a threat. He was summoned to the Forbidden City and curtly informed that he was being relieved of all of his duties. The official reason, the court claimed, was a foot disease. Yuan returned to his home in the southern Henan Province; Chinese history, he knew better than most, was cyclical, and he simply waited for his star to rise again.

Yuan's men followed him off the stage. One by one, the mission's graduates, with few exceptions, were dismissed by the court, stripped of their responsibilities, and sent home to sulk. Tong Shao-yi, upon his return from his disastrous mission abroad, learned that he no longer held any official position. He went home to his native village in the south. Having amassed a fortune in his years as a senior official, Tong had built himself a small estate, which included a tennis court and an observatory set in a vast park. He hadn't planned to live there for many years yet, not until he had retired at a ripe old age. Now forty-seven, he spent his days exercising, cataloging his collection of porcelain objects, and ambling through his property. Unlike most mandarins, who surrounded their properties with fences to keep out the neighboring peasants, Tong opened his estate to the public. Meanwhile, he, like Yuan, waited for his fortunes to turn.

Neither Tong nor Yuan had to wait very long. Like the Taiping and the Boxer rebellions, the uprising of 1911 began in fits and starts, igniting in a few sporadic locations and then spreading to consume the entire nation. It started by chance: on October 9 of that year, in the southern city of Wuchang on the banks of the Yangtze River, a bomb accidentally exploded in the offices of a secret society. Arriving to investigate, the police discovered the underground group's membership roster. The incriminating document listed the names of military officers organizing to fight rampant corruption; the officers, knowing that they faced imminent arrest and execution, staged a revolt. Within a few days, they had rallied 3,600 men to their cause. The government forces tried to dispel the rebels, but failed. The officials fled town. Wuchang was lost to the boy emperor. Across Hubei, local strongmen followed suit, driving out the Qing representatives and slaughtering unsuspecting Manchus. Less than two weeks later, the riots spread to Hunan in the south. By the end of the month, seven provinces were in rebellion against the throne.

Reading about these developments in his hotel room in Denver, Colorado, the exiled reformer Sun Yat-sen realized that his historic moment had arrived. Like Yung Wing, Sun was born in a small village in Guangdong and, also like him, left China at an early age. He developed a mild obsession with American politics—the Gettysburg Address, in particular, never failed to move him—as well as a number of other foreign tastes. Throughout Sun's life, for example, his acquaintances could never help remarking that he disliked rice and preferred beef bouillon. Sun traveled to Hong Kong, converted to Christianity, and took up the cause of reform. His good looks and ample charm made him a desirable companion for women and a natural leader for men, and before long Sun was engaged in the business of revolution. Not one for weapons and tactics—an attempted coup in 1895 failed miserably and forced him to flee China—his efforts consisted mainly of fund-raising, and he was particularly successful with Chinese expatriates in Europe and the United States who saw in the worldly Sun the sort of man China needed. The 1911 revolts presented the perfect opportunity. "This time," Sun admitted, "I did not expend an ounce of strength."[5] Thrilled with the developments, he bid the Rocky Mountains adieu and made his way to China.

There, affairs were rapidly spinning out of control. Watching rebels taking up arms in province after province, the Grand Council begrudgingly admitted that the only man who could stop the uprising was Yuan Shikai. A delegation of mandarins went to visit Yuan in his home, where, surrounded by his ten wives, he claimed that he was enjoying his retirement too much and had no desire to once again put on his uniform. The mandarins pleaded, and Yuan consented on two conditions: that he have complete control over China's armed forces as well as the right to legislate reforms as he saw fit. Desperate to quell the uprisings, the officials agreed.

Leading a charge on Wuchang, Yuan's well-trained soldiers quickly overran the antigovernment forces. But Yuan saw a path to victory that skirted the battlefield. He made a secret pact with one of the rebel leaders, agreeing to spare the revolutionary's life and show mercy to his men in return for political cooperation. On November 14, Yuan rode the train to Beijing where, in an exercise of his newly minted power, he formed a government and named himself its prime minister. The country, he announced, needed a strong constitutional monarchy in order to survive. Deferential, and powerless to resist, the regent abdicated.

Still, the uprising raged on, with rebels now taking hold of Nanjing, the imperial summer capital, in the south. Calling on his connections within the rebellion's leadership, Yuan campaigned for a unified republic. Sun, however, was not easily placated. Having arrived at Shanghai on Christmas Day, he quickly stood out among the rebels as the most competent and celebrated of them all. In addition to the many who'd been loyal to him throughout the years of failed attempts at revolution, Sun was winning acolytes with his charisma and his resolve. When one fellow rebel suggested that perhaps Yuan's offer wasn't so bad, and that perhaps China could be governed by a parliament and a prime minister, with a president serving only as the titular head of state, Sun erupted. "I will not stand apart like some holy excrescence while the great plans for the revolution are ruined," he shouted.[6] One by one, his opponents withdrew their objections. Sun would become the rebels' uncontested leader.

On December 29, the newly installed National Assembly convened in Nanjing to cast its vote for China's new president. It consisted of 870 senators, representing a wide array of ideological convictions, and was the result of a lengthy process of regional elections. The closest body to a parliament that China had ever had overwhelmingly elected Sun as provisional president. As night fell on New Year's Day of 1912, in a hall brightly lit not by lanterns but by electric bulbs, Sun was inaugurated as the head of a new leadership, pledging to "overthrow the despotic Manchu Government, consolidate the Republic of China and plan for the welfare of the people."[7]

Sun's authority, however, was fragile. He had no military power that could best Yuan's well-trained army. And the senators who supported him, Sun knew, could just as easily transfer their allegiances to Yuan, if the general's victory appeared to be inevitable. Ever the realist, Sun understood that he had no choice but to placate Yuan. On the day of his inauguration, Sun sent Yuan a telegram, informing him that while Sun had accepted the presidency, "it is actually waiting for you, and my offer will eventually be made clear to the world. I hope that you will soon decide to accept this offer."[8]

This was all Yuan needed to hear. He went to the Forbidden City and informed the court that Sun had agreed to hand over the presidency and that, since the republic's power had now been consolidated in him, the dynastic system was over. It was time for the six-year-old emperor to abdicate. Although imperial loyalists vowed to fight, their words mattered little. On February 12, 1912, the court issued its final edict. It was written by Lung Yu, Puyi's mother:

> It is clear that the minds of the majority of the people are favorable to the establishment of a republican form of government. The universal desire clearly expresses the will of Heaven, and it is not for us to oppose the desires and incur the disapproval of the millions of the People merely for the sake and privileges and powers of a single House. . . . We, the Empress Dowager and the Emperor, will retire into a life of leisure, free from public duties, spending our years pleasantly and enjoying the courteous treatment accorded us by the People, and watching with satisfaction the glorious establishment and consummation of a perfect Government.[9]

With these words, nearly two millennia of Chinese imperial rule came to an end.

The following month, Yuan was elected president by the National Assembly. Fireworks lit up the sky. Sun Yat-sen gave a speech, praising his successor as "the friend of the Republic, the devoted and valued servant of the cause."[10] A new constitution was drafted shortly thereafter, guaranteeing every Chinese citizen equality and protection under the law. A new presidential election, the assembly decided, would be held within ten months. Progress, it seemed to those present, might have at long last arrived.

Less than three years after they were relieved of their positions, graduates of the educational mission returned to power, taking up the most senior spots in Yuan's new administration: Tong Shao-yi was named prime minister; Liang Dunyan was appointed minister of foreign affairs, and Cai Shoaji and Liang Ju-hao were appointed his deputies; and Tsai Ting Kan, Yuan's trusted military attaché, was now senior adviser to the president.

Shortly after the republic was established, Tsai came to see the new president in private. He arrived to perform a symbolic ceremony. With just the two of them in the room, Tsai, the boy who had won a special dispensation to remove his queue in the machine shops of New England, took out a knife and cut off the queue of Yuan Shikai, liberating the great soldier from the last, formal vestige of Manchu domination. He would now answer to no one.

As his students shepherded China toward the future, Yung Wing did not have a chance to relish their success. Having fled China in the wake of the Hundred Days' Reform more than a decade earlier, he discovered, to his horror, that the American citizenship he had held for nearly fifty years had been revoked. With the influence of his American friends, Yung tried to appeal the harsh decision. Secretary of State John Sherman replied to

Yung's appeal. "Inasmuch as Yung Wing appears to have been granted his certificate of naturalization, a refusal to admit now his right to privileges which he has apparently exercised for many years would on its face seem unjust and without warrant," Sherman wrote. "Nevertheless, in view of the construction placed upon the naturalization laws of the United States by our highest courts, the Department does not feel that it can properly recognize him as a citizen of the United States."[11] Five decades after arriving in America as a student and three decades after returning to prepare for the arrival of 120 boys, Yung Wing took a boat to San Francisco and sneaked into the country illegally, like a petty thief. He arrived just in time to watch his youngest son graduate from Yale. Lacking citizenship in America and holding no official position in China, he could do little else. Having spent decades living off his earlier fortune, he was now broke. He stayed in boardinghouses, where the other tenants, swept up in the xenophobic spirit of the era, sometimes refused to dine at the same table with him. On May 29, 1912, a few months after the boys he trained so well stood at the forefront of China's first republic, Yung Wing died penniless and alone.

If they heard about their mentor's misfortune, his former students had little time to waste in mourning. Running railway lines, mining operations, and warships was one thing. Directing the course of a nation required an even higher level of responsibility and intellect. No matter: they were ready. Even in their earliest Hartford days, when the boys were so certain of their auspicious futures, few could have imagined that a day would come in which Ajax, the star of the Chinese Educational Mission, would become a leader of all of China, or that Liang Dunyan, orator extraordinaire, would administer the nation's foreign policy. They had hoped, of course, to make China modern and believed wholeheartedly—believed even when circumstances were against them—that the day would come when they could serve their nation with efficiency and talent. But the fall of the empire was more than any of them could ever have imagined; now that they had power, they were intent on using it to create a republic as democratic, as rewarding, and as innovative as the one they had come to admire as teenagers in America.

Yet China, whether ruled as an empire or a republic, proved to be especially resistant to the types of change the mission graduates had hoped to introduce. In Beijing, Tong Shao-yi found life at the highest echelons of government very taxing. As prime minister, it was his duty to appoint a cabinet, and that cabinet, he thought, should allow equal representation to all ideological convictions. Using every last bit of his considerable charisma, he pleaded, promised, and cajoled, desperate to fashion a fair and durable government. Yuan's ego, however, proved stronger than Tong's abilities, and Yuan did not take well to dissent or differing opinions. Soon, Tong found himself clashing with his old benefactor.

As soon as Yuan Shikai was inaugurated, his behavior became increasingly despotic. He was not above assassinating his political opponents. A number of Sun's supporters organized themselves into a new group—the Kuomintang, or Nationalist Party—and vowed to take up arms if Yuan failed to respect his promises to govern the republic according to democratic principles. A soldier at heart, Yuan interpreted all criticism as insubordination.

By June, three months after assuming office, Tong could endure the situation no longer. He had little desire to exist as a rubberstamp for Yuan's dictatorial decisions. Tong resigned, refusing Yuan's numerous exhortations to return to Beijing and resume his duties. Tong's cousin Liang Ju-hao followed suit. Not long thereafter, Sun and a few other Nationalists, including a promising young leader named Chiang Kai-shek, fled to Japan. With China's new government in shambles, the nation was once again in its familiar state of turmoil.

"The mistake we made," Tong told a British journalist years later, "was that we gave the president too much power. . . . We provided for a parliament and a representative government serving the people, theoretically at least, with all authority reaching from bottom to top. But the president was a bigger despot than the former emperors. With so much power concentrated in one person, it led to more abuses under the republic than under the Manchus."[12]

Yuan Shikai filled most of the vacant cabinet positions with sycophants. Still in Yuan's service, Liang Dunyan was rapidly losing faith in the former warlord. When Yuan railed against the Confucian classics, Liang grew upset. As a student in America, Liang, along with the other boys, had disliked spending summer vacations reciting the *Analects* and memorizing the ancient texts by heart in Hartford's "Hell House." As he grew older, however, Liang had discovered the merits of Chinese tradition, and he came to believe that there could be no China without Confucius. He urged Yuan to reconsider his position, but the general, who pressed on with his campaign to eradicate all vestiges of Confucian learning, ignored him. It didn't take long for Liang to resign. Heartbroken, he retired to his home. Yuan pleaded in vain that he return to office.

As the situation fell apart, Yuan Shikai became more unhinged. What China needed, he now believed, was not a paltry president who spent his days quibbling with insolent ministers and pleading with parliamentarians to adopt his point of view. Rather, it needed a strong man who could lead it to greatness. It needed another emperor.

In the fall of 1915, Yuan appointed a court: six dukes, eleven marquises, twelve earls, four viscounts, and sixteen barons, all selected from the ranks of his most unquestioning supporters. On December 23, he rode an armored car through the gates of the Forbidden City and ordered his chauffeur to drive him to the Temple of Heaven. There, he clambered out of the vehicle, removed his uniform, and donned a silk robe embroidered with dragons. Following a short ceremony, he was crowned emperor and given the name Hongxian, "Constitutional Abundance."[13]

Liang Dunyan, Tong Shao-yi, and Yuan's other former protégés were relentless in their criticism. The reserved Liang admitted to a foreign ambassador that he was "not too pleased" with Yuan, a shockingly candid sentiment.[14] Tong went much further. Yuan, he told anyone who would listen, local and foreign newspapermen included, was a "disgrace to the country." His old boss, he declared, decided to restore the monarchy "on the advice of six of the worst opium smokers" in public life.[15] That Yuan was a tyrant, that he relentlessly pursued his detractors, and that he might go after them for their criticisms mattered little to the members of the Cantonese Clique. The mission graduates had known disappointments before and were no strangers to the ebb and flow of fortune. But this was not just another setback. In sacrificing the dream of a republic on the altar of his own ambitions, Yuan had acted against everything that the graduates of the educational mission believed was just. They were faithful to their heritage, and, despite having been educated in liberal America and believing in Western notions of progress and technology, only one of the 120 boys of the mission had cast his lot with the revolutionaries who had fought to topple the antiquated Qing system. All of its burdens notwithstanding, the graduates still had reverence for tradition. Therefore, when the Mandate of Heaven was seized by a power-hungry soldier, Yung Wing's students let their anger show, the consequences be damned.

Sensing Yuan's growing isolation, the Japanese decided to make fresh demands. They pressured the new emperor to concede immense territories—including Shandong, Manchuria, and Fujian in their entirety—to Japanese control. Powerless to resist or negotiate effectively—the storied general was too preoccupied quelling the chaos racking his empire to once again trot his army into battle—Yuan gave Japan almost everything it wanted. More uprisings took place. China seemed on the verge of breaking up. Yuan, his body weathered by years of combat and drink, fell ill.

W. H. Donald, an Australian adviser to Yuan, came to see the emperor on March 18, 1916. "You must abdicate," he told Yuan. "You most stop this make-believe." Yuan's answer was simple. "I am tired," he said.[16] Then he walked out of the room. Three days later, he sent out an edict announcing that he was no longer emperor but president once more. The move did little to restore quiet, and Yuan now prepared to flee the country, enlisting Donald's help in arranging safe passage abroad. With Sun

Yat-sen's help, an agreement was reached to ferry the general to Japan. But it was too late: on June 6, Yuan died of kidney failure.

With Yuan gone, the various factions again wrestled for control of the government. On the first of July, Puyi was reinstalled on the throne in an attempted Manchu restoration. Liang, the onetime darling of Cixi, decided to cast his lot decisively with the imperial loyalists. He publicly came out in support of Puyi and served as his minister of communications. Foreigners who had known Liang only as an American-educated expert in international law and the management of railways were flummoxed by his show of loyalty to the embattled boy emperor. Few could believe that Liang, the product of Western schooling, would choose to align himself with the retrograde imperial party, especially as the restoration had been given little chance of succeeding.

On July 5, 1917, G. E. Morrison, a correspondent for the *Times* of London, wrote to Liang and expressed his friendly concern for the man he thought he knew: "There is no Chinese in China who was more generally respected by foreigners than you. It was then with the most painful feelings that I learned you had seen fit to ally yourself with this insane attempt to restore to China a Government of reaction. . . . There is not the faintest possibility of your Government continuing."[17] Morrison urged Liang to leave Beijing before it fell.

Two days later, Morrison dispatched another missive to Liang, who had refused to entertain any idea of abandoning his sovereign. Morrison had heard that Liang enjoined his former classmate Tsai Ting Kan to join him at the reestablished court of Puyi, and he could think of only one possible explanation, wrongly accusing Liang of having become addicted to narcotics:

"Misty as your faculties have become by the prolonged use of opium, you are surely not too muddled to realize how dishonourable is your conduct in causing the issue of an Imperial Decree appointing Tsai Ting-kan 'Deputy Imperial Commissioner of the Customs Administration,' a loyal friend to you ever since you were together in America. To make it appear now, as this edict does, that he is willing to serve in the present insane Government is to do that which you know to be untrue. Telegrams will be sent to-day to try to counteract the evil you are trying to do to your friend."[18]

But Tsai, like Liang, had come to see the virtues of China's ancient traditions and served the emperor willingly. On July 12, only eleven days into his restored reign, Puyi was removed from power by one of the numerous warlords then vying for power.

Puyi, as a private citizen, would go on to marry a Manchu princess in 1922. An official reception was held in Beijing for the newly wedded couple to greet foreign officials.[19] Although no longer emperor, Puyi had been residing in the Forbidden City. Nearly two hundred guests made their way to the throne room of the Palace of Cloudless Heaven, where they were escorted individually to bow and shake the hand of the former emperor and his bride. Among those ushering in the guests were Liang Dunyan and Tsai Ting Kan, both faultlessly loyal to the Confucian ideals of China that had so mystified them in Connecticut.

After Puyi's abdication, the country descended further into chaos. In 1917, Sun Yat-sen returned to China and mobilized the

Nationalists to try to unite the fragmented nation under his rule. He died of cancer in 1925, and Chiang Kai-shek emerged to take his place. For most of the 1920s, the Nationalists worked hand in hand with a fledgling political force, the Communist Party of China. In 1927, Chiang turned on the Communists, and that party's faithful were forced to embark on the yearlong, 8,000-mile march to China's desolate northwest, where they carried on the fight against their former allies. During that Long March, Mao Zedong, a young and brilliant commissar of the party's central committee, assumed leadership of the Communists. The rivalry between the Nationalists and Communists continued even during the Japanese occupation of Manchuria in 1931, when the Japanese renamed the province Manchuko and installed the twenty-five-year-old Puyi as its ruler.

With few exceptions, these tumultuous years left no mark on Yung Wing's former students. They had devoted their entire lives to traveling down the slow and tortuous road leading toward China's modernization. They had put up with narrow-minded mandarins and corrupt clerks. They had suffered long stretches of service in some of the empire's least rewarding positions and were stung by the suspicion and mistrust that accompanied success in the Qing's byzantine court. They had seen Western nations, even those fashioning themselves as champions of freedom, democracy, and self-determination, do their best to drain China of its independence and its wealth. They remained infatuated with the robust ideals they had witnessed in America, but they never lost their passion and commitment to China's ancient traditions and its customs. They wanted change, not revolution.

They wanted progress, and at every turn progress was denied. Mostly in their sixties in the 1920s, they no longer had the energy to fight. China, they agreed, had no future. All that was left was its past.

Tsai Ting Kan spent his days reflecting in his garden, writing and translating classical Chinese poetry. Liang Dunyan immersed himself in the lives of the ancient emperors and the *Analects*.

Tong Shao-yi in his later years devoted most of his time to China's past glories. Back home in his village on the South China Sea, he invested his energy and resources in increasing his now considerable porcelain collection. One Western observer wrote,

> It is perhaps the finest private collection in China. Pieces of Sung and Ming, of Clair de Lune, of Sang de Boeuf, of wonderful peach blow, and blue and white, were arranged around the walls on shelves, each with its carved black teakwood stand and its pink satin-padded box. [Tong] fondled each piece with the loving fingers of a connoisseur. . . . He lifted down a great cool green vase of sea nymph's pallor, with marvelous dragons twisting themselves around it in relief—imperial dragons, with five claws holding the precious jewel. "This is my favorite," he announced. "It is very rare, I have had my agents looking for the mate to it all over the country for five years. Wouldn't J. P. Morgan have loved to get hold of it?"[20]

But the artifacts of the past were not enough to fill a mind as dexterous and probing as Tong's. From time to time, he emerged from his estate to try once more to save his nation from destruction. There were rumors he might side with the Japanese occupiers, whose talent for modernization he openly admired. Someone—it is not precisely clear who, although Chiang Kai-shek emerges as the prime suspect—decided that Tong posed too much of a threat.

Knowing how much the former prime minister loved his porcelain, three men presented themselves at Tong's house on the afternoon of September 30, 1938, in the guise of antique dealers. They brought with them ten pieces of porcelain. Tong, now seventy-six years old, should have been preparing for his daughter's wedding later that day, but he couldn't resist looking at the collection on offer. As he examined the artifacts, one of the men surreptitiously removed all the matches from Tong's parlor, and then produced a cigarette and asked his distracted host for a light. Tong looked around. Usually, he kept matches strewn throughout the room, but now he couldn't find any. He dispatched his servant to get a fresh box from the pantry. It was just the opportunity the assailants had been waiting for. One of them reached into a large agate vase and produced an ax, striking Tong on the skull as hard as he could. Tong fell to the ground, bleeding, unable to make a sound. The three men collected their antiques, headed out the door into a car they had stolen earlier that day, and drove away.[21]

On the floor of his parlor, Tong was losing blood. The servant returned with the matches, and rushed to help his master. That afternoon, Tong was dead.

EPILOGUE

Traveling through China in the winter of 2009, we visited many of the locations where the events of this book take place. We walked through what was once Yung Wing's native village, sat at Tong Shao-yi's desk, and stood near the spot where Yuan Shikai declared himself emperor. The more we learned about the graduates of the Chinese Educational Mission, the more obsessed we became with a single, simple question: was theirs a happy story or a sad one?

There is much evidence to support either assertion. On the one hand, of the 120 boys who left China for New England, an overwhelming number reached positions of power and influence. For the sake of brevity and coherence, we chose to tell the story of some of the mission's most prominent graduates, but a great number of others led equally illustrious lives. There was Chow Chang Ling, who became the first Chinese to sit on the Legislative Council of Hong Kong and was honored as a Knight of the British Empire. Or Chow Wan Pung, who, as director of the Imperial Telegraph Administration and chief of the postal services, did much to connect China's disjointed provinces and revolutionize its antiquated communications system. Woo Yang Tsang, who had been nicknamed Alligator in New England, was the director of several of China's largest mines and introduced innovative technologies that propelled his industry toward an era of higher efficiency and profit. There were dozens more like them, pioneers who put their Western education to use in the service of their nation, men to whom modern-day China owes a great debt.

Some of the graduates, however, found themselves unable to achieve success in the years following their American adolescence. Li En Fu, for example, returned to the United States in 1884 and wrote a book about his experiences as a student of the educational mission, for which he earned a bit of fame. He married an American woman and had a family, but his vociferous criticisms of the anti-Chinese sentiment he found in the United States were more than most Americans were willing to take from a foreigner. Li's wife divorced him, and he spent the rest of his life working at a variety of odd jobs, at one point operating a poultry market. Luk Wing Chun also returned to America, where he completed his degree at Yale and later found work as the Chinese vice consul in New York City. In 1909, a deranged, unemployed Chinese man strayed into the consulate and fatally shot him. Even many of those who had seemed at one point to be blessed with fortunate lives died alone in misery: Liang Dunyan succumbed to pneumonia in 1924, sixty-six years old and broken, while Yung Leang, the irrepressible By-jinks Johnnie, lost everything he owned when a Japanese shell destroyed his house in 1931. Yung, at least, had the good fortune of living for twenty-three more years, surrounded by his children and grandchildren. Some weren't so lucky: Tsai Ting Kan, nicknamed Fighting Chinee, had nothing but his poems to keep him company when he died, aged seventy-four, in 1935.

Yet more than individual stories of failure or triumph, the story of the educational mission is the story of China's surge toward modernity. In America, its graduates had seen the virtues of democracy and the possibilities of progress, but learned soon after returning home that their ancient empire was steeped in its own traditions and governed by its own rules. If it was to march forward, it would do so on its own path and at its own pace. The mission graduates worked tirelessly to give China the tools it needed to bring about progress, and they worked equally as hard to protect its sovereignty from Western nations eager to subdue it. The problems they faced are the problems still facing China today.

It is impossible, then, to decide whether the story of the Chinese Educational Mission ends on a happy note or a sad one. As long as China continues to address the same challenges and concerns the mission's graduates faced, the story will continue.

A NOTE ON TRANSLATION

For the names of places, characters, and key Chinese terms, we have tried, as much as possible, to use the pinyin spelling system, which became the international standard in the 1980s and is now used almost universally. Our hope is that this will aid the curious reader who wishes to follow our characters on a map, find them in an encyclopedia, or cite their exploits in another work.

However, we have had to balance this desire with several other considerations. Most of our English primary-source materials date from a time when no such spelling standard existed, when Chinese names were brought into English more or less willy-nilly. The waters are further muddied by the fact that the romanizations of personal and place-names in our sources are often based on their pronunciations in Cantonese, the native language of most of the people around which our tale revolves, rather than in Mandarin, the language upon which the pinyin system is based. This has in some cases prevented us from finding the Mandarin equivalents of these names; in other cases, it seems inappropriate to substitute a Mandarin name for a place or person known to our subjects by its Cantonese name, or by an antiquated but commonly used English spelling. Our subjects, after all, were literate in English, and in some cases we would like to remain faithful to the way they represented themselves and their surroundings on paper.

To achieve this balance, we have constructed our own system of translation, making use of several available standards. When a person or place is known universally by a certain spelling, we retain that spelling: for example, Yung Wing is rarely, if ever, referred to in English by his Mandarin, pinyinized name, Rong Hong. Similarly, when a subject knows a place or a person by a certain name—and that place or person is not widely known by a pinyin name—we retain the nonstandard spelling in an effort to convey a sense of subjectivity and, at times, of local flavor. Occasionally, we have also taken into consideration what would have been the common names known to English speakers at the time that the events described in this book unfolded. While the city of Canton, for example, was never known to Chinese speakers as "Canton," nineteenth-century English speakers called it that, and as a result the name conveys a sense of place and time that the pinyin alternative, Guangzhou, does not.

As a result, we occasionally sacrifice consistency for flavor. We hope the sticklers will forgive us, and suggest they consult the endnotes for standard Mandarin names and pinyin spellings when appropriate.

A NOTE ON SOURCES

In telling the story of the Chinese Educational Mission, we are indebted first and foremost to its commissioners, graduates, and supporters, many of whom left behind biographies, diaries, and other invaluable primary sources. Particularly helpful were Yung Wing's *My Life in China and America* and Li En Fu's *When I Was a Boy in China*, as well as the correspondence of Dr. Joseph Twichell, collected in Steve Courtney's *Joseph Hopkins Twichell: The Life and Times of Mark Twain's Closest Friend*. Also in this category are two thorough unpublished theses written about the mission, Chris Robyn's "Building the Bridge: The Chinese Educational Mission to the United States: A Sino-American Historico-Cultural Synthesis, 1872–1881" and Anita Marchant's "Yung Wing and the Chinese Educational Mission at Hartford."

A number of archives, in America and China, have preserved an assortment of letters, journals, and photographs belonging or pertaining to our subjects. They include the Connecticut Historical Society; the Colebrook Historical Society in

Colebrook, Connecticut; Yung Wing's papers at Yale University; Liang Dunyan's papers in Renmin University; and the Zhuhai International Cultural Exchange archives.

Hu Jincao, a producer for CCTV and the creator of a documentary series about the mission, was kind enough to share with us her footage, her notes, and her insights. Jimmy Tong, a grandnephew of Tong Shao-yi, invited us into his home and shared with us recollections and documentation of his storied relative.

We are also indebted to the excellent works by Thomas E. LaFargue, whose encounters with the mission's graduates produced *China's First Hundred: Educational Mission Students in the United States, 1872–1881,* and to David G. Hinners, whose own family's connection to the mission informed his *Tong Shao-Yi and His Family: A Saga of Two Countries and Three Generations,* as well as to Stacey Bieler's *"Patriots" or "Traitors"?: A History of American-Educated Chinese Students.*

Struggling to see the expansive vistas of Chinese history in full, we found ourselves fortunate to have extraordinary works from which to learn. We are particularly indebted to Jonathan Fenby, whose *Modern China: The Fall and Rise of a Great Power, 1850 to the Present* is as thrilling as it is informative; to Jonathan D. Spence, whose *The Search for Modern China* is justifiably the seminal work on the subject; and to William T. Rowe, whose *China's Last Empire: The Great Qing* provided us a nuanced and immensely edifying framework of the politics and economics of the empire at its twilight.

On the lives and minds of Zeng Guofan and Li Hongzhang, we learned much from Samuel C. Chu and Kwang-Ching Liu's *Li Hung-chang and China's Early Modernization* and from

Kwang-Ching Liu's "The Confucian as Patriot and Pragmatist: Li Hung-chang's Formative Years, 1823–1866," published in the *Harvard Journal of Asiatic Studies*.

For the early years of Chinese immigration to America, with all its wonders and horrors, we turned to Peter Kwong and Dusanka Miscevic's *Chinese America: The Untold Story of America's Oldest New Community*, as well as to Iris Chang's masterful and heartbreaking *The Chinese in America: A Narrative History*.

Finally, since this book is a tale just as much of America as of China, we gained much insight into the economic thrusts of the nineteenth century from John Steele Gordon's *An Empire of Wealth: The Epic History of American Economic Power* and Stephen E. Ambrose's *Nothing Like It in the World: The Men Who Built the Transcontinental Railroad*. Like the nation they so aptly chronicle, their works, too, were marvels of industriousness and pluck.

ACKNOWLEDGMENTS

Having retraced the steps of the Chinese Educational Mission's graduates in China and America, we are indebted to the following people for showing us the way:

In Hong Kong, Qian Gang did much to set us on our path, providing advice and introductions, while the effervescent Anna Bisazza exposed us to the city's charm and its many happy valleys.

In Zhuhai, Yang Yi and Donald Tan helped us dig up the mission's roots, serving as both gracious hosts and knowledgeable guides. We were also fortunate enough to spend some time with Jimmy Tong, the great-nephew of Tong Shao-Yi, who told us stories about his famous ancestor.

In Beijing, Hu Jincao shared with us the fruits of her extensive research into the mission and its graduates. Her insights helped us turn 120 disparate experiences into one cohesive story.

In Connecticut, we benefited much from the bounties of the

Connecticut Historical Society and from the marvel that is Bob Grigg, Colebrook's historian and resident bard.

In New York, the remarkable talents of a few extraordinary individuals aided, comforted, and inspired us. Austin Woerner, our stellar translator, was blessed with the poet's ear and the scholar's eye, helping us capture the terrible beauty of the Qing court. Lisa Ann Sandell was, as always, a brilliant reader, and her comments gave our sprawling story much-needed shape. Krista Ingebretson patiently put up with our follies and shared with us her fantastic observations. Anne Edelstein, our incomparable agent, gave us her boundless wisdom, her unflagging support, and—most cherished—her true friendship, for all of which we are eternally grateful. Finally, we are thrilled and honored to be working with the magical people at W. W. Norton: the saintly Laura Romain, who diligently and skillfully shepherded this manuscript on its way to print; the luminous Winfrida Mbewe, who masterfully presented to the world a brighter side of us than we could ever present ourselves; and Amy Cherry, our editor, whose sharp mind and generous heart are too great to capture in words and to whom we are thankful for just about everything.

NOTES

1: The Freshman

1. The following account of the 1850 football game is taken from Charles Hallock, "Football Forty Years Ago: When Numbers Counted—The Notable Yale Game of 1850," *New York Times*, December 8, 1889, and from "Armenian vs. Chinaman; Another Reminiscence of Yale Football Forty Years Ago," *New York Times*, December 15, 1889.

2. Quoted in Jerome Karabel, *The Chosen: The Hidden History of Admission and Exclusion at Harvard, Yale, and Princeton* (Boston: Houghton Mifflin, 2005), 29.

3. Hallock, "Football Forty Years Ago."

4. Ibid.

5. Unless otherwise noted, all information pertaining to Yung Wing's life is taken from his autobiography, *My Life in China and America* (New York: Henry Holt, 1909), available online at http://web .pdx.edu/~lorz/texts.htm.

6. John K. Folger, *Education of the American Population* (Manchester, N.H.: Ayer Company Publishers, 1975), 3–5.

7. Chang Ho Chang, *Chinese Customs and Traditions* (Boston: Cheng & Tsui, 1987), 193.

8. Wang Wei, "Song bie," in *Xin yi Tang shi san bai shou*, ed. Qiu Xieyou (Tabei Shi: San min shu ju, 2006), 26–27; translation by Austin Woerner.

9. Discussion of the imperial examination system is taken from Ichisada Miyazaki, *China's Examination Hell: The Civil Service Examinations of Imperial China*, trans. Conrad Schirokauer (New Haven: Yale University Press, 1981).

10. Ibid., 17.

11. Yung Wing to Samuel Wells Williams, December 25, 1850, Yung Wing Archives, Yale University, New Haven.

12. Yung Wing Archives, Yale University, New Haven.

13. Yung Wing to Samuel Wells Williams, December 25, 1850, Yung Wing Archives, Yale University, New Haven.

14. Yung, *My Life in China and America*, 16.

2: The Qing

1. Yung Wing, *My Life in China and America* (New York: Henrl65y Holt, 1909), 45.

2. Ibid., 47.

3. Ibid.

4. Ibid., 48.

5. The conversation between Yung and his mother is based on the account ibid., 18–19.

6. William T. Rowe, *China's Last Empire: The Great Qing* (Cambridge: Harvard University Press, 2009), 150.

7. Ibid.

8. Why China, once a nation dedicated to innovation, had allowed itself to lag behind the West is a mystery that has bedeviled scholars for decades. While we cite the two most popular explanations to what has become known as the Needham Question—named after British sinologist Joseph Needham, the great chronicler of Chinese science and technology—there are those who believe

the question is beyond answering. For more on Needham, see Winchester, Simon. *The Man Who Loved China: The Fantastic Story of the Eccentric Scientist Who Unlocked the Mysteries of the Middle Kingdom* (New York: Harper, 2008).

9. Jonathan Fenby, *Modern China: The Fall and Rise of a Great Power, 1850 to the Present* (New York: Ecco, 2008), 6.

10. John King Fairbank, Katherine Frost Bruner, and Elisabeth MacLeod Matheson, eds., *The I.G. in Peking: Letters of Robert Hart, Chinese Maritime Customs, 1868–1907*, vol. 2 (Cambridge: Belknap Press of Harvard University Press, 1975), 118.

11. Thomas Buoye et al., eds., *China: Adapting the Past, Confronting the Future* (Ann Arbor, Mich.: Center for Chinese Studies Publications, 2002), 59.

12. Rowe, *China's Last Empire*, 151.

13. Georg Wilhelm Friedrich Hegel, *The Philosophy of History* (New York: Dover, 2004), 90–91.

14. Ibid., 116.

15. Quoted in Rowe, *China's Last Empire*, 167–68.

16. Quoted ibid.

17. Ibid., 166.

18. Ibid., 167.

19. Quoted in Franz Schurmann and Orville Schell, eds., *Imperial China: The Eighteenth and Nineteenth Centuries* (New York: Penguin, 1968), 139.

20. Quoted in Rowe, *China's Last Empire*, 172.

21. Quoted ibid., 173.

22. Jonathan Spence, *The Search for Modern China* (New York: Norton, 1990), 38–39.

23. Quoted in Jonathan Spence, *God's Chinese Son: The Taiping Heavenly Kingdom of Hong Xiuquan* (New York: Norton, 1996), 161.

24. Quoted ibid.

25. Yung, *My Life in China and America*, 19.

3: The Foreigners

1. Yung Wing, *My Life in China and America* (New York: Henry Holt, 1909), 20.
2. Peter Parker, in *Quarterly Report of the Medical Missionary Society in China*, 1838, 29.
3. Yung, *My Life in China and America*, 23.
4. Ibid.
5. Ibid., 25.
6. Ibid.
7. Ibid.
8. Ibid., 26.
9. Ibid., 27.
10. Herbert Allen Giles, *China and the Manchus* (London: Cambridge University Press, 1912), 83.
11. Quoted in Godfrey Elton, *Gordon of Khartoum: The Life of General Charles George Gordon* (New York: Knopf, 1955), 31.
12. Yung, *My Life in China and America*, 37.

4: Self-Strengthening

1. Yung Wing, *My Life in China and America* (New York: Henry Holt, 1909), 48.
2. Han-Yin Chen Shen, "Tseng Kuo-fan in Peking, 1840–1852: His Ideas on Statecraft and Reform," *Journal of Asian Studies* 27, no. 1 (1967): 72.
3. Quoted in Franz Michael, "State and Society in Nineteenth-Century China," *World Politics* 7 (1954): 425.
4. Quoted in Stanley Spector, *Li Hung-chang and the Huai Army: A Study in Nineteenth-Century Chinese Regionalism* (Seattle: University of Washington Press, 1964), 14.
5. Kwang-Ching Liu, "The Confucian as Patriot and Pragmatist: Li Hung-chang's Formative Years, 1823–1866," *Harvard Journal of Asiatic Studies* 30 (1970): 19.

6. Jonathan Fenby, *Modern China: The Fall and Rise of a Great Power, 1850 to the Present* (New York: Ecco, 2008), 22.

7. Yung, *My Life in China and America*, 50.

8. The conversation is quoted ibid.

9. Ibid., 51–52.

10. Ibid., 52.

11. Ibid., 55.

12. Kwang-Ching Liu, "The Confucian as Patriot and Pragmatist," 15.

13. Samuel C. Chu and and Kwang-Ching Liu, eds., *Li Hung-chang and China's Early Modernization* (Armonk, N.Y.: M. E. Sharpe, 1994), 23.

14. Kwang-Ching Liu, "The Confucian as Patriot and Pragmatist," 19.

15. Yung, *My Life in China and America*, 57–58.

16. Ibid., 58.

17. Quoted in Kwang-Ching Liu, "The Confucian as Patriot and Pragmatist," 32.

18. Quoted ibid., 33.

19. Quoted ibid., 34.

20. Yung, *My Life in China and America*, 60.

21. Ibid., 63.

22. William Speer, *The Oldest and the Newest Empire: China and the United States* (Pittsburgh: Robert S. Davis, 1877), 681.

23. Quoted in Hu Jincao, *Boy Students*, Documentary Television Series, Beijing, China, CCTV, 2004.

24. Quoted in Thomas E. LaFargue, *China's First Hundred: Educational Mission Students in the United States, 1872–1881* (Pullman: Washington State University Press, 1987), 36.

25. Yung, *My Life in China and America*, 65.

5: The Arrival

1. "Progress of the Fair Trial—Arrival of Chinese Students," *New York Times*, September 15, 1872.

2. University of California, San Francisco, "A History of USCF," http://history.library.ucsf.edu/1868_goldrush.html.

3. Iris Chang, *The Chinese in America: A Narrative History* (New York: Penguin, 2003), 29.

4. Ibid., 41.

5. Mark Twain, *Roughing It* (New York: Library of America, 1984), 820. While the word "Chinaman" is nowadays tainted with the stain of racism, Twain, as is clear from the context of his passage, did not mean it to be negative.

6. The discussion of Chinatown draws on Chang, *The Chinese in America*, 46–50.

7. Quoted in John Steele Gordon, *An Empire of Wealth: The Epic History of American Economic Power* (New York: Harper Perennial, 2004), 218.

8. The discussion of Central Pacific's Chinese workers draws on Chang, *The Chinese in America*, 57–63.

9. Ibid., 56.

10. Quoted ibid.

11. Ibid., 64.

12. The discussion of the transcontinental railway is drawn from Stephen E. Ambrose, *Nothing Like It in the World: The Men Who Built the Transcontinental Railroad* (New York: Simon and Schuster, 2000); National Park Service, "Golden Spike," http://www.nps.gov/history/history/online_books/hh/40/hh40q.htm; and PBS, "American Experience: Transcontinental Railroad," http://www.nps.gov/history/history/online_books/hh/40/hh40q.htm.

13. Quoted in Ambrose, *Nothing Like It in the World*, 366.

14. P. S. Dorney, "A Prophecy Partly Verified," in *The Overland Monthly*, vol. 7, no. 39 (March 1886): 233.

15. Yan Phou Lee, *When I Was a Boy in China* (Boston: D. Lothrop, 1887), 33.

16. Quoted in Gordon, *An Empire of Wealth*, 175.

17. Quoted ibid., 176.

18. "Our Celestial Visitors," *Hartford Evening Post*, September 25, 1872.

6: The Forbidden City of Willard Street

1. "The Chinese Students," *Hartford Courant*, October 11, 1872.

2. "Our Celestial Visitors," *Hartford Evening Post*, September 25, 1872.

3. Quoted in Witold Rybczynski, *A Clearing in the Distance: Frederick Law Olmsted and America in the Nineteenth Century* (New York: Scribner, 1999), 32–33.

4. Steve Courtney, *Joseph Hopkins Twichell: The Life and Times of Mark Twain's Closest Friend* (Athens: University of Georgia Press, 2008), 146.

5. Yan Phou Lee, *When I Was a Boy in China* (Boston: D. Lothrop, 1887), 34.

6. Thomas E. LaFargue, *China's First Hundred: Educational Mission Students in the United States, 1872–1881* (Pullman: Washington State University Press, 1987), 35.

7. Edward Hart Fenn, *Friendship Albums, 1874*, Connecticut Historical Society Archives, Hartford, Conn.

8. "The Chinese Students," *Hartford Evening Post*, June 4, 1874.

9. Quoted in Chris Robyn, "Building the Bridge: The Chinese Educational Mission to the United States: A Sino-American Historico-Cultural Synthesis, 1872–1881" (M.A. thesis, Chinese University of Hong Kong, 1996), 25.

10. "The Celestials," *Hartford Union Post*, September 26, 1872.

11. "The Chinese Students," *Hartford Evening Post*, August 20, 1873.

12. Quoted in Anita Marchant, "Yung Wing and the Chinese Educational Mission at Hartford" (M.A. thesis, Trinity College, Hartford, 1999), 16.

13. William Lyon Phelps, *Autobiography, with Letters* (New York: Oxford University Press, 1939), 83–86.

14. Ibid.

15. Quoted in "The Chinese Students," *Hartford Evening Post*, June 4, 1874.

16. "Yung Wing Marries a Connecticut Lady," *New York Times*, March 2, 1875.

7: The Return

1. The discussion of the Centennial Exhibition draws largely on Visitors' Guide to the Centennial Exhibition and Philadelphia, May 10th to November 10th, 1876 (Philadelphia: J. B. Lippincott, 1876).

2. Centennial Exhibition Digital Collection, Exhibition Facts, http://libwww.library.phila.gov/CenCol/exhibitionfax.htm.

3. Centennial Exhibition Digital Collection, Foreign Countries, http://libwww.library.phila.gov/CenCol/exh-foreign.htm.

4. William Dean Howells, "A Sennight of the Centennial," *Atlantic Monthly* 38 (1876): 93.

5. Centennial Exhibition Digital Collection, Machinery Hall, https://libwww.freelibrary.org/CenCol/tours-machineryhall.htm.

6. Quoted in Hu Jincao, *Boy Students*, Documentary Television Series, Beijing, China, CCTV, 2004.

7. Ibid.

8. Quoted in "Young John at the Centennial," *Hartford Evening Post*, August 24, 1876.

9. Quoted in Hu Jincao, *Boy Students*.

10. Yung Wing, *My Life in China and America* (New York: Henry Holt, 1909), 70.

11. Ibid.

12. Ibid.

13. Hu Jincao, *Boy Students*.

14. "Chinese Educational Mission: Introductions to the Chinese Students by the Commissioner," *Hartford Daily Courant*, April 27, 1880.

15. Yung, *My Life in China and America*, 71.
16. "Too Muchee She," *Hartford Daily Times*, June 11, 1877.
17. The discussion of the boys' graduation ceremony, and their speeches, is taken from "Hartford Public High School," *Hartford Daily Times*, April 18, 1878; and "The High School," ibid., April 20, 1978.
18. William Lyon Phelps, *Autobiography, with Letters* (New York: Oxford University Press, 1939), 12.
19. Ibid.
20. Iris Chang, *The Chinese in America: A Narrative History* (New York: Penguin, 2003), 125.
21. Quoted ibid., 126.
22. Quoted ibid., 130.
23. Quoted in Steve Courtney, *Joseph Hopkins Twichell: The Life and Times of Mark Twain's Closest Friend* (Athens: University of Georgia Press, 2008), 205.
24. Quoted in William S. McFeely, *Grant: A Biography* (New York: Norton, 1982), 474.
25. Quoted in Courtney, *Joseph Hopkins Twichell*, 205.
26. Quoted ibid., 205–6.
27. Quoted ibid., 206.
28. Quoted ibid.
29. Quoted in Hu Jincao, *Boy Students*.
30. Quoted in Courtney, *Joseph Hopkins Twichell*, 207.
31. Quoted ibid., 205.
32. Quoted ibid.
33. Quoted ibid., 148.
34. Carrington Diaries, Colebrook Historical Society, Colebrook, Conn.
35. Quoted in Stacey Bieler, *"Patriots" or "Traitors"?: A History of American-Educated Chinese Students* (Armonk, N.Y.: M. E. Sharpe, 2004), 10.
36. Hu Jincao, *Boy Students*.

37. Quoted in Thomas E. LaFargue, *China's First Hundred: Educational Mission Students in the United States, 1872–1881* (Pullman: Washington State University Press, 1987), 124.

8: The Prisoners

1. Anonymous, Connecticut Historical Society Archives, Hartford, Conn.
2. Yung Leang, date and recipient unknown, Connecticut Historical Society Archives, Hartford, Conn.
3. Huang Kaijia to Fannie Bartlett, January 28, 1882, Connecticut Historical Society Archives, Hartford, Conn.
4. Yung Leang, date and recipient unknown, Connecticut Historical Society Archives, Hartford, Conn.
5. Anonymous, Connecticut Historical Society Archives, Hartford, Conn.
6. "Chinese Custom," *Hartford Evening Post*, January 9, 1882.
7. Huang Kaijia to Fannie Bartlett, January 28, 1882, Connecticut Historical Society Archives, Hartford, Conn.
8. Quoted in George Rogers Haddad, *The Romance of China: Excursions to China in U.S. Culture, 1776–1875* (New York: Columbia University Press, 2008), 302.

9: "One Vast Jellyfish"

1. *Memoirs of the Viceroy Li Hung Chang* (London: Constable, 1913), 256–57.
2. Quoted in David G. Hinners, *Tong Shao-Yi and His Family: A Saga of Two Countries and Three Generations* (Lanham, Md.: University Press of America, 1999), 8–9.
3. Quoted in Ann Paludan, *Chronicle of the Chinese Emperors: The Reign-by-Reign Record of the Rulers of Imperial China* (London: Thames & Hudson, 2009), 213.
4. Quoted in Jonathan Fenby, *Modern China: The Fall and Rise of a Great Power, 1850 to the Present* (New York: Ecco, 2008), 46.

5. Quoted ibid., 47.

6. Quoted in Hinners, *Tong Shao-Yi and His Family*, 9.

7. William Elliot Griffis, "The Statesmanship of Yuan Shi Kai," *North American Review* 204 (July 1916): 70.

8. Ibid., 10.

9. Quoted in Marius B. Jansen, *The Making of Modern Japan* (Cambridge: Belknap Press of Harvard University Press, 2002), 464.

10. Quoted in James Martin Miller, *China: Ancient and Modern* (Los Angeles: Sanderson-Whitten, 1900), 288–89.

11. Quoted in Vladimir, *The China-Japan War: Compiled from Japanese, Chinese, and Foreign Sources* (Whitefish, Mont.: Kessinger Publications, 2009), 161–62.

12. Quoted in S. C. M. Paine, *The Sino-Japanese War of 1894–1895: Perceptions, Power, and Primacy* (Cambridge: Cambridge University Press, 2003), 214.

13. Henry Cabot Lodge, ed., *The History of Nations: Japan* (New York: P. F. Collier and Son, 1913), 271.

14. Although there are several conflicting accounts of Admiral Ting's suicide, this one was personally recounted by Yung Leang in his older age. Quoted in Thomas E. LaFargue, *China's First Hundred: Educational Mission Students in the United States, 1872–1881* (Pullman: Washington State University Press, 1987), 87.

15. David C. Evans and Mark R. Peattie, *Kaigun: Strategy, Tactics, and Technology in the Imperial Japanese Navy, 1887–1941* (Annapolis, Md.: Naval Institute Press, 1997), 524–25.

16. Quoted in J. O. P. Bland, *Li Hung-chang* (New York: Henry Holt, 1917), 174.

17. "A Pathetic Proclamation: Chinese Emperor's Autograph Explanation of Japan's Victory," *New York Times*, May 24, 1895.

18. Quoted in Fenby, *Modern China*, 55.

19. Zhongguo Jindai Shi, "China 1895–1912: State-Sponsored Reforms and China's Late-Qing Revolution," *Chinese Studies in*

History 28 (Spring–Summer 1995): 50–51.

20. Luke S. K. Kwong, *A Mosaic of the Hundred Days: Personalities, Politics, and the Ideas of 1898* (Cambridge: Harvard University Press, 1984), 178.

21. Charles Beresford, *The Break-up of China* (New York: Harper and Brothers, 1899), 272.

10: The Hundred Days

1. Quoted in "The Reforms in China: Epitome and Discussion of the Emperor's Dress," *Meriden Daily Republican*, November 2, 1898.

2. Quoted in *Fortnightly Review* (London) 72 (1899): 45.

3. Ibid.

4. "The Reforms in China."

5. Luke S. K. Kwong, *A Mosaic of the Hundred Days: Personalities, Politics, and the Ideas of 1898* (Cambridge: Harvard University Press, 1984), 178.

6. Quoted in Charlotte Franken Haldane, *The Last Great Empress of China* (London: Constable, 1965), 145.

7. Ibid., 146.

8. "The Reforms in China."

9. Yung Wing, *My Life in China and America* (New York: Henry Holt, 1909), 75.

10. Ibid., 78.

11. Francis H. Nichols, *Through Hidden Shensi* (New York: Charles Scribner's Sons, 1902), 193.

12. Quoted in David G. Hinners, *Tong Shao-Yi and His Family: A Saga of Two Countries and Three Generations* (Lanham, Md.: University Press of America, 1999), 11–12.

13. Jonathan Fenby, *Modern China: The Fall and Rise of a Great Power, 1850 to the Present* (New York: Ecco, 2008), 80.

14. Jonathan D. Spence, *The Search for Modern China* (New York: Norton, 1990), 232.

15. Quoted in Fenby, *Modern China*, 86.
16. Quoted in Joseph Esherick, *The Origins of the Boxer Uprising* (Berkeley: University of California Press, 1987), 289.
17. Quoted ibid., 302.
18. Quoted in William Francis Mannix, ed., *Memoirs of Li Hung Chang* (Boston: Houghton Mifflin, 1913), 244.
19. Quoted in Der Ling, *Two Years in the Forbidden City* (New York: Moffat, Yard and Co., 1917), 362.
20. Nichols, *Through Hidden Shensi*, 230–31.
21. Quoted in Ng Lun Ngai-ha, *Interactions of East and West: Development of Public Education in Early Hong Kong* (Hong Kong: Chinese University Press, 1984), 118.

11: Sunset

1. Liang Dunyan Online Archive, Renmin University, http://www.daxtx.cn/liangdunyan/index.htm.
2. "Arsenic Killed Chinese Emperor, Reports Say," CNN, http://www.cnn.com/2008/WORLD/asiapcf/11/04/china.emperor/index.html?eref=rss_world, retrieved April 2, 2010.
3. Quoted in J. O. P. Bland and E. Backhouse, *China under the Empress Dowager* (Boston: Houghton Mifflin, 1914), 292.
4. Quoted in Frank Dorn, *The Forbidden City: The Biography of a Palace* (New York: Scribner, 1970), 292.
5. Quoted in Joseph Esherick, *Reform and Revolution in China: The 1911 Revolution in Hunan and Hubei* (Berkeley, Calif.: Center for Chinese Studies, 1998), 225.
6. Quoted in Shinkichi Eto, *China's Republican Revolution* (Tokyo: Tokyo University Press, 1994), 142.
7. Quoted in Jerome Ch'en, *Yuan Shih-kai* (Stanford: Stanford University Press, 1961), 123.
8. Quoted in Jonathan D. Spence, *The Search for Modern China* (New York: Norton, 1990), 267.
9. Quoted in Elsie F. Weil, "The Boy Emperor of China," *Asia:*

Journal of the American Asiatic Association 17 (March–December 1917): 448.

10. Marie-Claire Bergère, *Sun Yat-sen* (Palo Alto: Stanford University Press, 2000), 220.

11. John Sherman to Charles Denby, April 14, 1898, no. 1567, National Archives, Record Group 77.

12. Quoted in David G. Hinners, *Tong Shao-Yi and His Family: A Saga of Two Countries and Three Generations* (Lanham, Md.: University Press of America, 1999), 38.

13. Jonathan Fenby, *Modern China: The Fall and Rise of a Great Power, 1850 to the Present* (New York: Ecco, 2008), 136.

14. Liang Dunyan Online Archive, Renmin University, http://www.daxtx.cn/liangdunyan/index.htm.

15. Quoted in Hinners, *Tong Shao-Yi and His Family*, 41.

16. Quoted in Earl Albert Selle, *Donald of China* (New York: Harper and Brothers, 1948), 179.

17. Quoted in Lo Hui-Min, ed., *The Correspondence of G. E. Morrison*, vol. 2 (New York: Cambridge University Press, 1978), 607.

18. Quoted in Peter Thompson and Robert Macklin, *The Life and Adventures of Morrison of China* (Sydney: Allen & Unwin, 2008), 403.

19. Reginald Fleming Johnston, *Twilight in the Forbidden City* (Vancouver, b.c.: Soul Care Publishing, 2008), 297.

20. Quoted in Hinners, *Tong Shao-Yi and His Family*, 41–42.

21. Ibid., 49.

INDEX